FROM ANTICIPATION TO ACTION

A Handbook of Strategic Prospective

by Michel GODET

(Translated from the French by Clare Degenhardt
Revised by Valerie Shepherd)

To Harry Rothman
one of the best
in the field of strategic
management
En cordial hommage

The designations employed and the presentation of the material in this publication do not imply the expression of any opinion whatsoever on the part of the UNESCO Secretariat concerning the legal status of any country or territory, or of its authorities, or concerning the delimitations of the frontiers of any country or territory.

Published in 1993 by the United Nations
Educational, Scientific and Cultural Organization
7, place de Fontenoy, 75352 Paris 07 SP
Printed by UNESCO

ISBN 92-3-102832-4

Printed in France

FOREWORD

In an age of anxiety and a period of transition, all institutions crave insight into the future. The globalizing of the world's economies is creating new complexities for business planning and aggravating uncertainties about the business environment. The imminence of the millenium is, for many, a social milestone, a point at which the future of nations will be seen to be bright and optimistic or in decline. In every sector, stock-taking, anticipation, and plans are the order of the day as we approach that transition.

This attention to the future is surely favourable to the human enterprise. But the anticipation of the future is sterile unless it is accompanied by systematic, well–grounded, comprehensive actionable plans. Since the seminal work of the Marquis de Condorcet at the time of the French Revolution, the Western world has learned that we can identify long-term trends and that we can anticipate many of the consequences of new developments. Further, it is clear that our actions influence the future. But more important is the recognition that we can consciously act to influence the future in directions in which we wish it to evolve.

Surely no one but a fool would claim that we can see the future with crystalline clarity or that we can take actions which will determine the future. All we need is to agree on this modest claim: that we can see the future to a degree that is useful for planning and that we can take actions which will make desirable outcomes more likely and undesirable outcomes less likely.

Central to the current look to the future is the concept of alternatives, that in view of all the complexity ahead of us, it makes little sense to say "this will happen" or "that won't happen". Taking complexity into account, we need to recognize a range of alternative futures as the basis for planning and systematic actions.

Professor Godet's work is an outstanding example of the integration of anticipation and planning for action. But his strengths as an analyst and as a planner go well beyond that. Too much of the study of the future - even today in this globalizing world - is parochial and provincial. Few British or American futurists, planners, and forecasters pay much or any attention to work done outside their national boundaries and even less attention to work done outside their native tongue. One of the accomplishments of Professor Godet is to work across cultures and across languages to give his work a value which is enhanced by his catholicity of perspective and broad embrace of materials.

By being cross-national in its orientation, Professor Godet's work is an unusual, if not unique, contribution to the management and futures literature. It draws on a wide range of experience and illustrations and offers a broader demonstration of techniques practised by corporations and other organizations than is generally found in other sources. Godet's work is an attractive integration of theory, the historical evolution of management and planning techniques, and the practical tools of the trade, all amply illustrated. Again, unlike other works in the field, Professor Godet offers a felicitous combination of technique and substance.

Beside the public of national and regional planners which is classical for UNESCO, the primary audience for Professor Godet's book are business and other organizational planners. The secondary, and nearly as important, audience are professors teaching courses in business schools in relation to planning and the future. Along that line, it might be noted that many American business schools have their curricula under reexamination and are moving to integrate futures thinking into the Master of Business Administration programme. Professor Godet's work should be a special, positive contribution to that new move.

The book should also find a substantial audience among individuals without planning responsibilities, who, out of curiosity or concern, seek a better understanding of the choices before us and the tools for exploring those choices.

Joseph F. Coates
Coates and Jarratt, Inc.
Washington, DC

SUMMARY

The future is not written anywhere. It has still to be built. Prospective thinking has nothing to do with the determinism of futurology (crystal ball) and of forecasting (modelling). Determination is essential in strategic prospective, and this implies not only reactivity, but also pre-activity and pro-activity.

What are the mainstreams of future thinking? How can errors in forecasting be avoided? This 'Handbook of Strategic Prospective' presents the main concepts and tools available to face uncertain futures and to master change. Most of the techniques used to build relevant consistent and likely scenarios in strategic management are described by means of concrete case studies. In other words this book is a plea for more rationality and pro-activity in thinking (a come-back of planning).

The author would like to thank Ms Valerie Shepherd for undertaking the revision of the English translation.

FROM ANTICIPATION TO ACTION

Contents

by Michel GODET

A Handbook of Strategic Prospective

CHAPTER I

FOR ANOTHER FUTURE

1. Dreams create reality

1.1. The dangers of being reactive and the benefits of being preactive and proactive
1.2. Using intuition and reason for planning and action
1.3. From anticipation to action by means of appropriation
1.4. Contingency and change : 1001 keys to excellence
1.5. Towards a revival of planning

2. Schools of prospective : models which endure despite fashion

2.1. The post-industrial school, between optimism and pessimism
2.2. The neo-Malthusian school of thought
2.3. Long waves and crises as bearers of hope
2.4. Bifurcations, determinism and creativity of chaos
2.5. Mutineers and mutants as the bearers of change

3. Schools of strategy : contradictory fashions, complementary models

3.1. The heuristic school : from common sense to the simplistic
3.2. The rationalist school : from success to misuse, pending a revival
3.3. Stop bad American soaps and Japanese curios

4. Spreading the cultures of prospective and strategy

5. One logic in ten chapters

1. Dreams create reality

This book is, above all, a manual of prospective and strategy ; its main aim is to provide simple, operational tools for the conspirator of the future, which potentially means all of us. What does this mean ? How can we reconcile intuition and reason ? How can we move from anticipation to action ? What are the keys to excellence ? What should we make of the successive fashions and models which dominate prospective and strategic thinking ? These are the main themes which we shall address in this introductory chapter, before outlining the book's format.

1.1. The dangers of being reactive and the benefits of being preactive and proactive

Unfortunately, anticipation is not widespread among managers. When all is going well they can manage without it, and when things are going badly it is too late to see any further than the end of one's nose : one has to react, and quickly.

However, reaction alone leads nowhere (remember Seneca's comment : 'There is no favourable wind for the man who knows not where he is going'). In other words, if there is no future direction the present is empty of meaning. This emptiness is frightening ; in the absence of a plan, too many managers thus find a constantly renewed outlet in the intoxication of action. Too many managers pedal like crazy from one stage to another, according to an itinerary imposed by the whim of circumstance. Absorbed in their efforts, with their noses at the handlebars, they no longer have the time to think. Eventually, in full swing and on the verge of exhaustion, they lose their balance. Let us reiterate : action in the short-term reality has no meaning unless it takes place in the long-term context of a plan, because 'the future is the raison d'être of the present'.

Prospective is above all an attitude of mind (anticipation and will) and a way of behaving (with imagination and hope) mobilized in order to ensure quality and control of our present and future existence. Prospective reinstates desire as the productive force of the future. If it has no future direction the present is empty of meaning. Thus, dreams do not oppose reality, they create it, and a plan animated by desire is the driving force for action.

1.2. Using intuition and reason for planning and action

Whilst reflection must not paralyse action, pilotage with vision/while keeping a look-out cannot replace strategy. It is because of past lack of anticipation that the present is full of questions, which yesterday were insignificant but which today are urgent and which have to be settled now, to the detriment of what is important for the future.

So it is time we stopped opposing pilotage with vision (intuition) and strategic pilotage (reason). Both are necessary ; it all depends on circumstances. A person cannot be reduced to a rational mind (the left brain) ; he is also driven by the emotional faculties (the right brain). Rational and heuristic schools of strategic thought are only apparently in opposition ; in fact they are complementary. If one or other is denied, a person's behaviour becomes crippled, because he now has only a debilitated thought faculty.

A sound initial reflection, imbued with relevance and coherence, reinforces the efficacity of action and reaction in the face of events. In the fire of action the time for reflection is limited to a few moments of intuition and reflex thought. Intuition is the lightning flash which springs from the right brain through the synthesis of information and analysis stored in the left brain ; hence the importance of initial reflection and of accumulating such reflection. The same applies to reflexes - they are better after intensive training.

Being reactive should not be confused with being flexible. The first is improvised as an organization's appropriate response to external hazards. The second is kept up as an intrinsic capacity of the organization to react and adapt to the environment without losing its direction. In other words, internal flexibility is the condition for external reactivity. The first derives from physical condition, the second from reflexes.

1.3. From anticipation to action by means of appropriation

Intellectual and emotional appropriation is a compulsory stage if anticipation is to crystallize into effective action. Thus we discover the three components of the Greek triangle : prospective thought gives content to mobilization, maintains motivation (motives for action) and nourishes strategic will.

We can define these three components as 'Logos' (thought, rationality, discourse), 'Epithumia' (desire in all its noble and not so noble aspects), 'Erga' (action and realization). The marriage of passion and reason, of heart and mind, is the key to success in action and to individual growth (the body).

Let us give the same message in colour : the blue of cold reason associated with the yellow of warm feeling produces the green of brilliant action. In the Greek triangle we find old debates which are still current. Thus men of thought complain about not having a grasp on action, and men of action complain that they lack the time for reflection.

One day we realized that the best ideas were those that people discovered by themselves. The phenomenon is well known : a good idea will move up the company hierarchy more easily if the boss believes it comes from him ; one should adopt this same reasoning with people one wishes to convince.

Any thinking which is not appropriated by those concerned and which relates to change will have difficulty crystallizing into effective strategic action. On the other hand, there must be a 'content' to be appropriated. Individual and collective motivation and mobilization are stronger and last longer when there is willingness to be drawn upon for a future project. The Greek triangle has its head at the base, in order to show that reason is not enough to ensure balanced action, and that passion is a necessary stage.

THE GREEK TRIANGLE

◊ PROSPECTIVE THOUGHT
◊ STRATEGIC WILL
◊ COLLECTIVE MOBILIZATION

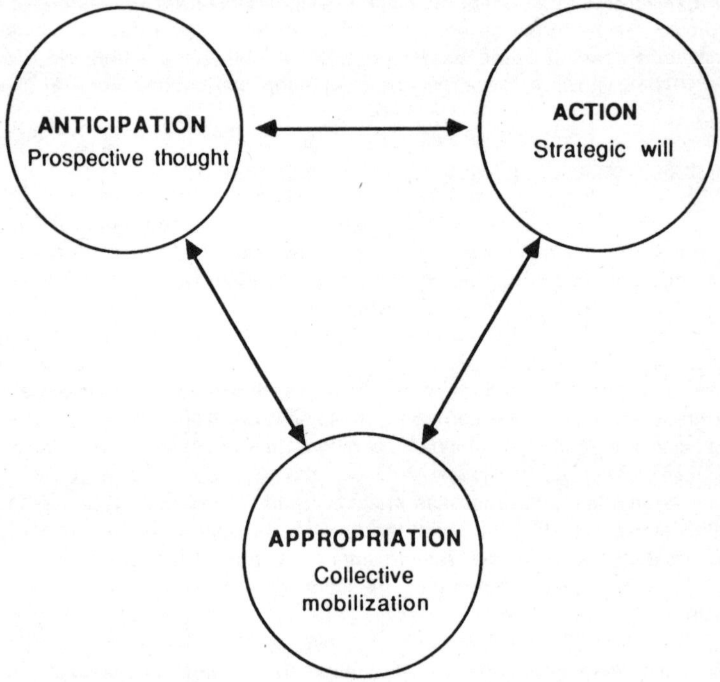

PROSPECTIVE GIVES CONTENT AND DIRECTION
TO COLLECTIVE MOBILIZATION

1.4. Contingency and change : 1001 keys to excellence

According to the principle of contingency[1], there are no universal key factors of excellence which are valid in all circumstances. For example, zero stock and Just-in-Time have been profitable aims for some companies, but also very expensive or even ruinous for others.

Management theorists should recall that statistics teach us not to confuse correlation with causality. It would appear that the authors of "*In Search of Excellence*" forgot this distinction. In their X-ray of successful US companies in 1980, they noted that these companies had various points in common which they immediately termed 'secrets of excellence'. Colinearity is not causality, however ; they should have examined whether poor performance companies also demonstrated these same characteristics. In fact, the majority of companies cited in "*In Search of Excellence*" experienced difficulties during the 1980s. Should we conclude from this that the secrets of excellence were actually the secrets of failure ?

Certainly not - it is simply a matter of recognizing the principle of contingency and admitting that there are combinations of human, organizational, technical and financial factors which are effective in a particular given context but which will not be so in other contexts. These combinations are multiple and change over time.

The only key factor of success whose permanence we can vouch for is precisely this principle of change, 'the source of diversity'. Blaise Pascal noted that 'boredom is born out of uniformity'. Variety is an indispensable stimulant for motivation - without it effectiveness is weak ; with it anything is possible. Remember the experiments of Elton Mayo in the 1930s : by increasing and then decreasing the light intensity in the factories of Western Electric he increased output each time.

A far-seeing manager is one who regularly introduces factors to break habits. In order to remain motivated a person needs to be permanently diverted and stimulated by challenges. Such challenges are more mobilizing if they are new, and more relevant if they form part of a coherent trajectory. This is how we should understand apparently disjointed attempts to mobilize the intelligence of organizations : leadership by objectives, participative management ; quality circles, company plans... All these attempts are marked by success and failure. In addition, reactivity and management in real time -which, as we have seen, it would be dangerous to make a religion of- can prove necessary and even miraculous in certain precise circumstances.

A universal key to excellence does not exist - it must be permanently remodelled according to environmental developments, counteracting the habits which fix organizations in the deep sleep of rigidity. What brought success yesterday could perhaps be the cause of failure tomorrow. In order to adapt to a changing world, we need to know how to change structures, behaviour and habits.

[1] Contingency : that which could not be, or which could be otherwise ; in other words, the opposite of necessity.

1.5. Towards a revival of planning

Any exclusive practice quickly becomes abusive, so managers must be careful to avoid becoming addicts of reactivity and real-time management. In plain language, we say yes to reactivity, but on the condition that it does not become an end in itself. Tactics, ie contingent decision making, should not take the place of strategy. From this point of view, the expression 'strategic reactivity' is a source of misunderstanding, as normally reactivity should be placed at the service of strategy. The same applies to so-called 'strategic management', a beautiful pleonasm, since by definition the aim of management is to put the organization at the service of strategy.

Strategic planning has been laid to rest by strategic management ; does this not point to an unconscious camouflaging of the lack of objectives and the loss of direction which characterize modern societies ? Not knowing where we want to go and why, we take pleasure in commentary - ie, in analysis of tactical ways and means to adapt in the face of change. The ship no longer has a prow, but the captain knows all the secrets of the tiller and the ship's instruments ; preactivity and proactivity are alien to him, he knows only the reactivity of strategic management.

Jean Cocteau put it so well : 'Fashion is what goes out of fashion'. Soon reactivity will have had its hour and we shall rediscover, perhaps with new words, the virtues of strategic planning - a skillful mix of voluntarism and flexibility. For this comeback to happen, the concept of the plan will first have to be definitively liberated from the bureaucratic corsets in which it has wrongly been laced.

2. Schools of prospective : models which endure despite fashion

It is not by chance that prospective is less sensitive to the effects of fashion than strategy. As a matter of fact the horizon of prospective is usually long term (defined as the horizon at which many things could have changed), whereas the horizon of strategy is generally shorter : fashion in clothing changes every year ; fashion in housing does not.

Although fashion is too ephemeral for prospective, it has nevertheless experienced different schools of thought over recent decades. Eric Philippart (1986) has written an excellent synthesis on this subject. Inspired by him we distinguish here four schools : post-industrial, neo-Malthusian, long waves, and bifurcations and chaos.

2.1. The post-industrial school, between optimism and pessimism

This school of thought, born in the 1960s, a time of rapid growth, is symbolized by the work of Daniel Bell (1973), "*The Coming of Post-Industrial Society : a Venture in Social Forecasting*". The book's sub-title is not neutral ; it conveys the idea that change, particularly technological change, can be accelerated and controlled by forecasting and planning. The methods exist - Erich Jantsch (1967) made a survey of them at OECD. This school of thought, on the whole highly optimistic, had been championed several years earlier by a book by Herman Kahn and Anthony Wiener (1967) on the year 2000 (ie, the equivalent of 2025 today). Kahn remained extremely optimistic until his death. His last book was "*The Resourceful Earth : a Response to Global 2000*" (ie, a response to a report to the US President published in 1980, which was very pessimistic about future ecosystems).

Alvin Toffler is probably part of this school of thought. A talented journalist, he received tremendous media exposure with "*Future Shock*" (1971), which was subsequently enhanced with his new books, particularly "*The Third Wave*" (1980). The key to success is simple : extrapolate technological change and announce the best sometimes, and often the worst. As a good journalist, he knows that 'bad news is good news'. So in "*Future Shock*" he wrote :

'We are at the dawn of an international revolution which will overthrow parliaments and houses of congress in the coming decade. But this raising of shields against the ravages of the ill-managed application of technology could crystallize into a pathological form, like a futurephobic Fascism under whose regime men of science would replace Jews in the concentration camps'.

We shall make no further comment !

None of this was very serious, but it did have the merit of making people think. Forecasting and planning's infatuation with controlling the future came to an end with the oil shocks and the economic crisis. However, several years later, at the end of the 1970s, the champions of the third industrial revolution which it was believed would ensue thanks to new information technologies, biotechnologies and new materials, rekindled the flame of the post-industrial society. Daniel Bell kept silent, and technological determinism was reborn out of his ashes. It was a vehicle for unfounded cliches about the society of tomorrow, such as the qualifications required for future professions. Tomorrow's jobs would be in the services, linked to the major trends of modern societies (ageing, leisure, security), which meant, in particular, care in the home, house maintenance, gardening - all jobs where competition and demand for quality would impose high standards of professionalism, which should not, however, be confused with high qualifications.

2.2. The neo-Malthusian school of thought

This school of thought was characterized by the Club of Rome, founded in 1968 by industrialists, academics, high-level civil servants... In a way this school of thought is also the heir of the 1960s wave of rationalism. It rested on the technique of system dynamics, developed at MIT by Jay Forrester. The first report of the Club of Rome by Meadows (1972), "*The Limits to Growth*", had an explosive impact. Exponential growth could no longer continue, resources would run out and the world would collapse under demographic pressure. The report did not really pose the right questions, but it did have the merit of provoking a great debate, although it was quickly eclipsed by the economic crisis.

OECD's "*Interfutures*" Report, produced under Jacques Lesourne in 1978, showed that there were not really any physical limits to growth, but more particularly problems of regulation on the global scale in an interdependent world where, according to Daniel Bell's famous phrase : 'Governments have become too small for the big problems, and too big for the small problems .

Ecology was part of these big problems, and the "*Global 2000 report*" (1980) began with the following terrible prediction : 'if current trends continue, the world in the year 2000 will be more polluted, more congested...'. In an interview in 1982 Gerald Barney, the author of the report, revealed to us that this first phrase had been censored - that is, remodelled ; the original version was 'if current policies continue... , which is not at all the same thing. The diagnosis was much less fatalistic but also more accusatory of those who govern us. So the authors of "*Interfutures*" were right - it was regulation which was lacking.

Since the end of the 1970s there have been two other schools of thought : long wave theory and bifurcation theory.

2.3. Long waves and crises as bearers of hope

The theory of long waves re-established Kondratiev's analyses which explained successive waves of growth and recession by waves of innovation. Each phase of the growth-recession cycle would last for about 25 years. Thus, after the high growth of 1950-1974, there would be a trail across the desert until the 1990s. Then would begin the era of a fifth Kondratiev cycle supported by the technological revolution which had been latent since the 1970s. This theory of technological long waves spawned the neo-Schumpeterian gurus, well represented by the works of Christopher Freeman (1974) and Scherer (1981), or in France the so-called regulation school. These works generally emphasized socio-organizational obstacles, ie, the rigidities opposing transformation of production structures and curbing the structural changes which the new technologies would necessitate.

Part of my own earlier work to a certain extent descended from this line - but not totally, for I emphasized above all the actors (in crisis) facing systems (undergoing change). From this perspective, crisis is perceived both as the consequence of rigidities and as the main lever to overcome them by changing our habits, structures, and behaviour. Crises are bearers of hope and capitalism is a perpetual hurricane of creative destruction (to quote Schumpeter). The titles of my books over the years - "*Demain les crises*" ("*Tomorrow Crises*") (1980), "*Crises are Opportunities*" (1985), and (with Jacques Lesourne) "*La fin des habitudes*" ("*The End of Habits*") (1985) - provide a good resume of my interpretation of crises and change.

But there is a fundamental difference between this work and that of the supporters of long waves and some of their gurus. I have always challenged technological determinism, which in our modern societies has taken over from the religious determinism of the past (with the technological fairy replacing God).

There is no fatalism. There are, on one hand, forces of change and, on the other, forces of inertia. Often these are in opposition and we speak of resistance to change or (economically, socially) non-viable change, depending on which is in favour. Structures and behaviour are characterized by strong inertia which curbs adaptation and evolution and then becomes rigidity if change (whether desired or not) has not been prepared for well in advance.

If long waves exist, they are socio-organizational rather than technological, ie they are linked to the non-linear rhythms of societies and people. Unlike people, society shows no regularity between cycles of sleep and intense activity. Random external and internal circumstances can precipitate evolution in an unexpected direction and, for example, give power to certain actors who, armed solely with their will and their plans, manage to overturn the course of events and cause bifurcations.

The collapse of the communist regimes in the countries of Eastern Europe provides a good example of bifurcation - it was unforeseen and nothing enabled us to forecast it, even though the forces which led to the splitting up of the empire had been spotted a long time ago (I refer to the work by Hélène Carrère d'Encausse (1979), "*L'empire éclaté*" ("*The Empire Explodes*").

It was assumed that these forces were only at work over the very long term and scenarios of violent disturbances and repression were imagined, but never scenarios of almost calm evolution, with a forced march towards pluralist democracy and the market economy. Barely a few months ago it was supposed that German reunification would inevitably be accompanied by the neutralization of Germany and the finlandization of Western Europe... Today's reality has overtaken yesterday's fiction. It is Eastern Europe that is westernizing and the former East Germany which is joining NATO. We rejoice at all this. However, the new equilibrium is unstable and could lead to other dangerous bifurcations, particularly in Russia and the new republics where internal diffuculties are weakening the reformist forces. We should not forget the lesson of history : external war often served as an outlet for internal contradictions.

The prospectivist will bear in mind that one should remain modest in the face of the future - that nothing is ever hopeless or established, and that probably part of what is still fiction today will be reality tomorrow. Which part, where and how ? We shall not reply recklessly, but say simply that one must remain ready to face any eventuality, which means, for example, not letting down one's guard on the subject of European defence.

2.4. Bifurcations, determinism and creativity of chaos

At the time when these upheavals are occurring (still contingencies), the bifurcation and chaos theories from the hard sciences (mathematics, physics, biology) are encroaching into the social sciences.

It all began at the end of the last century with the work of the mathematician Poincaré (1889-1908). He showed that certain systems of parametric equations had no stable solution, but an infinite number of unstable solutions, which could go from one extreme to another as a function of the parameters and of time. This is Poincaré's 'mathematical indeterminism'. Thus, there exist sets of equations which are sensitive to the initial conditions whose solutions diverge in a chaotic manner. It is also to Poincaré that we owe the notion of the 'diagram of bifurcations'.

We note in passing that there is a double uncertainty here : uncertainty over the measurement of the initial conditions and uncertainty over the consequences of this lack of precision for the calculation of the solutions. In such systems, determinism would be hidden, would have all the appearance of chance, and would in any case remain indeterminable (if only because of the lack of precision of the original measurement). Much later these ideas were taken up again by Lorenz (1961) in simulating weather forecasting models. He showed that a slight initial fluctuation could reverberate in an exponential and chaotic way over time. This idea was made famous by the image of the 'butterfly effect', according to which the simple beating of a butterfly's wing in one part of the world could in an extreme case cause a storm in another part some weeks or months later. Thus we once again have the idea of a 'deterministic chaos'.

In the 1970s Ilya Prigogine and Isabelle Stengers (1979) used the theories and experiments of thermodynamics and physical chemistry to go further and develop the concepts of 'order through fluctuation' and 'creative chaos' (Prigogine, 1990). They showed that, 'far from the initial conditions of equilibrium', there appeared bifurcations leading to other equilibria. Near these critical points, slight internal or external fluctuations in the system can be decisive in determining whether movement is towards one branch of evolution or another. Transposed to social systems, these slight fluctuations could be, for example, chance disturbances or individual actions. At these critical points 'fluctuations are dangerous', whereas otherwise they could remain insignificant.

This reading of social systems based on analysis of the evolution of physical systems is interesting for prospective in that it reconciles determinism on the one hand (the system has a history which conditions its future possible trajectories, and leads to one diagram of bifurcations rather than another), and freedom on the other (in the bifurcation zone insignificant actions, caused by chance or by free will, can set off major upheavals). Outside these critical points, fluctuations are not events. In these new interpretations of evolution, chance, necessity and free will, alternately and together, play a determining role.

Other scientists from biology, such as Henri Atlan (1979), participated in this movement, implicitly taking up once again Darwin's principle of natural selection, adaptation and diversity (1859). Certain chance mutations (fluctuations) within living systems constitute events. Events can also result from fluctuations in the environment and cause new adaptations -'complexity through noise'- that is, a superior variant of the organism/superior mode of diversity in the system. Chance is the driving force of evolution, and noise becomes information. In short, this is 'chance as organizer'.

Is it possible to adapt these descriptive theories of the evolution of physical or biological systems to explain the transformation of social systems ? With the current state of knowledge we have to answer in the negative, which is just as well. It is not that we are veiling our faces in horror and retreating into some kind of obscurantism (rejecting science and its advances). It is simply that the real world is much too complex for us to hope that one day we will be able to find an equation to explain its hidden determinism. Even if we could, the inherent uncertainty over any measurement, especially social measurements, would mean that, at least in our minds, the range of possible futures would remain wide open ; rightly or wrongly, this is our mental image of the famous 'diagram of bifurcations'.

So we have to act as if chaotic determinism did not exist and take action in order to move in the direction of those evolutionary branches which seem desirable to us. We prefer Pascale's bet and the myth of Sisyphus tirelessly pushing his rock to the fatality of determinism. The expression 'chaotic determinism' seems doubly unacceptable to us, since it renders human will powerless in the face of the dual games of necessity and chance.

Bifurcation and chaos theory above all demonstrate, *ex post*, that change in structure corresponds to one solution of a system of differential equations - for a given value of the environmental parameters. However, *ex ante* the question remains, what will be the value of these environmental parameters and their eventual evolution ? This problem has to be overcome in order to determine whether the future which will materialize out of the range of possible futures is a rupture, a disaster, or not.

This is precisely the aim of prospective - to determine what could be the values of the environmental parameters, taking account of forces at work and actors' plans, ie, what are the possible, realizable and desirable scenarios regardless of any offence these might cause.

Bifurcation and chaos theory relaunched 'La querelle du déterminisme' (the quarrel about determinism), to quote the title of the collective work published by the journal "*Le Débat*" (1990). The resolute rejection of determinism in the social sciences should not, however, lead to a restraint on research in fundamental science. Rene Thom, the author of catastrophe theory[2], seems to be isolated in this quarrel. Yet he is right to say that : 'Determinism in science is not a given, it is a conquest. The enthusiasts of chance are apostles of desertion' (cf. his article in the issue of "*Le Débat*" (1990), entitled 'Halte au hasard, silence au bruit' (Let us halt chance and silence noise).

Many European readers did not come across this debate, which is now so fashionable, until the highly publicized success of the book on chaos theory by American journalist James Gleick (1987). The bestselling management authors sensed that it was a goldmine, and in 1989 Tom Peters published "*Chaos Management*".

---

[2] The phrase 'catastrophe theory' has made a fortune, but it is often misunderstood, because of the very strong impact on the imagination of the word 'catastrophe'. For Thom, a catastrophe is the disappearance of one equilibrium and the establishment of a consecutive one with a continued modification of potential. Simple examples are provided by the passing from a liquid state to a solid or gaseous state, or the metamorphosis of the chrysallis into a butterfly (it is the same but it is completely different). On this subject we share the views of mathematician Ivar Eckeland (1984) :

Catastrophe theory has no vocation to be normative or even to predict ... it does not announce anything, not even catastrophes ... the success of this theory rests partly on an initial misunderstanding caused by the magic of words.

In 1986 Eric Phillipart wrote : 'In the USA, the utilization of these concepts seems still to be limited to the adoption of new metaphors (without attempting to demonstrate the validity of this procedure) as an easy way of giving discussions otherwise lacking in great originality the appearance of novelty'.

In Europe chaos theory is favoured by the media. It is true that the vocabulary lends itself to journalistic emphasis and whets the appetite with words which make us dream, such as 'strange attractors', 'fractals', 'bifurcation cascades', 'the butterfly effect', etc... or which inspire fear, such as 'noise', 'disorder', 'catastrophe', 'chaos'.

It is always good to enrich one's vocabulary, especially when these concepts echo well established mathematical conventions or physical mechanisms. The scientists who write on these subjects generally respect the potential and the limits of these concepts. They only venture to transpose them into the social domain as questions, and with extreme caution.

They will nevertheless be reproached for not always giving the same meaning to the same words - giving rise to misunderstandings which cause epic quarrels between specialists about chance, determinism, etc... Unfortunately, in the field of social sciences the 'fluctuation' in the movement of ideas brought about by bifurcation and chaos theory has only added to the disorder and confusion in 'houses' where the housekeeping of ideas leaves much to be desired.

We are still a long way from the 'science of complexity' hailed by some experts (cf. Roy Amara, 1984). Meanwhile it is primarily complication that we are confronting. In fact, complexity has become a great cooking pot into which we haphazardly throw all the concepts we find on the table of advanced ideas (epistemology, information theory, thermodynamics, dissipative structures, bifurcations and of course chaos, not to mention self-organization). To give the resulting soup a reputation of good cuisine we invoke the names of all the saints (scholars, intellectuals) who protect these concepts. But we forget that they are not all from the same church. Thus, the so-called 'science of complexity' is rather like a new religion which claimed to be superior because it borrowed from Islam, Christianity, Buddhism, etc ... It is an idea that we should ponder over no longer that we would over esperanto.

Representational models do not escape the vagaries of fashion, and fashion always relies on models. This is as true for prospective as it is for strategy and management - except that prospective has a greater propensity for models, and strategy has a greater sensitivity to fashion.

2.5. Mutineers and mutants as the bearers of change

Where should we place prospective in relation to these schools of thought ? It has to be said that prospective constitutes an unclassifiable mosaic which borrows the most illuminating aspects of various readings.

From religious determinism prospective retains the fact that the question of why (the clockmaker) is not raised by the answers to the question of how (the clock).

Science is advancing but the idea of God does not recede, it continues to assert itself as a defence against the absurd.

The theory of evolution has brought to prospective the principles of natural selection and adaptation, which have lost none of their modernity, for both individuals and for organizations facing international competition, as Hubert Landier has shown clearly (1987). The mechanisms exist ; it is up to us to make use of them for our own benefit, to adapt to and to transform our environment.

Actors are not disarmed in the face of systems, they can act either to drive or to restrain evolution. The inertias of structures, behaviour and habits are such that often it is necessary to destroy former organizations in order to create new ones.

From chaotic determinism prospective will retain bifurcations and the possibility that certain mutineers or mutants may be bearers of change : 'Not any individual, idea or behaviour, but the "dangerous" ones, that are able to use for their own benefit those non-linear relations which would ensure the stability of the former average state' (Prigogine and Stengers, 1979).

How are we to recognize bifurcation points : 'Which events, which innovations will remain without consequence, which others are capable of affecting the whole system and determining irreversibly the choice of evolution ; where are the zones of choice, and the zones of stability ?' These are the questions which make up the daily menu of prospective. When we identify the range of possible futures are we not also recognizing the diagram of bifurcations ? Are not the parameters of bifurcations also the key variables of prospective analysis ?

Since determinism is indeterminable, we must act as if nothing had been set in motion, as if only the rebellion of free will could overturn the tyranny of chance and necessity.

For some years we have noticed that scientific work has been converging on the concept of self-organization. What are we to make of this new fashion of self-organization ? Is its success due to the fact that it is both suggestive and fuzzy ? It is as much an echo of Fourierism or workers' struggles as it is of cybernetics (Von Foerster) or Prigogine's 'order through fluctuation'. Now it is penetrating economic science (cf. Jacques Lesourne 1990). In its new acceptance it forms part of the galaxy of concepts mentioned above.

What is it all about ? For Jean-Pierre Dupuy (1982) 'The self-organizing process seems to be result of interaction between an autonomous structure and chance events which are extraneous to it. Because it thus allows adaptation to the new and to production again self-organization achieves, at least locally, a reversal of time's arrow'.

This 'reversal of time's arrow' is no more than what prospective means by 'The future is the raison d'être of the present'. In other words, we can say that desire as the productive force of the future is also the main driving force of self-organization.

3. Schools of strategy : contradictory fashions, complementary models

Fashion has a short memory. Many ideas on organizational management and strategy are worthy of the famous comment recalled by Georges Yves Kervern (1986) : 'Good ideas and new ideas, unfortunately, are not the same thing'. In fact, in strategic circles new things are often not interesting and interesting things are often not new, as we can see if we look back to the sources of military strategic thinking (Clausewitz, General Beaufre...), and to the founders of managerial thinking at the beginning of this century (Fayol, Taylor, Mary Parker Follet).

On this subject, Michel Crozier (1990) remarks that, despite its inadequacy, 'fashion offers new ways of responding to the new problems' which regularly appear and as a result of which former problems go out of fashion. Of course these new problems are partly generated by the excesses of previous fashions. Thus, fashion is renewed and destroyed by the successive waves of rigour and imagination which by turns are elevated as dogma.

It has to be said that this succession is only apparent to specialists, and that consumers dress themselves from one source and another in strategy's ready-to-wear boutiques, depending on their history, their resources and the information available to them. Some still choose goal-oriented planning or strategically segmented profit centres (linking the product with the market), others go for company plans together with quality circles. In order to be like the Japanese, some even go so far as to turn the company into a place of regimentation and psychological conditioning. Heads of companies believe themselves to be messiahs and hammer out their 'ten commandments'.

The reality is simply a mixture of all this, confused rather than intelligent, where we juxtapose the pieces of the puzzle but do not really manage to put them together. The right and left brain form a whole which cannot be dissociated. Warm values (enthusiasm, charisma, desire, plans, will) and cold values (reason, analysis, calculation, forecasting) are not in opposition but complement and mutually reinforce each other.

This fact resurfaces throughout the literature on management. We can quote the excellent Riboud report (1988) "*Modernisation, mode d'emploi*" ("*Modernization : directions for use*") : 'Today there are companies perfoming well in all branches of industry, even the most vulnerable. It is firstly a question of people with indisputable professional credibility and proven charisma. Today, motivation of people is the *sine qua non* condition for effectiveness and profitability... People are motived if their deep-seated aspirations are respected. To do this, managers must listen to them and, through negotiated agreements, arrange with them proposed objectives and positive sanctions. They should neglect neither the aspiration to be nor the aspiration to have'.

This complementarity does not prevent division, or rather a dialogue of the deaf, between, on one hand, supporters of a rationalist approach (economic analysis, operational research, segmentation, portfolio analysis, planning) and, on the other, supporters of an approach fittingly called heuristic by Marie-José Avenier (1985), because one of its fundamental principles is to act and then to learn from action. We shall stick to these terms which are very close to those suggested by other authors, such as Thomas Durand (1985) and Alain Charles Martinet (1984).

3.1. The heuristic school : from common sense to the simplistic

The heuristic approach excited worldwide interest with the success of the book by Peters and Waterman (1982) "*In Search of Excellence*", and in France with the first book by Herve Serieyx (1982) "*Mobiliser l'intelligence de l'entreprise*" ("*Mobilizing corporate intelligence*"), and his second book, written with Georges Archier (1984), "*L'entreprise du troisième type*" ("*The company of the third kind*"). These books insist, rightly, on the importance of the human factor -which managers must know how to motivate, mobilize, make responsible- the indispensability of listening to the customer, and the necessity of (perceived) quality of products and services.

For supporters of the heuristic approach, thought should not be allowed to paralyse action. They claim that the clever methods of the rationalist approach have often led to failure. They prefer to proceed by trial and error, by an incremental approach, developing what works and abandoning what doesn't. So far so good, but care should be taken not to throw the baby out with the bathwater.

The deficiencies of strategic pilotage must not lead to pilotage by sight. There must be a meaning to the mobilization of people ; it is not an end in itself, flexibility and piloting by sight lead nowhere. Moreover, rationalists were quickly able to poke fun at their detractors. In fact, in autumn 1984 a famous "*Business Week*" article tempered initial enthusiasm for the secrets of excellence : a significant proportion of the companies presented by Peters and Waterman in 1982 as successful examples of collective mobilization were in difficulty. Here was proof that the gymnastics of collective mobilization are not sufficient to ensure flexibility and performance in all circumstances : in addition anticipation of change and planning of strategy and innovation are necessary.

A sound initial reflection, imbued with relevance and coherence, reinforces the efficacity of action and reaction in the face of events. In the fire of action the time for reflection is limited to a few moments of intuition and reflex thought. Intuition is the lightning flash which springs from the right brain through synthesis of information and analysis stored in the left brain ; hence the importance of initial reflection and of accumulating such reflection. The same applies to reflexes - they are better after intensive training.

Accused of gross simplification, some champions of the heuristic approach reply that their message is still too complex. Carried away by their 'passion for excellence', they turn it into a religion and their book becomes a catechism where company heads are transformed into mythical heroes playing the role of apostles. They thus forget that enthusiastic mobilization around charismatic leaders is not an end in itself, and that flexibility cannot replace strategy. The Gospel according to Saint Mac had the fate it deserved at the pen of Georges Yves Kervern (1986).

The Gospel grew by 610 pages in one fell swoop with Tom Peters' book, "*Chaos Management*" (1989). The author does not beat about the bush. This book, he writes :

"... throws into question all the concepts of management. Today, flexibility and a passion for change must replace our inclination for mass production, destined for mass markets and based on the possibility (long past) of making relatively reliable forecasts... tomorrow's champions will move ahead of chaos'.

This is total delirium - all the more paradoxical as the success of this kind of book is precisely the result of the effectiveness of a system of mass production and distribution (sales in garage and airport kiosks). In the form of pilotage by sight the heuristic approach is quite insufficient and may lead to worse just as easily as better.

3.2. The rationalist school : from success to misuse, pending a revival

As Marie-José Avenier has quite correctly written (1985) 'If there is a dearth of literature on the operating modes of pilotage, we are, on the other hand, witnessing a veritable burgeoning of practical tools'. These planning tools are well-known : life cycle, the experience effect, strategic segmentation, portfolio analysis, multicriteria choice, etc... the panoply has recently been enriched by competitive analysis, value chains and competence trees, and it's not finished yet, since scenarios from elsewhere (prospective) are now disembarking on Planet Strategy.

These rational methods found great success in the 1960s and 1980s. They had the great merit of imposing a common language and relevant modes of reasoning which allowed generations of managers to be trained in strategy. Since then the concepts of segmentation, of milch cows and of stars have been part of all managers' vocabularies.

The champions of the rational methods often went too far, however. They were tempted to present one scenario or another as the universal key to strategic analysis. Reality rebels against panaceas and always contradicts theory with solid counter-examples.

Thus, for example, according to the experience effect cited by the Boston Consulting Group, companies having the strongest market share should be the most competitive. How then can we explain the better performance of smaller companies with a weak market share ? The answer is probably to be found in the area of innovation and in the diversification which it permits. Is not the accumulation of experience with a given technology and mode of production a source of rigidity, a brake on evolution ?

The effects of volume, quality and innovation all, to a greater or lesser extent, play a role in profitability, as the authors of the PIMS method (databank on the performance of companies which can be used for simulation) have shown cf. Pierre Buigues (1983) and Alain Thietard (1984).

The Gospel according to Saint Mac by G. Y. Kervern
Annales des Mines - Gérer et Comprendre - March 1986

'Good ideas and new ideas, unfortunately, are not the same thing'. This cruel phrase, which certain professors amuse themselves by writing on their students' work, would not be cut of place describing the writings of the Apostles of Excellence, the celebrated Thomas J. Peters and Robert W. Waterman, both educated at the school of Mc Kinsey and admired advocates of what could be called The Gospel according to Saint Mac, which has sold in its millions. The Gospel runs to 806 pages ; 306 pages for the Old Testament, *"In Search of Excellence"* (Intereditions, 1983) ; 446 pages for the New Testament, (*"The Passion for Excellence"*), (Intereditions, 1985), Tom Peters' last born.

Among those ideas which are good but not new, we find ourselves confronted with 'what every chief executive should know' : be a good boss, take care of your clients, look after your staff, be vigilant about quality, simplify as much as possible, do what you know how to do, decentralize, and use small motivated groups for innovation.

These are the much-vaunted wonders of excellence which everybody is talking about today as if this were a historic discovery in the annals of management. We can certainly rejoice that these basic truths have been esteemed so highly. We may deplore the fact that they are sometimes ignored by certain chief executives. We can be glad that our US competitors have a tendency to ignore them. We may tremble at the idea that the Japanese are putting them scrupulously into practice. But do we need to pay $12 000 for each conference devoted to the articulation of these holy principles ?

Among those ideas which are new but not good, at least two are currently enjoying a great *succès d'estime*, in California at any rate :

- mistrust of human reason
- mistrust of respect for rules.

These two ideas have culminated in the paradigm of the 'skunk'. For the authors of *excellence*, a skunk today refers to individuals who pursue a highly creative activity on the margins of a company's formal systems.

There are two rules in the skunk catechism :

- act first, ask questions later ;
- 'cheating' is OK, and more efficient.

The skunk thus has short ideas. His drug is action, his slogan KISS (Keep It Simple and Stupid). The word 'stupid' is very important since it accurately sums up the mistrust of the rational model which forms a basis for that 'coming revolution'. Let's pray that this KISS, apologist for the rough and ready and the stupid, does not turn out to be the KISS of Death for Science and Management.

Each tool of the rationalist approach is partly true but also partly false. The degree to which it will be one or the other depends on many other factors, internal and external to the company, which cause the latter to be understood as an element of a system, of a network, or even of a network of actors and system. In this context, Georges Yves Kervern and Jean Pierre Ponssard have noted (1990) : 'The search for rationality therefore becomes the search for a language adapted to an imperfect state of knowledge which it is nevertheless in one's interest to share in order to structure collective action'. In other words, the rational approach must pollinate the heuristic approach to give action the intelligence, analysis and thought which it lacks. In this way we find the complementarity between these two currents, mentioned above, which it is useless to oppose. Strategic pilotage needs the compass, instruments and maps of the rationalist school of thought.

3.3. Stop bad American soaps and Japanese curios

The rationalist and heuristic schools have a tendency to follow fashion and to forget the experience of the past. Thus the SWOT approach of looking at external strengths, weaknesses (human, technical, financial), external opportunities and threats, which we owe largely to the pioneering work of Igor Ansoff (1965) has appeared out-of-date to some people. It's all very well to speak of value chains, competitive environmental chains, strategic positioning, or the mobilization of people ; to start with, one should really know one's products, one's markets, one's costs and one's human, technical and financial resources. The strategic diagnosis's prescription depends above all on the conclusions of this classic check-up. This is how celebrated books speak of business strategy, without saying a word about financial or human aspects.

Speaking frankly, after many and careful readings, I am convinced : most best-sellers in the field of management are the equivalent of American TV serials. These 'products', usually 'made in the USA' repeat the obvious, which is applicable to everybody, and from general conclusions draw simplistic examples which are easy to understand without any great effort. They are sold in airports like magazines. Let us hope that these intellectual sandwiches don't spoil the appetite of those just starting out. For the rest, they are not dangerous, since they contain virtually nothing worth remembering.

Most commonly in these works, usually several hundred pages long, an avalanche of uninteresting maxims of the type, 'the boss puts his desk in the middle of the typing pool' (Tom Peters and Nancy Austin) substitutes for demonstration. But, you will say, this definitive comment is particularly applicable to the heuristic school. Alas, not really !

In fact, certain stars of the rational school, like Michael Porter, only partly escape criticism. It is not the content which is wanting, it is the spirit of synthesis - and the reader finds him or herself drowning in a tide of analytical details. Thus, for example, in the interplay of actors in the competitive environment (Michael Porter, 1980), it takes some time to realize that the author is repeating the same thing over and over again by considering, each time, each one of the actors in relation to all the others. Reasoning is diluted by the encyclopedic volume of the writing. The prudent and efficient reader contents him or herself with the summaries. At the same time, in-depth criticism is becoming rare. One needs to go right to the end and keep a clear head to notice, for instance, that the firm is scarcely ever approached from the angle of its financial reality and human identity !

Mischievous tongues are proposing a remedy for the tedium of American soaps on management : wait for the next episode (book), which will have the same defects but the advantage of starting with a short resume of the previous episode. The latest vogue to date consists of marrying management with chaos [theory] (Tom Peters (1989)). We already discussed what we think of this unconsummated marriage (cf. schools of prospective).

As with a firework display, we must end this introduction with the finale announced right at the beginning. This involves one of the most famous Japanese curios, a 'true lie' which made directors tremble, shook politicians and filled the front page of magazines : everyone gulped it down and it continues to circulate worldwide.

Let's tell this incredible tale. Everything started with those terrible comments attributed to the Japanese President Matshushita : 'We are going to win and the industrialized west will lose. You can no longer do much about it because you carry the seeds of your defeat within yourselves. Your organizations are Taylorist, but worse still, so are your heads ... whereas we are post-Taylorists'...[3].

Widely quoted since the middle of the 1980s, these comments provided a salutary electric shock to the brain : Japan's advance could be explained by its management model, which must first be understood in order then to draw inspiration from it. However, it has been known since 1987 that this text is a 'true lie' - its author, H. Serieyx, revealed it in his preface to a book by Isabelle Orgogozo (1987) and confirmed it in 1989 in a new book entitled "*Zéro Mépris*" ("*Zero Scorned*").

Thus the Japanese system of management would have become a real fashion based on a false model. It would be a kind of rumour, but it is well known that, in order to circulate, rumours need to echo realities. We know that Japanese courtesy is falsely modest and often hides suppressed arrogance. The text was plausible. What a shame ! For once a Japanese seemed to be telling us a few home truths.

The story would have stopped here if I hadn't been invited by the Management Centre of Europe in June 1990 to speak to 300 managers from around the world who had come to Paris for the sole purpose of listening to eminent people such as Henry

[3] This text was cited by G. Archier and H. Serieyx in *L'entreprise du Troisième Type*, Seuil, 1984 - with the subtitle *'A Japanese President's speech'*, then, without quite knowing how, rumour attributed it to President Matshushita. For the sake of completeness, the rest of the text is given here. The ideas and style of Herve Serieyx are easily discernible. *'You are totally persuaded that you make your businesses function well by distinguishing bosses on one side, executives on the other, thinkers on one side, those who sit tight on the other. For you, management is the art of making the bosses' ideas pass conveniently into the hands of the workers. We are post-Taylorists, we know that business has become so complicated, so difficult, and the survival of a firm so problematic in an increasingly dangerous, unexpected and competitive environment, that a firm must mobilize the intelligence of everyone every day to have a chance of making it. For us, management is precisely the art of mobilizing and stacking up all this total intelligence in the service of the company project'.*

Kissinger make pronouncements on the prizes to be won and lost today. Among the speakers, I had the opportunity to listen to R. T. Pascale (1984), Harvard professor, recognized as one of the best specialists on Japan and its management model. Surprise was followed by inward shock -in the middle of his speech, he let loose, in English, the infamous quotation attributed to President Matshushita. What was I to think ? What was to be done- but sound the alarm and check what was going on ? By questioning Pascale's assistant, I discovered that he had only been using the quotation for two or three years, while his last interview with President Matshushita had taken place in 1982. Persevering, I pushed curiosity so far as to (discreetly) challenge R. T. Pascale himself. Visibly embarrased -to his credit- he told me that in fact 'he had one day read this 10-line text' (the English version is word for word the same as the French). He added, in connection with something else that he 'had met president Matshushita in 1982 and that the latter, who was very old, spoke English almost inaudibly'. However, what he 'believed he understood from the President, corresponded exactly to what he had later read as one of his pronouncements'. Perhaps Joan of Arc has rivals across the Atlantic !

To clinch the matter I nevertheless reported all this to H. Serieyx, who laughed heartily and swore to me that we were definitely dealing with a 'true lie' (and not 'a false true-lie'), and that he had not translated some obscure US journalist. H. Serieyx specified that the quotation had been in circulation and published since 1978, after an authentic trip to Japan, in a business review.

Will this denial succeed in snuffing out the rumour ? Rumour is already playing for time by putting the denial in doubt. Who knows Hervé Serieyx in the USA ? Not, in any case, Professor Pascale's assistant, who happens to be French-born : 'Never heard of him' was her comment. Americans are ignorant of work not written in English, ie the greater part of the world's writing...

This true-false text is only one of a number of Japanese pronouncements used as references or bogies[4]. We are dealing with a real management fashion based on a false model. What share does reality have in the images we receive of Japanese management ?

In order to explain the formidable competitiveness of Japanese firms, we should first cite the will to work to escape the privations of the 1950s, the memory of which is still fresh in people's minds. Japan has no other resources than people and their labour. 'Just in time' production methods were developed there because of the acute lack of space and the cost of maintaining physical stocks caused by the very high price of land (four-fifths of Japan comprises uninhabited wooded mountains). This is why Japanese factories are so compact, which requires great efforts in organizing production but ultimately improves productivity. This model should not be engraved on tablets of stone ; the South Koreans are often more competitive than the Japanese, with huge factories where zero stock is not the rule.

Concepts of productivity and quality have been imported from the USA where, in the 1950s, productivity was the highest in the world. Since no-one is a prophet in his own land, it was at Japan that the Americans W. E. Deming and J. M. Juran, considered the fathers of the concept of quality, aimed their applied ideas, cf. Dimitri Weiss

[4] I have written a book on this subject, with Pierre Noel Giraud (1987) entitled *Radioscopie du Japon*.

(1988). At first, it was a question of small groups responsible for improving processes and products at the most general levels. But the idea of 'total quality', ie literally of quality 'of everything together', soon became indispensable and was treated as a collective goal for which responsibility was shared, rendering the very notion of quality control useless (when speaking of the same thing, US authors tend to use the word 'excellence'). If quality has had such success in Japan, it is also for preventative reasons : Japanese products are exported worldwide without the need to develop costly networks of after-sales service.

Other pillars of the Japanese management system have been advanced to explain the success of its companies. First and foremost, employment for life, which in reality only involves a fifth of wage-earners but testifies above all to the attachment and quasi-feudal loyalty of employees to their company.

The Japanese does not exist as an individual but as a member of a group, a clan. This is the context in which we should re-locate another pillar of the Japanese management system : consensus. Group pressure is essential to explain the apparent social harmony which reigns in Japanese society and companies. Certain sayings like 'hammering down the nail which sticks out' illuminate the conditions under which the famous consensus is achieved. In addition to the official control of hierarchy : 'being beaten on the head', there is the unofficial but omnipresent control of colleagues : 'being pulled by the feet'.

How could people not stay in line under such conditions ? In each case it is a question of doing as the others do : not leaving the office before one's colleagues, not behaving differently. Thus the famed consensus is less the result of negotiation than the fruit of a collective self-censuring where each renounces his or her own ideas for fear of compromising the harmony of the group, which, in any case, would not forgive them for it.

Nor is it at all surprising that trade unions avoid unreasonable social conflicts and that the 'good' union leaders are rewarded with promotion. Indeed this occurs to such an extent that, in order to become a manager, it is useful to have had union responsibilities at one time or another.

Another cliché of the Japanese model : the performance of manufacturing industry thanks to a longer working day than elsewhere. The official statistics are more theoretical than real, for the constraints of production and group life are such that, 'spontaneously' many employees stay late in the evening and come back on Saturdays -or even Sundays- to achieve their targets. Group pressure is such that it is better to do as one's colleagues and give up a significant proportion of one's leave.

Motivation and mobilization are thus at the heart of the system. At Honda, for example, the prize goes to whoever makes the most proposals for improving productivity. This motivation determines the significant bonuses (worth several months' salaries) which are paid twice a year.

Thus, contrary to common wisdom, the Japanese miracle resides neither in management advances nor technology, but rather in the organization of production, in the most concrete sense of the term. It is a question of doing well what one has to do with order, method, tidiness and, of course, the all-important well motivated staff. None of this is outside our grasp ; the Japanese electronic industries set up in the UK are already performing better than those in the Japan itself. However, the US example demonstrates that simply transferring a model (or rather its image) to another reality does not automatically work : production by the tightened/stretched flow just in time method has shown itself to be more costly than useful in numerous companies. For its part, Germany testifies to another reality : the Germans are as efficient as the Japanese, yet work less than the French.

Ultimately, the principal virtue of the true-false Japanese management model is to have unleashed a veritable mental revolution in our companies (quality circles, company projects, self-training, the cult of business). Future historians will perhaps recognize Japanese methods, as well as the salutary role they have played in the West.

4. Spreading the cultures of prospective and strategy

At the end of this introductory chapter, we are resolutely optimistic. Indeed, debate and dispute over prospective and strategy are fertile and fashions help models to progress and ideas to advance.

We may end by confirming the evidence. If the recipes presented by American business schools and management best-sellers were as useful as claimed, American businesses would be performing better and US industry less sick. Companies are not the only ones affected by the plotting of a desired future. Authorities, local communities and associations have already got the forward planning itch. The democratization of prospective is only just beginning.

It is safe to bet that prospective and strategic cultures will spread widely through organizations... This democratic diffusion cannot fail to raise the level of debate. US soaps and Japanese curios will be abandoned for books by classic authors and reflection on the strong and durable performance models which are burgeoning around us in Germany, France, Italy and Spain. These models are based on long-term, planetary visions and ambitions, efficient management of the (technical, financial, human) means of production to achieve objectives, highly intelligent utilization of the human lever, and all done with respect for identity and in harmony with culture. In a word, the movement being sketched out is indeed that 'of a European school of strategic management'[5]. As Fernand Braudel said (1980) 'What unites Europe is its diversity'. The common characteristic of this European school is precisely the variety of organizations and behaviours which are proving effective. Thus the principle of contingency is the essential basis of this school, which has always existed, but which is only just beginning to recognize itself.

[5] This was the title chosen by AFCET and AFPLANE for their international colloquium held 1-2 February 1990. Proceedings are available from AFCET, 16 Bd Pereire, Paris 75017.

5. One logic in 10 chapters

The field covered by this manual is above all that of prospective. Developments in company strategy aim primarily to propose a synthesis of widely scattered material. By relying on this synthesis, it will be possible to illuminate the complementarities and synergism between the two approaches. In this sense, this work retains the logic of " *Scenarios and Strategic Planning*" (Michel Godet, 1987, Butterworths).

The first two chapters deal with the fundamental principles of anticipation. As the future is not written anywhere and has still to be built, prospective thinking has nothing to do with the determinism of Futurology or Forecasting. The critique of quantification and extrapolation of trends is necessary to improve the complementarity between approaches : planning needs forecasts with scenarios.

The following chapters list the methods of the prospective tool box, illustrated by case studies. In this way we present the necessary mathematical procedures for identifying the key variables of the future, analysing the interplay of actors, reducing uncertainty and finally building scenarios and defining strategic options.

The third chapter is devoted to the scenarios method, whose logical sequence (delimitation of the system retrospective analysis, actors' strategy and constructing scenarios) has become established after dozens of prospective studies.

However, this entirely literary logic is an insufficient weapon for tackling the analysis, comprehension and explanation of increasingly complex systems. Hence the need to call on the more formalized tools of systems analysis defined by Y. Barel (1971) in the following manner : 'Systems analysis, in most cases, consists in bringing out the fact that the goal examined must be re-placed in a wider context than its original system. The term "analysis" serves to underline the usefulness of breaking down complex problems into their constituent parts'.

In the chapters which follow, we shall present some of these formalized tools to which one can turn at one or other stage of the scenarios method.

- Structural analysis and the Micmac method, particularly useful for delimitation of the system and for determining the essential variables, are presented in chapter IV.

- Analysis of the past and of future projects are valuable supports for understanding the interplay of actors whose analysis by the MACTOR method is the basis of chapter V.

- Morphological analysis, useful for scanning the field of possibilities and identifying the key dimensions of the scenarios, is presented at the beginning of chapter VI.

- Expert methodologies (Delphi and cross impact) allow us to assess the likelihood of different hypotheses acting on the variables and key dimensions for the future. Chapter VI is specially devoted to one of these : SMIC methodology.

By presenting these different tools and methodological supports, we will at the same time better understand how to utilize the scenarios method. Let's be clear, however, that, although the sequence is logical, it is not essential to follow it from A to Z : everything depends on the degree of knowledge one has of the system studied and the goals being pursued. The scenarios method is a modular approach and can, where necessary, be limited to the study of particular modules, eg :

- structural analysis of, and search for, key variables ;
- analysis of actors' strategy ;
- surveying experts on key hypotheses for the future.

One of the biggest constraints of the scenarios method is time. In general 12 to 18 months are needed to carry out the logical procedure in its entirety ; half of this time will be spent on construction of the base. If only three to six months are available, it is preferable to concentrate one's thoughts on the module which seems most important.

The complete scenarios method has only been applied in just under half the cases quoted in chapter III. In order to illustrate the modular character of the tools of prospective, they are presented via different case studies. All the same, for reasons of confidentiality it has not been possible to present an example which is a complete and detailed example in all stages.

The outlook is clear, the scenario system will continue to play a reference role but will seldom be carried through from A to Z. That can only be the business of specialists undertaking long and exacting work.

The prevailing winds are blowing in the direction of a democratization of prospective. Prospective is itself moving to embrace the appropriation of methods and is imposing openness and simplicity. This is a strong trend which ought to reinforce still further the infatuation for prospective workshops and to favour the modular use of tools : as needed, as appropriate to particular problems, circumstances and temperaments.

It is then appropriate 'to identify and evaluate possible strategic options'. Chapter VII presents the problematique of the decision-making and evaluation process and develops the principal methods of multicriteria choice available, notably the Multipol method, a particularly simple and easy-to-use tool.

Chapter VIII concerns itself with 'marrying prospective and strategy' (by showing how the meeting and integration of these two approaches was inevitable). This chapter also provides the opportunity to return to the sources of strategy and management. On the way, we discover that these concepts are as old as the hills and that modern authors have invented nothing - the essentials had already been said and written a long time ago by forerunners such as Henri Fayol, Frederic Winslow Taylor and Mary Parker Follet. One lesson may be drawn from this retrospective : there are a thousand and one keys to excellence.

Chapter IX attempts a synthesis. It demonstrates that people are at the heart of the difference between organizations which win and those which lose. It also describes the metamorphosis of structures and behaviours which is indispensable if old habits are to be broken and a true mental revolution is to be launched.

The final chapter entitled "The dawn of the 21st century" proposes a review of the main trends and uncertainties which organizations will have to face in the future.

CHAPTER II

FROM DETERMINISM TO DETERMINATION
FROM FORECASTING TO STRATEGIC PROSPECTIVE

" The future cannot be forecast, it is prepared"
Maurice Blondel, philosopher

Prospective is neither forecasting nor futurology, but a mode of thinking for action and against fatalism. Prospective recognizes that the future is the "raison d'être of the present", that it is multiple and uncertain, and that it is a way for everyone to take control of their own futures. This chapter looks at the role of such qualitative prospective analysis in the context of business planning and forecasting . Scenario-building emerges as more vital than ever for forecasting and strategic management.

1. An action-oriented anti-fatalistic thinking

Those who claim to foretell or forecast the future are inevitably liars, for the future is not written anywhere - it is still to be constructed. This is fortunate, for without this uncertainty, human activity would lose its degree of freedom and its meaning - the hope of a desired future. If the future were totally foreseeable and certain, the present would become unliveable. Certainty is death.

Thus, the first aim of prospective thought is to illuminate the choices of the present by the light of possible futures. Good forecasts are not necessarily those which are realized, but those which lead to action to avoid the dangers and arrive at the desired objective.

The frequent errors that occur in forecasting and the notable absence of forecasts of crises, bear witness to the crisis in forecasting itself . The impossibility of seeing ahead into the future solely by means of using past data, explains the futility of classical economic models, which fail to include qualitative and unquantifiable parameters, such as projects entertained by, and the behaviour of the principal actors. The future must be studied with a view to illuminating the present; that is the basic idea which inspires *la prospective* .

Such prospective analysis involves taking a view which is global, qualitative and voluntarist (a concept created by G. Berger in the late 1950s). It is neither forecasting, with an excess of deterministic quantification, nor futurology, a concept fashionable mainly in the English-speaking world and which embraces all aspects of research into the future without specific reference to the criteria of globalism and will. Futurology has had rather a bad press in western Europe, where it is widely seen as a throwback to the crystal ball or a variant of science fiction. At the same time, the concept of prospective analysis has found acceptance mainly in the Latin world (southern Europe, Latin America).

Another significant difference between the two cultural worlds is that the concept of 'technological forecasting' has not been accepted on the European side of the Atlantic as being capable of providing a sufficiently global insight into social developments; rather, it is seen as restricted to trends in science and technology and their consequences, on the implicit premise that science is no more than a product of society and as such cannot suffice to explain it.

The concept of forecasting is not self-contained, but is subject to fluctuation from one period and from one society to another. To oversimplify, there are three attitudes to the future (passivity, adaptation and voluntarism); in practice, however, these constantly overlap and intermingle.

The passive attitude to the future is a legacy of religious fatalism. The 1739 edition of Richelet's dictionary contains the following : 'Prévision : se dit de Dieu et signifie connaissance de ce qui adviendra'. According to this view, the future is inevitable and virtually predetermined, having already been written by the hand of God, so that man has no alternative but to submit to his destiny; this being the case, it serves no purpose to encumber the present with future misfortunes, since tomorrow will be tomorrow and there is nothing that can be done about it.

With the advent of the industrial revolution and the sharp acceleration in the pace of change during the 20th century, people came to realize that the pages of history, whether or not written in advance, were turning faster and faster. If change was inevitable, it was perhaps also predictable, in which case it could be worthwhile anticipating it so as to be ready for it when it came, and to take advantage of the opportunities that it offered. An adaptative attitude to the future thus developed as a reaction to rapid change, bringing in its train a phenomenal development in economic, technological and social forecasting accompanied by excessive and sometimes blind confidence in the new gods of mathematical model-making and econometric methods.

This adaptative attitude is essentially reactive rather than pro-active, resigned rather than voluntaristic, since it has not purged the original sin of determinism and inevitability. Curiously, fatalism has cast off its religious habits to assume the mantle of a new idol - science and technology. Technological forecasting seems to have become the modern substitute for divinely inspired prophecy. The passive 'wait and see' attitude has been transmuted into blind faith in the unlimited powers of a technological good fairy, who will solve all problems, including those for which she is responsible.

Such technological optimism, which has now become so widespread, has also triggered a reaction generating its antithesis - technological pessimism (the world is doomed, we are playing with fire, the problems that technology cannot solve are those which are of its own making), which is just as heavily impregnated with determinism.

In the face of the accelerating pace of change, the uncertainties of the future, and the increasing complexity of phenomena and interactions, resignation is no longer an acceptable response. An antifatalistic, pre-active and pro-active attitude is essential.

People are not fated to accept relationships which are necessary, determined and outside their control. They create relationships through their own will and their actions.

At the root of all prospective is an assumption of freedom in the face of multiple and indeterminate futures. Prospective has nothing to do with the determinism of futurology and crystal ball gazing. Nor is prospective the same as forecasting, which is too greatly affected by quantification and extrapolation of trends. Prospective does not see the future simply as a continuation of the past, because the future is open to the games of many players, who are acting today in accordance with their plans for the future.

So, prospective is a way of thinking which throws light on present action by looking at possible futures. In modern society, anticipation is imperative because of the combined effects of two main factors :

- firstly, the acceleration of technical, economic and social change, which necessitates long-term vision : 'the faster you drive the further your headlights must shine' ;
- secondly, factors of inertia inherent in structures and behaviour mean that we must sow the seeds of change today if we wish to harvest them tomorrow.

Although the world is changing, however, the direction of this change is uncertain. For a company or local authority, change carries numerous uncertainties (economic, technological and social) which it must integrate into its strategy. Prospective does not claim to eliminate this uncertainty through illusory prediction, but aims simply to reduce it as far as possible, and to take decisions based as little as possible on hypothetical futures (which is a lot in itself).

2. A critique of forecasting

2.1. Definitions

Confusion between projection, forecasting, prospective analysis and planning is a source of many forecasting mishaps and misunderstandings The following definitions should serve to reduce such problems (see Table II-1).

- *Projection* is the extension into the future of past developments using certain assumptions for the extrapolation or variations of trends. A projection constitutes a forecast only where it is based on probability.
- *Forecasting* is the assessment, with a degree of confidence (probability), of a trend over a given period. The assessment will generally be expressed in figures and based on past data and a number of assumptions.
- *Exploratory propective analysis* is a panorama of possible futures, or scenarios, which are not improbable in the light of past causalities, and the interaction between the intentions of interested parties. Each such scenario (a coherent series of assumptions) may be the subject of an assessment expressed in figures, ie a forecast.

- *Planning.*, to quote Ackoff (1973),'consists in conceiving a desired future and the practical means of achieving it'. It therefore calls for a normative prospective approach. It should be made clear that the plan (an instrument of discipline and consistency) is only one stage in the planning process (an instrument of dialogue). The plan must be simultaneously informative(diagnosis), indicative (remedies) and directive (ends and means). Too many people fall into the classic trap of confusing planning with forecasting, mistaking a divergence from a predetermined objective for a forecasting error.

Summary definitions of the main concepts used in the literature on the future are given in Table II-1.

Conjecture Probable hypothesis	*Prospective analysis* All-embracing, qualitative, and quantitative, voluntarist, multiple scenarios (largely a Latin concept)
Projection Extension into the future or variation of past trends	*Forecasting* Assessment with a degree of confidence : quantitative,deterministic
Prediction Statement of fact before the event (Delphic oracle)	*Futurology* All aspects of research on the future (an Anglo-Saxon concept)
Prophecy Prediction by divine inspiration	*Scenarios* Coherent series of assumptions

Planning
'Consists in conceiving a desired future and the practical means of achieving it'
(Ackoff, 1973)

Table II-1

The historical paradox is that forecasting developed at a time when it was easiest and least necessary. In practice, econometric models, backed up by computers, were being used to demonstrate things that anyone could easily find out for himself; everything was more or less directly related to the gross national product; GNP itself was rising by about 5 % a year. Basically, time was the best 'explanatory' variable.

The year 1973 marked the turning-point at which the future ceased to resemble the past, making the need for a prospective analysis (to take account of breakdowns in trends) more immediate. Such breakdowns are associated with new behaviour patterns, so that models based on past data and relationships are powerless as predictors.

This is not the place for a detailed survey of the causes of errors in forecasting, but attention can be drawn to three factors :

- inaccurate data coupled with unstable models ;
- excessive quantification and extrapolation;
- explanation of the future in terms of the past.

2.2. Inaccurate data and unstable models

Economics does not obey rules as rigorous as those applied in the more 'exact' sciences such as physics. Statistical data are often supplied without any estimate of the extent of errors which may have been made in compiling them. What purpose is served by sophisticated calculations made to the nearest hundredth or thousandth when the figures to the left of the decimal point cannot be relied upon ? In the USA, according to O. Morgenstern, even the GNP figure can only be regarded as accurate to within 10% either way, and there is no reason to suppose that errors are always in the same direction; even the direction of variations in GNP may be in doubt. Economists -and others- should always ask themselves about the sensitivity of their results to minimal changes in input data.

Given its relative importance, the anodyne notion of stability requires careful study. Various viewpoints are possible.

Let us suppose a static framework. Given a matrix A where coefficient $a(ij)$ represents the number of goods i produced in region j. Each $a(ij)$ is purchased in this region in the proportion $x(j)$. We therefore make the unrealistic assumption that for $x(j)$ is an average value j, independent of i so that the national output of goods i effectively consumed is $b(i) = \Sigma\, a(ij) \quad X(j)$.

The following problems can be raised : given $A = (a(ij))$, $b = (b(ij))$, what will be the value of X ? If A varies by $(\Delta) A$, what will be the corresponding variation $(\Delta) X$ of X ? Or again, if b varies by $(\delta) b$, what will be the corresponding variation $(\delta) X$ of X ? In other words, the problem is the one of the study of the stability of X as a function of the minute variations $(\Delta) A$ of A and $(\delta) b$ of b.

We need not recall the rather restrictive theory of 'appropriating' matrices for problems involving linear equations. The following well-known example amply illustrates this :

$$A = \begin{bmatrix} 10 & 7 & 8 & 7 \\ 7 & 5 & 6 & 5 \\ 8 & 6 & 10 & 9 \\ 7 & 5 & 9 & 10 \end{bmatrix} \qquad b = \begin{bmatrix} 32 \\ 23 \\ 33 \\ 31 \end{bmatrix} \qquad X = \begin{bmatrix} 1 \\ 1 \\ 1 \\ 1 \end{bmatrix}$$

$$A = \begin{bmatrix} 10 & 7 & 8 & 7 \\ 7 & 5 & 6 & 5 \\ 8 & 6 & 10 & 9 \\ 7 & 5 & 9 & 10 \end{bmatrix} \qquad b+\delta b = \begin{bmatrix} 32 \\ 23 \\ 33 \\ 31 \end{bmatrix} \qquad X+\delta X = \begin{bmatrix} 9.2 \\ -12.6 \\ 4.5 \\ 1.1 \end{bmatrix}$$

$$A+\Delta A = \begin{bmatrix} 0 & 7 & 8.10 & 7.20 \\ 7.8 & 5.45 & 6 & 5 \\ 8 & 5.98 & 9.89 & 9 \\ 6.99 & 4.99 & 9 & 9.98 \end{bmatrix} \qquad b+\delta b = \begin{bmatrix} 32 \\ 23 \\ 33 \\ 31 \end{bmatrix} \qquad X+\Delta X = \begin{bmatrix} -81 \\ 137 \\ -34 \\ 22 \end{bmatrix}$$

(i) Whatever the problem under consideration, it is essential to carry out a full study of the stability factor without which it is impossible to give significance to the results.

(i i) Most, if not all, static linear models are in fact devoid of interest ; because of the way real-world values are subdivided, the coefficients obtained are known with a margin of error so large as to make the final results useless.

Excerpt from C. I. Bruter, 'Two observations as to the relationship between economics and mathematics', Proceedings of the AFCET Symposium, 1977, p. 58.

2.3. Excessive quantification and extrapolation

Most forecasting methods are based on extrapolation of trends, which assumes that 'all things will be equal' in other spheres. This is quite unrealistic when the environment is increasingly subject to change and the phenomena to be taken into account are increasingly complex and interdependent. In these circumstances, uncertainty about the future is reflected in divergences from a trend.

This makes econometric models powerless to anticipate major long-term structural changes, although their users regularly attribute their forecasting errors to 'hidden' variables.

Piecemeal forecasting which takes account of only a few (usually economic and quantified) explanatory variables and ignores changes in balances of power and the emergence of new trends is more misleading than useful. Its inaccuracy is attributable largely to the fact that the economic sector is becoming self-contained, so that economic forecasting is divorced from social and political forecasting, while at the same time it is tending increasingly to be broken down into technological forecasts, population forecasts, and so on.

It is therefore clear that it has become necessary to take a global view; the pace of change is accelerating, there is increasing interdependence and interaction, and nothing can any longer be taken for granted. The time has come for forecasting based on quantification to be replaced by an overall prospective approach taking account of all the qualitative parameters (whether or not quantifiable) which may have an immediate or remote impact on whatever phenomenon may be under examination.

Adopt a global vision for local action

Prospective thinking must be global - hardly any problems can be isolated ; in fact, we are witnessing quite the opposite trend - a growing interdependence, even entanglement, of problems. We cannot hope to find solutions which are not global, even if the point of application of these solutions is local. Moreover, the complexity of elements and relationships to be taken into account, and the need to put them into a global perspective, makes analysis particularly difficult. This is why it is necessary to use methods of systems analysis.

2.4. Future explained in terms of the past

The prospective approach accepts that there is a multiplicity of possible futures at any given time and that the actual future will be the outcome of the interplay between the various protagonists in a given situation and their respective intentions. How the future evolves is explained as much by human action as by the influence of causalities. The future should not be seen as a single predetermined line, an extension of the past; on the contrary, it is plural and indeterminate. The plurality of the future and the scope for freedom of human action are mutually explanatory; the future has not been written, but remains to be created (see Figures II.1 and II.2).

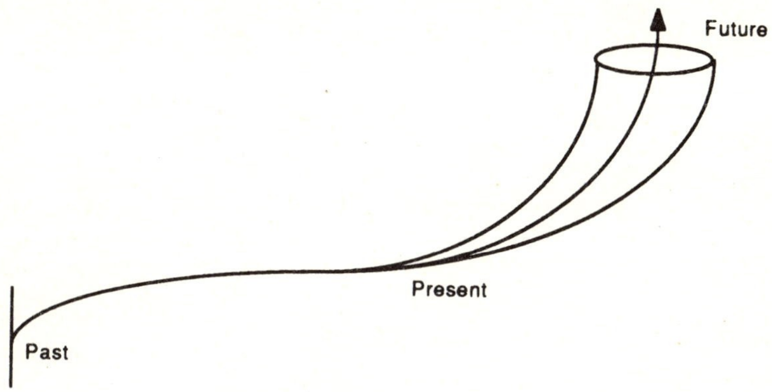

Figure II-1

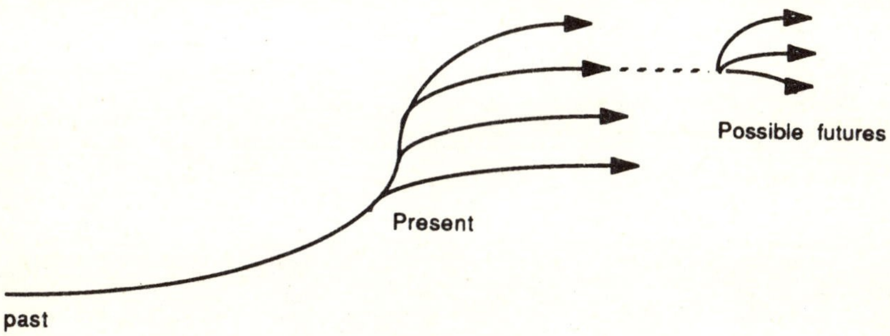

Figure II-2

The prospective approach has evolved from the realization that the future is the product of both causality and freedom; that which is undergone in the future is a result of past actions (and of course unforeseeable natural phenomena); that which is willed explains present actions. In other words, the future is explained not only by the past but also by the image of the future imprinted upon the present. For instance, an individual 's consumption at a given time is not determined solely by his past income (savings), but also by the future income that he anticipates (credit), as Milton Friedman has clearly demonstrated in his theory of continuing income.

The eye of the future illuminates the present; seen in this light, the future is today's *raison d'être*.

	Classical forecasting	Prospective approach
Viewpoint	Piecemeal 'Everything else being equal'	Overall approach 'Nothing else being equal'
Variables	Quantitative, objective, and known	Qualitative, not necessarily quantitative, subjective, known or hidden
Relationships	Static, fixed structures	Dynamic, evolving structures
Explanation	The past explains the future	The future is the *raison d'être* of the present
Future	Single and certain	Multiple and uncertain
Method	Deterministic and quantitative models (econometric, mathematical)	Intentional analysis Qualitative (structural analysis) and stochastic (cross-impacts) models
Attitude to the future	Passive or adaptive (future *comes* about)	Active and creative (future *brought* about)

3. Usefulness and scope of prospective

3.1.Usefulness and credibility of prospective analysis

The usefulness of prospective analysis depends largely on the aims pursued by those who conduct or commission such studies. The objectives that prospective analysis can serve include :

Strategic objectives :

- guidance of present action (the plan) in the light of possible and desirable futures, eg by aiming for maximum flexibility in the face of uncertainty;
- staking out possible futures so as to be able to take a selective view of the multitude of current events, identifying those which point to the future, ie 'events whose present dimensions are minute, but whose potential consequences are enormous' (P. Massé, 1967).

Tactical objectives :

- using warnings in an attempt to pre-empt or foster future developments (inflation rate, economic growth rate, ...);
- testing a hypothesis or theory, eg in order to justify a decision and forestall possible criticism;
- cultivating a purposeful and dynamic image;
- developing communication within an organization or between it and the outside world; and
- challenging received ideas and unconstructive behaviour (scepticism, blind faith, shortsightedness).

Given the wide range of objectives pursued by those who carry out or commission prospective analysis, little purpose can be served by inquiring into its credibility; prospective analysis is not neutral, but depends on subjective choices regarding the approach employed with regard to specific problems, the assumptions tested, the aims pursued. Because of the uncertainty of the future it is necessary to make judgments and then back them; only after a series of such judgments has been proved right or wrong, can the credibility of prospective analysis be assessed.

3.2. What ingredients go into making an accurate forecast ?

An immediate observation is that the "correct" forecast is not necessarily the one which turns out to be true. When we anticipate a future problem, we normally set in motion actions that ensure that it will not take place or that its effects will be mitigated.

A second observation is that an accurate forecast is not necessarily a useful forecast. In forecasting, as in statistical testing, three types of error can be identified :

- retaining a hypothesis which ultimately is not substantiated ;
- excluding a hypothesis or an event that does in fact transpire ;
- not asking the right questions, i.e not incorporating in the prospective thinking the hypotheses or events that are going to play a predominant rôle in the future ;

This third risk occurs regularly in forecasting and can best be explained by the "lamp-post effect" - where the drunk who has lost his keys looks for them under the lamp-post, since that is where the ground is lit.

3.3. What makes a good expert ?

We have a simple answer to this question, but nonetheless it does not solve the problem : the best experts are generally a minority ; this leaves the question open as to who, among the minorities, has it right.

In practice, in many fields, particularly those of a technological nature, expert predictions are often the main source of information.

The success of methods like Delphi (where a convergence of opinion is sought through a somewhat directed, even manipulated consensus) can readily be explained. Such methods are appropriate when it comes to obtaining decisions through consensus, but they are more often misleading than useful as forecasts[1].

As an illustration of this point, the reader should reflect on the results of an evaluation of experts made several years ago (Exhibit II.2).

An assessment of experts' forecasting performance

In a 1976 "Futures" article, George Wise, of General Electric's R & D Centre, analysed the accuracy of forecasts made in the USA between 1890 and 1940 on technological progress and the impact of innovation. His analysis was based on 1 556 forecasts of technological advances (some of which materialized, others which did not) in 18 specific areas of technology ; and the anticipated social, economic or political effects of these changes.
He drew five conclusions :

- experts producing long-term forecasts (10 years and upwards) are wrong more often than they are right ;
- experts are slightly more accurate in their forecasts than non-experts ;
- forecasts made by experts in a field outside their speciality are no less accurate than those of experts specializing in the field concerned ;
- forecasts concerned with the continuance of the technological status quo at a given moment are no more accurate than forecasts concerned with technological innovation ; and
- the effects of technological development are less easy to forecast than the developments themselves.

Some guidelines for prospective analysis

- Do it in-house rather than rely on outside bodies.
- Select a 'new consultant' in preference to one of the traditional type.
- The traditional type seeks to shock the client with his preliminary diagnosis, making him feel guilty so that he allows himself to employ an outside team organizing a major assignment.
- The new type seeks to become a catalyst for communication and new ideas within the undertaking, setting up and helping to run in-house prospective analysis workshops or studies broadening the horizon beyond the confines of the undertaking.
- Approach problems from several angles, according to their complexity.
- Be sceptical of certainties.

Exhibit II-2

[1] Bearing in mind that "convergence" is not necessarily (i.e., rarely) indicative of statistical consistency, as we shall see when we develop the SMIC Prob-Expert cross-impact method.

3.4. The absence of neutrality of information and forecasts

Information about the future, the present or the past, is rarely neutral : it usually serves specific interests. How many studies and analyses are lying hidden in drawers because they are politically undesirable? How many pertinent reports are emptied of their substance by selective use of words ? How many realities are ignored because they do not fit preconceived ideas? Information is manipulated simply because it is a major source of power.

'To inform someone, to give him information which he does not possess, is to divest it from oneself, to relinquish those trump cards which could be sold and to make oneself vulnerable in the face of takeover attempts. Total communication is impossible. To enter into a relationship with another person, to seek to open up to him, is at the same time to hide and to protect oneself behind fortifications and to oppose him. Briefly, any relation with another person is strategic and contains a power component, however buried or sublimated it may be'[2].

Prospective information does not escape from this influence and the consequent pollution ; there seems to be an unending stream of alternately alarmist and reassuring reports on population, environment, energy, arms, etc... all mutually contradictory in their conclusions. By its nature, prospective information is relatively more durable, but is less of a burning issue than headline news.

Nevertheless, we scan these futures to illuminate and guide present action. The future is an emerging landscape with unknown contours; the constraint is that, despite the unknown horizons, we have to take decisions today that commit us for the future. Even if the information is degraded we have to take out our bets now, to create the future rather than to submit to it.

4. Pluralism and complementarity

4.1. Problems and methods

The problem of specification, identification and calculation of the parameters for a model are classic problems for econometrics. Three problems in particular have received insufficient consideration, despite the fact that the manner in which they are solved conditions the validity of any forecast.

The problem of identifying explanatory variables. Let the variable to be explained be x, whose development is to be investigated and forecast.The first immediate question is, what are the variables that have to be taken into account in order to explain x? Some of these explanatory variables will be readily identifiable on the basis of thorough knowledge of their past influence on the variable, while others will be more difficult, either because the nature of their influence is not sufficiently well known or because it has not yet manifested itself fully.

[2] M. Crozier and E. Friedberg (1977, pp 107 et 181).

It is not sufficient to identify these variables. It is necessary to specify the form of the relationship function (linear, exponential, power, lag, etc). This requires drawing upon theoretical knowledge, experience and intuition. It calls for a good knowledge of the past (analysis of correlations) but, above all, imagination and creativity. This is why the problems of specifying and identifying variables and relationships also necessitate the use of qualitative methods (eg brain-storming, synectics, data analysis, morphological analysis, structural analysis).

The problem of estimating future values of explanatory variables. When the explanatory variables have been specified and identified, and the parameters of the function have been estimated, the next problem in the forecasting process is to make a quantitative estimate of the future values of the explanatory variables. This problem can be expressed as follows : either, what will be the value of each variable at instant t, or alternatively, by what date will each variable have reached a given magnitude ?

This type of question is often dealt with by extrapolating or more or less arbitrarily fixing the values of the explanatory variables, whereas in theory each of these variables should be explained together and in turn. However, this would make for an endless and heavily looped model and, given the constraints imposed by known data and available time and resources, it would not be possible to go very far along such lines. This is why estimates of the future values of explanatory variables are generally obtained by the use of simple or sophisticated methods of extrapolation (analogies, logistical curves); in short, it is as though each explanatory variable explained itself over time, with time acting as a pseudo-explanatory variable.

The problem of uncertain estimated values. An estimate does not become a forecast until it can be supported with a certain degree of confidence. In coping with this problem of establishing the probability, the uncertainty, the forecaster has little to go on apart from the intuitive judgments of experts when applying methods of the Delphi or cross-impact type.

Selection of forecasting methods. No miracle forecasting method capable of solving all problems exists. In practice, because there are so many different types of forecasting problem, each forecaster will have a more or less complete box of tools from which he makes a selection according to the nature of the problem at hand, his objective and the constraints (data and time available) within which he has to work.

In the absence of an all-purpose tool, a 'kit' has to be made up from the tools available to meet the requirements of each forecasting problem, an appropriate methodological response which should include improvisation wherever necessary.

Finally, it should be remembered that, in industrial prospective analysis, the choice of a method for forecasting the development or sales of a product depends on certain criteria, such as the life cycle of the products concerned (birth, growth, maturity, decline -see Figure II.3). It is found for instance, that conventional econometric methods are particularly appropriate forecasting tools for products in their mature phase, when plenty of past series are available. In the early stages of a product's development, on the other hand, methods of the Delphi or cross-impact type are more appropriate (note : more appropriate, not 'appropriate').

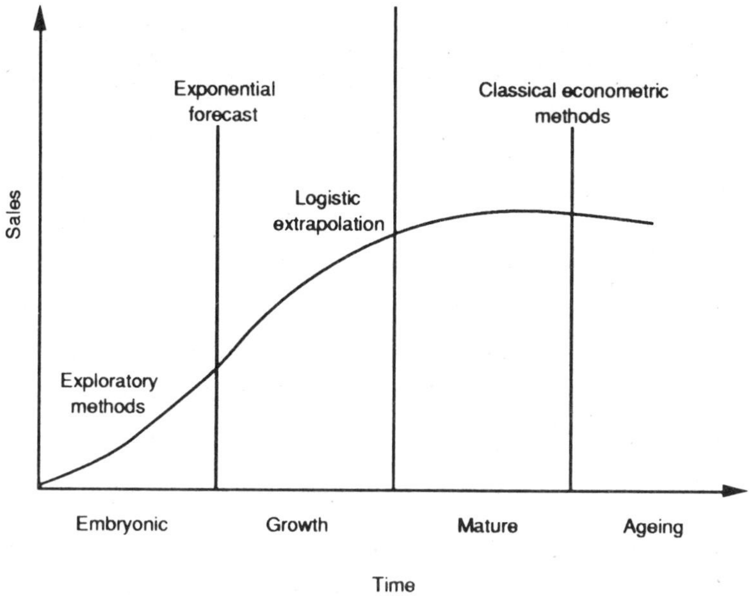

Figure II-3

4.2. Planning needs forecasts with scenarios

The dangers of excessive quantification (the ever present tendency to concentrate on things which are quantifiable to the detriment of those which are not) should not lead to a rejection of statistics, but merely to cautious use of them. The statistics (mathematical, econometric) contained in forecasting models are essential to an assessment of the consequences of scenarios. The validity of a forecasting model is determined by that of the assumptions (economic, political, etc) upon which it is founded; the purpose of prospective analysis is to fill in the background, providing the sets of assumptions which will give the model its validity, ie its consistency with future reality. The complementarity between prospective analysis and forecasting has led to the creation of 'new forecasting'. The contribution of prospective analysis meets three essential needs of forecasting :

(a) the need for explanation : determination of known or hidden essential variables makes for improved selection of indicators;

(b) the need for assumptions : construction of scenarios - coherent set of probable assumptions based on explanatory variables - is the process which lends validity to a forecasting model; and

(c) the need for quantification : forecasting according to scenarios provides a means of quantifying the results and consequences of prospective analysis and taking account of that which cannot be quantified.

Using the following notation of the above model $y = f(X_i)$, the contribution of prospective analysis is to supply, in the form of scenarios, consistent sets of probable assumptions based on the explanatory variables X_i and the function f relating them. These assumptions provide the background for application of a forecasting model to enable calculation of the desired final result, y.

This 'new forecasting' is a synthesis of prospective analysis and forecasting, which are two complementary approaches ; it incorporates the rules and constraints of econometric techniques in the coherent framework provided by scenarios. This scenario is outlined in Figure II.4.

Researchers would therefore do well to make the distinction between forecasting and prospective analysis more often. The value of a forecast is no more than that of the underlying assumptions. More often than not, several coherent sets of assumptions (scenarios) can be considered fairly probable, so that a forecast should never be published without giving an indication of the estimated probability of the corresponding scenario[3].

Attention should also be drawn to the dangers of only considering the scenario which is thought to be the most probable. Finally, it should be noted that some scenarios may correspond to breakdowns in past trends. Such scenarios are outside the scope of projection and cannot be calculated according to the conventional forecasting methods.

New forecasting

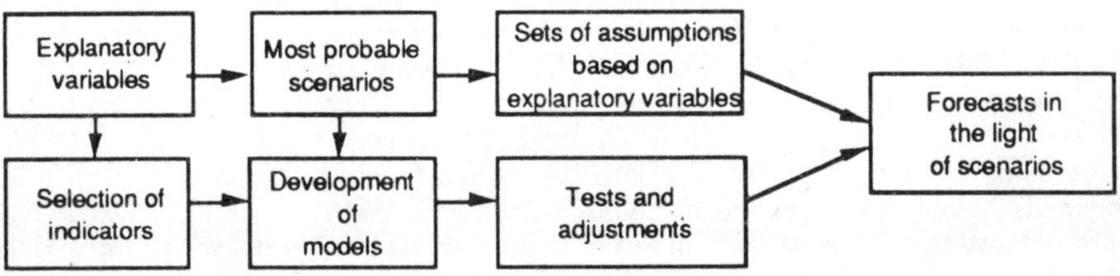

Figure II-4

4.3. Proposals for solving the crisis in forecasting

There can be no sensible planning without exhaustive consideration of possible futures and debate on desirable futures and the means of bringing them about. If this debate is to be organized on a proper footing in the light of all relevant information,

[3] If one takes N assumptions, there will be 2^N sets of possible assumptions covering a period leading up to a given date, the sum of the probabilities of the corresponding scenarios being equal to 1. Assume that $N = 2$ and that the four possible scenarios have the following probabilities : S1, probability 0,4 ; S2, 0,25 ; S3, 0,15 ; and S4, 0,20. Clearly, the most probable scenario (S1) is in fact the least probable outcome - the most probable outcome is that any one of the three other scenarios will be borne out.

statistical forecasts corresponding to each of the alternative scenarios envisaged must be available on a regular basis.

It is at the *interface* between *prospective* consideration of possible and desirable futures and quantification by means of forecasting models that the greatest difficulties are encountered in national and corporate planning exercises.

How can statistics be produced in the face of uncertainty ? How can scenarios and models be integrated with each other ? These are two of the questions which inevitably arise ; as yet there are no satisfactory answers, and they are eminently suitable subjects for research.

As a contribution to the necessary research effort, the following comments are offered to the researchers concerned. First, economists are too inclined to forget that a *model is not reality, but one of a variety of possible means of gaining an insight into reality.*

They should therefore make it their practice, in the interests of prudence and neutrality, to broaden their methodological options (by testing several models and different approaches, each acting as a failsafe system for the others).

It is not acceptable to restrict the range of possible futures in the name of logic and constraints deriving from a model built on the past. Variants should not be determined according to the nature of models, but scenarios should be taken as the starting-point for the construction of models which are most appropriate for the representation of the development to be explored. In other words, it is truly essential to adjust the models to the reality to be constructed rather than the reverse : the means should not be allowed to outweigh the ends

Second, the fact that a model is sophisticated and contains thousands of simultaneous equations does not necessarily mean that it gives a better description of reality. Such exhaustiveness is all the more misleading when factors which are unquantifiable, not well known, or controversial have been left out. In fact, such complex models are becoming increasingly incomprehensible to users who have not been involved in their development (trade union representatives, company economists, researchers working in other fields, etc). This detracts further from the reputation of modelling, which has already suffered seriously as a result of the large numbers of forecasting failures.

This defect in forecasting is felt particularly keenly by public and private undertakings which have to take decisions affecting their future by feeling their way without any clear frame of reference or coherent objectives. These undertakings are disarmed because they have nowhere to turn other than to forecasting centres which are ill-prepared or ill-placed to quantify the uncertainty resulting from the multiplicity of possible scenarios.

Third, some people take the view that, since the standard planning period is five years, long-term prospective analysis (ten years or more) is a lower priority than short - and medium-term forecasting. This opinion is groundless, since the timescale of prospective analysis should be determined by that of the plans of interested parties or of possible breakdowns in trends, which could occur in the near future. Present action should be guided by the possible futures, since, when fog and uncertainty abound, an excellent compass-setting is a fundamental pre-requisite for survival.

4.4. Key concepts for a methodology

One can conclude that quantitative forecasting and qualitative prospective studies are two approaches, where the "qualitative" and the "quantitative" must be complementary.

Constructing a forecasting approach by scenarios such as that proposed here is not a simple task, since there is a lack of methods. This methodological gap reflects insufficient past research into the topic as well as a breakdown between the two networks- that of the forecast model-builders and that of the "prospectivists", i.e. the futures analysts.

In practice, it would be desirable to bring together economists, sociologists, historians, etc, on the same forecast, even though the models may match less well with figures than with reality. In short, the global view of prospective must be based on pluralism and complementarity of approaches. This is the price to be paid if forecasting is to find its way out of crisis.

5. Practical advice for future thinking

How to implement future thinking ? We can recommend from experience four ways to improve the relevance and efficiency of prospective analysis.

5.1. Ask the right questions and mistrust conventional wisdom

Everybody remembers Woody Allen's famous remark : 'The answer is yes, but what is the question ?' As there is no right answer to a wrong question it is essential to pose real questions. Unfortunately common wisdom generates numerous false problems ie, clichés proved wrong by the facts.

Light creates shadow. If present-day projectors are so powerfully trained on certain problems, this is in order to hide more effectively other problems which people prefer not to see. Today's dominant conventional wisdom and fashionable ideas must be regarded with mistrust, for they are generally a source of error in analysis and forecasting.

In order to see things more clearly and to ask the right questions, one should not hesitate to think against the flow, even if this means displeasing others. This is an important challenge, for there is little chance of prescribing the appropriate remedy if one is mistaken over the diagnosis.

In general, the majority of experts are conformists (it is easy to take refuge in the majority and leave the task of explaining to others) and conservative[4]. Very often, good forecasts, i.e., those which see things accurately, are achieved by a minority of experts who demonstrate daring and imagination.

The most difficult thing is, of course, to know how to pick out the 'good' minority point of view from the rest. For the practitioner of prospective, the lesson is clear : although it may be difficult and risky a priori to defend one new idea among other possible ones, he must not be afraid to attack dominant ideas. It is in this spirit that we were able, for example, to :

- announce as early as 1978 both a new oil crisis and the energy surplus which would render nuclear energy less necessary[5] ;
- dispute the thesis of the industrial decline of Europe in relation to the USA and Japan[6] ;
- cast doubt on current clichés about the Japanese model[7] ;
- question the often evoked thesis of Germany's decline - at a time when Germany has become the world's leading exporter of manufactured products[8] ;
- denounce the myth of technology as the lever with which to emerge from crisis[9].

The day before yesterday (in the 1970s) energy was blamed as the cause of all our ills ; yesterday (the 1980s) technology was going to save us ; now, the priority is training (renamed, for today's circumstances, 'non-material investment'). After having fallen victim to the technological mirage, we are now suffering from 'diploma disease'[10]. It seems that human societies pass from one mirage to another in order to avoid confronting the forest of real problems, which are of a socio-organizational nature : technological and educational changes imply social change and a revolution of the mind.

This point applies equally to companies. It is often in structures, behaviour and quality of personnel that we should seek to understand the situation of companies in difficulty. Otherwise, how are we to explain the fact that other companies, facing the same market and environmental constraints, enjoy a high degree of success ?

---

[4] As O. CLarke emphasized, 'When an eminent and aged expert says that something is impossible, there is a good chance that he is mistaken'.

[5] 'Energy horizon keeps receding?, The Times, 5/9/ 1978.

[6] There is no proof of Europe's industrial decline', Le Monde, 21/12/1982 ; 'Europe : the aft wind', Le Monde, 5/2/1986 ; The USA : Renaissance or concealed decline ?,'Futures, June 1985.

[7] Ten unfashionable and controversial findings on Japan', Futures, Vol 19, n° 4, August 1987, p. 371-384.

[8] See also, 'Germany : paradoxical power', Futures, August 1989, Vol 12, n° 4.

[9] 'From the technological mirage to the social breakthrough', Futures, June 1986.

[10] 'Worldwide challenges and crisis in education systems', Futures, June 1988.

Over the last two decades we have also noticed that errors of forecasting are often based upon two mistakes :

- overestimation of the pace of change (of technologies);
- underestimation of inertial factors (structures, behaviours).

Therefore, when thinking about the future, we suggest it is useful to start by identifying factors which are unlikely to change.

5.2. Think in the long term and imagine first what will not change

Fernand Braudel repeatedly demonstrated the necessity of long-term vision (encompassing several decades, or even several centuries) in understanding the evolving rhythm of societies, economies or ecosystems. For example, 14th century Europe experienced a series of epidemics and famines which caused the total population to fall by about 40%, but which also halted the excessive deforestation caused by the previous rapid population growth. This major crisis was to be followed by the Renaissance and finally, several centuries later, by the progress of the Age of Science and Enlightenment. In a sense we are still being carried along on these waves of innovation, which have continued to accumulate for almost six centuries.

So crises -the consequence of rigidities- are often favourable moments for undertaking necessary adaptations and wide-reaching reforms which would otherwise have been held in check by multiple resistances to change. Crises bring opportunity for social and organizational change ; unfortunately in many cases crises are necessary for change to happen.

History does not repeat itself. With the passage of time, however, societies retain disconcerting similarities in behaviour, which lead them, when faced with comparable situations, to react in almost identical, and consequently foreseeable ways. Most events which are destined to happen have already taken root in the distant past. So the past holds forgotten lessons, which can teach us much about the future.

A good prospective study therefore almost always implies considerable analysis and retrospective thought as a preliminary. This may represent two-thirds of the time invested in such a study. A priori, the past has the advantage of being less cluttered and calmer than the present ; however, it too is liable to many different interpretations. Thus, looking at the past remains a difficult task, for it means reconstituting scattered and often controversial information.

We should not underestimate the importance of factors of inertia in relation to forces of potential change. In prospective, there is often the tendency to imagine what could eventually change, while forgetting systematically to record what has at least a good chance of remaining unchanged. Large organizations are characterized by strong inertia, which means that unless there are discontinuities, changes inevitably take a long time. This makes it imperative to prepare for changes well in advance.

5.3. Use simple, adaptable methods to stimulate thought and facilitate communication

There is no universal tool ; no one method is a panacea ; available data are both overabundant and incomplete. Furthermore, a model is not reality, but a means of looking at reality. All these considerations lead us to point out that the scope of each method or model is relative.

The imperfection of the tools, the inaccuracy of data, and the subjectivity of interpretations are unavoidable realities, which prompt us to opt for pluralistic and complementary approaches. As far as possible, the results of a model should be tested for their sensitivity to a variety of data inputs and to the use of another tool. Only sufficiently robust results should be considered credible.

The main interest of methods is not only that they provide results, but also that they should be the occasion for structured thought and intelligible communication on a given theme. From this point of view, our recommendation to researchers and practitioners is clear ; the container matters little so long as one is intoxicated by the content- communication. The most important thing in a study (whether it be prospective, strategy or marketing) is not so much the resulting report, as what has happened in the minds of those who have been involved in the thought process it has engendered.

This fact has important consequences for practising researchers and advisers, whose work should increasingly consist of 'making people do, rather than doing', of letting each person discover the problems and solutions in his own language rather than revealing ready-made truths in a scholarly but alien language. This new advice is to former advice what psychoanalysis is to conventional medicine. It relies on appropriate methods, ie, methods which are simple enough to remain adaptable.

What is too simple is stupid and wrong, what is too complex is usefulness. The idea is to use tools which are simple enough to be appropriable by the users and customers of the results. Such appropriation is necessary to turn anticipation into action (see the Greek Triangle).

Strategic management must use relevant, consistent and likely scenarios in order to better adapt and reach the strategic goals. To construct scenarios and strategies, we need appropriate tools.

For this reason, we have elaborated a toolbox which classifies problem-solving methods as follows :

1. Asking the right questions and identifying the key variables : futures workshops and structural analysis with MICMAC method (see chapter IV) ;
2. Analysing trends and actors' strategies : retrospective studies and MACTOR method (see chapter V) ;
3. Reducing uncertainties to likely scenarios : morphological analysis, experts methods (Delphi, cross-impacts),(see chapter VI) ;
4. Identification and assessment of strategic options : multicriteria analysis and MULTIPOL method.

Last but not least, we have good news for users; Most of these tools are now available on diskettes (PC and MAC). However, users must be cautious and choose proper tools for each problem. Researchers too often apply the same tool indiscriminately to any problem just because they know it !

5.4. Start with prospective workshops.

In most cases, the collective prospective approach begins with a one- to two-day residential seminar which proves the best way to address the problem under study . The working group is introduced to tools and methods that may prove useful and the group members can become acquainted with each other. They not only receive training in methodology, but think productively about the problem under study. After the seminar, the group members are in a better position accurately to assess the problem and to adopt an appropriate working method. This method will not be fully validated until several weeks have elapsed.

An example of a prospective workshop in action : the Vierzon township facing its future

After thirty years of local communist government, all indicators were in the red. The inhabitants were deserting the town, as were the firms, with record levels of unemployment and strike action ; urban planning was haphazard. In June 1990, local town-council elections brought in a new majority (an intelligent blend of dissident socialists, determined liberals and grass-root ecologists). A fortnight later, the new town council decided to give the inhabitants a say and to organize extra-municipal commissions on the town's future. For two days some 80 persons (town council officers, trade union representatives, industrial executives, shop-owners, teachers, senior citizens, civil servants...) gave thought to the future of their town and drafted some proposals. The two plenary sessions attracted about 300 people and the committee delegates presented their ideas and suggestions, both in the public session but also to the media and to the town council members... a mobilization process was under way, with the aim of seeking a better future for Vierzon. This process can and should continue. It would be a pity merely to be content with the intellectual stimulus arising from the workshops. From this point on the image of Vierzon is no longer the same. Previously it was simply witnessing its own decline ; now it intends to control its future. More to come ....

The rules of the game are easy : the group divides into sub-groups, each choosing as its theme one of the following four topics :

1. anticipating and acting on change ;
2. eliminating erroneous preconceived ideas ;
3. arbitrating between short- and long- term policy decisions ;
4. competence trees : past, present and future dynamics.

The framework for the workshops can be restricted to just a few overhead transparencies. The workshops can schedule their work sessions into 2 to 4 hour modules.

Prospective workshops may involve groups ranging in size from 10 to 100 persons who have "common life experiences" and who wish to think together about possible and/or desirable changes, with a view to better controlling them and re-directing them. The ideal number of participants would appear to lie somewhere between 25 and 35. It is then possible to have a limited number of sub-groups, each with 5 or 6 persons, sharing the work assignments. It is advisable to have at least two sub-groups working on 'Anticipation of Change' (so that they can compare their findings) and there must always be one group working on 'Preconceived Ideas'. In this way certain unspoken assumptions will be voiced and this particular group will play the role of watchdog (and punch-ball) for all the other groups.

Workshops can serve as 'launching-pads' for new thought processes and as a way to take control of change. In certain cases, however, the usefulness of such workshops can be even more immediate. Thus, for a consulting group, it may prove advisable to translate future challenges (as identified by the prospective workshops) into associated objectives, to identify sub-objectives, possible actions, projects, other studies that would contribute to these objectives (using the 'tree of relevance' method), and to compare this potential overview with the reality of the studies and projects under way. This approach also enables rapid identification of any ongoing actions whose aims are imprecise, as well as major challenges which require new action.

STRATEGIC PROSPECTIVE WORKSHOPS

(organizations involved with the author since 1985)

---

* Renault (automobile consortium)
* Bongrain (agro-food)
* Chanel (cosmetics)
* L'Oréal
* EDF-GDF (electrical and gas utilities)
* French Army Command
* Ministry for Education, France
* Federation for private education, France
* Moselle regional amenities board
* Montpellier town council
* Vierzon town council
* Sollac (steel products)
* Adidas
* Bull and ICL

The summing-up sessions which follow the workshops enable everyone to gain a better insight into the key problems that should be given priority treatment. This enables the group to define a commonly agreed working method (i.e., whether they should use given tools or not) which is compatible with time constraints, available resources, lead-times and finally with the agreed objectives.

5.5. Practical guidelines for prospective groups.

* *Composition and modus operandi of the group*

The group mandate must be carefully defined (outlining the problems set, the aims, the source of the study, the target audience and the lead-times). Drafting of interim documents and the final report should be the collective responsibility of the group.

The group should ideally be steered by a "pilot", chosen from among the group. The pilot's role will be to lead and coordinate the assignment of individual tasks among the group members. The pilot will be required to provide leadership throughout the entire study, i.e., he should not be changed. It is his role continuously to review lead-times and to make necessary adjustments, primarily revising means and tools rather than objectives.

* *Meetings : scheduling and content*

The best frequency appears to be : three or four closely spaced meetings to begin with, then at least three annual meetings once the study is under way and finally three to four meetings to conclude. It is also advisable to establish ahead the schedule of meetings and the agendas by about five to six sessions.

Every meeting must have an agenda and minutes must be taken. For each session, all group members should file a status report for each session on the work for which they are responsible. At the end of each meeting, individual assignments should be detailed and the agenda for the following session approved.

* *Competence, group action and "sub-contracting"*

One should consult specialists both before selecting methodologies, and particularly before launching an application ; similarly, one should consult external and internal experts (for technical expertise and operational specialities) ; each interview should be conducted by two team members and the conclusions written up immediately. If need be, certain specific technical (or other) points could be sub-contracted out.

* *Role of the group leader and occasional external experts*

It is not always easy to put together a study group (bringing together a wide variety of talents and temperaments). The most difficult point is choosing a group leader capable of investing a considerable amount of his available time, both during working hours and off-duty should this be deemed necessary. The group leader prepares the meetings, takes notes, drafts the minutes, and must involve all members of the group by assigning the individual tasks. The group leader must also plan ahead and draw up a programme for the ensuing phases, identifying the problems and the most appropriate methods as he or she sees it.

It is in this way that the external expert's role can prove useful. His input is not only methodological ; he can be called upon to react to group ideas and even to be provocative on occasion. The presence of the external expert is not required for all meetings and it is the group leader who determines when it is most relevant to call upon his services.

* *Choice of method : efficiency, motivation and communication*

There is no *a priori* choice of method ; however, making a choice is vital if the meetings are to be effective. Where there is no method, there will be no common language, no valid exchanges, no coherence, no organization of ideas. Method is not an end in itself and one should not be shackled by its results ; method is merely an aid to make the group's thinking more relevant.

A rigorous method is also conducive to group cohesion and motivation ; interim status reports - which should be circulated - and visibility of progress also contribute towards motivation. Lastly, the choice of a method will be dependent on the type of problem under study (cf. start-up seminars), on time constraints and on the simple wish to see results published. The tools should be sufficiently simple to remain within the grasp of both the end-users and the target population.

Efficient running of meetings is not something that can be improvised. To quote Dr. Victor Bataillard -author of the COM-Tables- the following common deviations were noted :

- "Endless discussions on minor points which make participants lose sight of the main objectives.

- Those who direct the debates prefer listening to themselves rather than listening to others.They are convinced that the meeting was a success, whereas others in the group have been unable to express their views.

- The debate focuses on points which are unclear and which interest only a fraction of the audience.

- Major contributions are not included in the minutes, nor recorded in any other way, especially when they are not initiated by the most important person present.

- The people running the meeting do not keep to the agenda.

- The people in charge of the meeting prefer indulging in small-talk rather than running the meeting".

In order to run a meeting efficiently, several methods can be used such as COM-Tableaux, METAPLAN, CREAPLAN. They all have points in common, apart from their Germanic origin (a concern for efficiency, even in creativity) . For example, the clever utilization of coloured cards of varying shapes and sizes : (rectangular, oval, circular), of green cards for positive ideas, and orange cards for critical points, of adhesive stickers, etc...

According to such methods all participants are allowed to express themselves freely but briefly in writing (no more than three lines or seven words per card) or in a presentation not exceeding 30 seconds. Ideas that are beyond the scope of the themes under debate are posted up for later discussion. Differences of opinion are identified by a lightning symbol. Each group member contributes to the logistics for the entire group. The results -as posted up- to a large extent reflect the ensuing minutes of the meeting.

CHAPTER III

THE SCENARIOS METHOD

The scenarios method which we discuss here was largely developed at the time the author was in charge of the Department of Futures Studies with the SEMA Metra Consulting Group, from 1974 to 1979.

With hindsight, it is now clear that setting up such an approach in *prospective*, with twenty or thirty actual applications undertaken in companies and public administration, contributed to :

- stimulating strategic thought and communication within companies ;
- improving internal flexibility of response to environmental uncertainty, and providing better preparation for possible system breakdowns ;
- reorienting policy options according to the future context on which their consequences would impinge.

In the course of this chapter we review the origins of scenarios methods, define the main concepts on which they are based, and set forth the aims and the logic of the underlying process.

1. Origins and definitions

The future is multiple and several potential futures are possible ; the path leading to this or that future is not necessarily unique. The description of a potential future and of the progression towards it comprises a 'scenario'. The word 'scenario' was introduced into futurology by Hermann Kahn in his book *The Year 2000*, but the usage there was primarily literary, imagination being used to produce rose-tinted or apocalyptic predictions previously attempted by authors such as Anatole France (*Island of the Penguins*), or George Orwell (1984).

In France, the OTAM team was the first to use a scenarios method, in a study of geographical futures undertaken for DATAR[1]. Since that time, this method has been adapted to industrial futures, notably in a study of 'chemical-agricultural' futures carried out by C. Kintz and G. Ribeil at SEMA in 1977[2].

The US researchers, Gordon, Helmer, Dalkey, and others, have developed several rather more formal methods to construct scenarios. All these are based on discussions among experts : Delphi, cross-impact matrix, etc. Developments are regularly published in journals, *Futures*[3], and *Technological Forecasting and Social Choice*[4].

---

[1] DATAR, 'France in year 2000 : a scenario of the unacceptable', Projects and Research in Prospective, N°20, Paris, la Documentation Française, 1971.

[2] See also 'Three scenarios for employment by the year 2000', in 'Employment or the obsession with the future', *Futuribles*, 1977.

[3] *Futures*, Butterworth, Heinemann, Oxford, U. K.

[4] *Technological Forecasting and Social Choice*, Elsevier, New York, USA.

In practice, there is no one scenarios method, but rather a variety of methods of construction (some simplistic, others sophisticated). However, a kind of consensus seems to have been reached ; the term 'scenarios method' only applies to an approach which includes a number of specific steps (systems analysis, retrospective, actors' strategies, elaboration of scenarios) which interrelate as discussed below.

The following concepts can be defined :

- *An invariant* : a phenomenon assumed to be permanent up to the horizon studied. Example : climatic phenomena.

- *Strong trend* : a movement affecting a phenomenon in such a way that its development in time can be predicted. Example : urbanization.

- *A germ* : a factor of change hardly perceptible at present, but which will constitute a strong trend in the future. In fact, a germ variable is what Pierre Massé (1967) described as a harbinger of the future : 'A sign which is slight in terms of present dimensions but huge in terms of its virtual consequences'.

- *Actors* : those who play an important rôle in the system through variables which characterize their plans and which they, to some extent, control. Example : the consuming countries, the producing countries, the multinationals, etc are actors in the energy system.

- *A strategy* : a set of tactics (set of conditional decisions) determining each actor's acts relative to his plan under every possible contingency.

- *A conflict* : may result from the confrontation between opposing strategies of the actors, and may take the form of an outbreak of tension between two trends (overcrowding and lack of space, constrained time and free time). The outcome of these conflicts determines the evolution of the balance of power between actors, or strengthens the weight of one trend or another.

- *An event* : the notion of an event is defined by E. Borel in the following manner : 'An event is an abstract entity whose only characteristic is to happen or not to happen'. An event can be considered as a variable taking only one of two values, in general '1' if the event happens, and '0' if the event does not happen ; such an event will be called an isolated event.

- *Randomness, subjective probabilities* : we refer to the long established but still relevant work of Professor Ville (1937). A phenomenon is said to be random[5] when it can take a certain number of values, to each of which is attached a subjective probability. We 'can consider the calculation of the probability of an isolated event as a subjective judgement, insofar as the considered event is classified in a category of events which subjectively have the same degree of probability. It is thus the expert who, in passing his judgment, establishes his categories'. A subjective probability is a

[5] 'Any event in the past or future of which we possess only partial information (ie we are incapable of confirming or otherwise whether the event took or will take place) shall be considered a random event. To attribute a probability to this event is equivalent to assigning to all or part of the information a number denoting the degree of randomness' (Ville, 1937).

gamble[6] which is almost always listed if we consider an event which will in fact either occur (probability one) or not (probability zero), but which must be considered as won if, among all the events to which we have attributed *X* chances in 100 of occurring, there are actually *X* in 100 which occurred at the given time[7].

2. Types of scenarios and strategies

Scenario : 'A totality made up of the description of a future situation and of the sequence of events which facilitates evolution from the original situation to this future situation'. To this definition, proposed by J. C. Bluet and J. Zemor (1970), we would add that the set of events must demonstrate a certain coherence.

Classically, a distinction is made between the following :

Possible scenarios, ie, everything that can be imaged ;
Realizable scenarios, ie, all that is possible, taking account of constraints ;
Desirable scenarios, ie, which fall into the possible category, but which are not all necessarily realizable.

According to their nature or their probability, these scenarios may be termed 'reference', 'trend-based', 'contrasted' or 'normative'.

In principle, a *trend-based scenario*, whether or not it is probable, corresponds to the extrapolation of trends at all points where choices are to be made.

Often the most probable scenario continues to be termed 'trend-based', although it may not correspond to a pure and simple extrapolation of trends, as its name suggests. Certainly, in the recent past, when the world changed less rapidly than today, the most likely development was in fact the continuation of trends. For the future, however, the most probable scenario in many cases seems to entail a severe breakdown of current trends.

The extrapolation of trends can lead to a situation which contrasts markedly with the present, as was shown by a study carried out for DATAR (1971), published in *Metra* under the title 'Trend-based scenario for France', and by Documentation Française under the title 'Scenario of the unacceptable'. In this case the trend-based scenario is based on extrapolation of trends, but is not the most probable scenario.

Since then, following the repercussions of this study, a certain amount of confusion of language set in. We therefore propose to use the term 'reference scenario' to refer to the most probable scenario, whether or not it is trend-based.

---

[6] 'A judgment of probability must be capable of embodiment in a gamble and the overall success of a certain number of these wagers will be the measure of the relevance of the judgment'.

[7] When a person says, 'I estimate the probability of an (isolated) event at 75 %', we follow Ville in understanding this judgment to mean, 'If you were to note all the events to which I would assign a probability of 75 %, and if you were to observe, for a large number of cases, the frequency with which the supposed event did in fact occur, I predict that the frequency would be in the vicinity of 75 %'.

A *contrasted scenario* is the exploration of a deliberately extreme theme, the a priori determination of a future situation. Whereas the trend-based scenario corresponds to an exploratory approach towards the evolution of a future situation, the historic contrasted scenario corresponds to a normative, imaginative, anticipatory approach ; a scenario for a future situation is chosen that generally contrasts markedly with the present (eg. coastal France, France with a population of 100 million) ; then one examines in reverse the course of events, ie, the evolutionary scenario, which could lead to this situation.

Practice has also given rise to another definition of the contrasted scenario, also corresponding to an exploratory attitude, examining the evolution of events to arrive at a situation. In this case, the contrasted scenario is defined as a highly unlikely course of events, and it is precisely its generally highly contrasted nature that makes it unlikely. This is the definition which we shall adopt here. However, this does not mean that we are abandoning the normative for the exploratory ; in our view, this distinction is only of operative interest. In fact, once the evolution and the situation are described, in one direction or the other, the corresponding course of events is both exploratory and normative.

It is among the realizable scenarios, which have a higher than zero probability, that we find contrasted (unlikely) scenarios and the field of development where the most probable scenarios are found. As regards *desirable scenarios*, these are found somewhere within the possible zone, and are not all necessarily realizable.

From anticipation to action

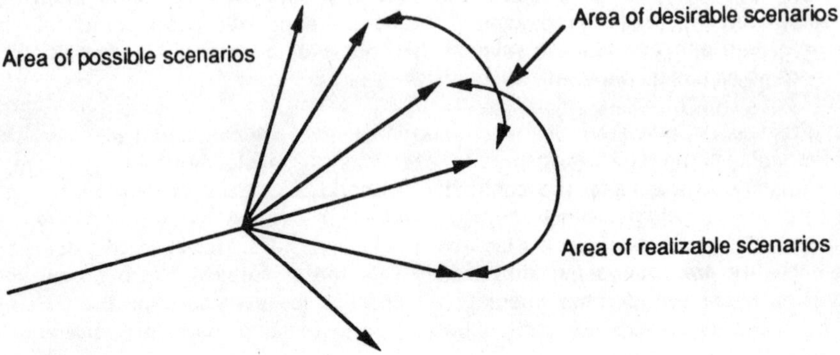

Figure III-1

Classification of scenarios according to probability and overall vision

Probability / Vision	Scenarios: Likely	Scenarios: Unlikely
Exploratory, from the present to the future	Extrapolation-based reference scenario (may or may not be trend-based)	Extrapolation-based contrasted scenario
Anticipatory, imag- -inative, normative (from the future towards the present)	Anticipatory reference scenario	Anticipatory contrasted scenario

Table III-1

Some areas of application of the scenarios method
(total or partial application by the author since 1975)

* Air transportation parameters
* Long-haul passenger demand
* Aircraft construction
* Shipbuilding in Portugal
* World petro-chemical industry
* Off-shore industries
* European automobile industry
* The cosmetics industry
* The dairy-produce sector
* Fairs and exhibitions in France
* Distribution of industrial products
* Distribution of electrical goods
* Demand for public transport
* Transportation modes in the Paris region
* Demand for environmental products
* Nuclear power sector
* French water networks
* Migration in the EEC
* Motivation of business executives
* The Three Valleys ski region, France
* The postal services
* Insurance sector
* The Bank of France
* Household consumption of banking products
* Videotex
* Geopolitical developments
* The Sahel region
* The Paris region
* The William Saurin company (agro-food)
* Aluminium
* Personal weapons
* Tourism and leisure
* Mail order services
* Noise
* Power distribution networks
* Building
* Steel industry

There is often confusion between scenarios and strategies. While scenarios depend on the type of vision adopted (exploratory, normative or retroprojective) and on probability, strategies depend on attitudes adopted in the face of possible futures.

Apparently, it is the concept 'normative' which gives rise to this confusion. In the case of scenarios the word 'normative' is used in a retroprojective sense, whereas it naturally refers to the notion of norms and objectives when we are talking about strategy. In other words, there are no scenario-objectives, but only strategies.

It is important not to confuse the dimensions or key components of the scenarios (demographic, technological, economic political, social...) with the configurations that each of these components can present. This is where morphological analysis comes in.

A system made up of four components, each having four configurations, will in principle have 256 (4^4) possible states. How can we navigate in this morphological space without being swamped by the sheer number of possible combinations ? One answer is provided by the combined utilization of the methods of morphological analysis and probabilization of combinations of configurations (interplay of hypotheses) through the SMIC method.

3. Objectives of the scenarios method

Increasing uncertainty, growing interdependence, the quickening pace of change in certain areas (political, technological, industrial, etc), and the noticeable lack of action in others (demographic, energy, socio-cultural) are all factors which call for a futures approach when considering present actions. Specifically, the following are required :

- *alternative scenarios* for future development, along with identification of the associated problems and opportunities, given the objectives which have been selected ;

- *the possible actions* required to remedy such problems or take advantage of such opportunities ;

- *the consequences of possible actions* given the scenario envisaged and the objectives selected.

The scenarios method specifically tries to conceive all possible futures and to explore the paths leading to them in order to clarify present actions and their possible consequences.

The objectives of the scenarios method are :

- *to detect* the priority issues for study *(key variables)*, by identifying relationships between the variables of the specific system under study through systemic analysis ;

- *to determine*, especially in relation to key variables, the *main actors* and *their strategies*, and the means at their disposal for bringing their projects to a successful conclusion ;

- *to describe*, in the form of *scenarios*[8], the development of the system under study, by taking into account the most probable evolutionary path of the key variables and by using sets of assumptions about the behaviour of the various actors.

The scenarios method comprises two phases : the construction of the database ; and, on this basis, the setting out of scenarios which lead to the generation of forecasts.

We can, in fact, use the techniques of classical forecasting within the framework defined by a scenario to convert it into quantitative terms.

The complementarity between the scenarios of *prospective* and the models of forecasting work operates in one direction but not in reverse : models have to be tested in the framework of the interplay of probable, coherent, hypotheses supplied by the scenarios, and not the other way round. In other words, designating the variants arising from simulation with a single model as scenarios, *is not prospective*.

By taking the different scenarios into account, we can then evaluate the consequences of previously decided orientations and, with the aid of multicriteria methods, we can deduce the priority strategic actions to be taken in order to exploit the expected changes, thus helping to devise the strategic plan (see Figure III-2). It will be seen in Part Two of this book that the choice of strategic options, taking environmental scenarios (external diagnosis : threats and opportunities) into account is preceded by the stages of an internal audit (strengths and weaknesses) and competitive positioning. See Figure III-3 for a diagrammatic of the scenarios method described below.

3.1. Construction of the base

The first stage attempts to construct the 'base', ie an 'image' of the present state of the system, which will serve as a starting point for the futures study. This image must be :

- detailed and comprehensive, both quantitatively and qualitatively ;
- broad in scope (economic, technological, political, sociological, etc) ;
- dynamic, clearly identifying past trends and harbingers of the future ;
- explanatory of mechanisms of change and of actors (movers of the system).

[8] Scenarios develop :

- on the one hand, the situation of the phenomenon being studied and its environment for a chosen horizon, as well as the best route to it (*reference scenario*) ;
- on the other hand, the extreme situations within which the phenomenon is located (*contrasted scenarios, both pessimistic and optimistic*).

Objectives of the scenarios method

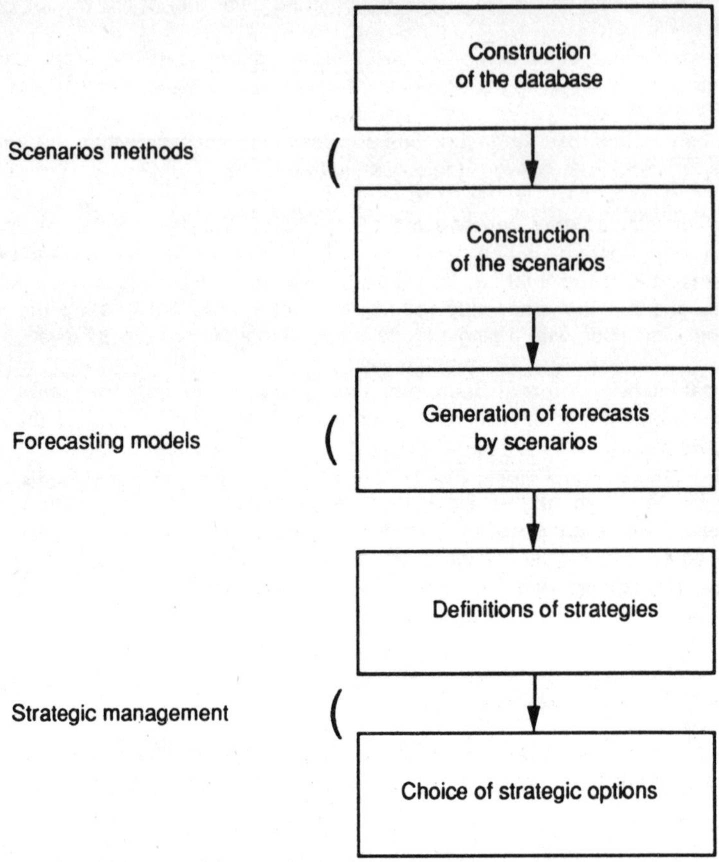

Figure III-2
From scenarios to strategy

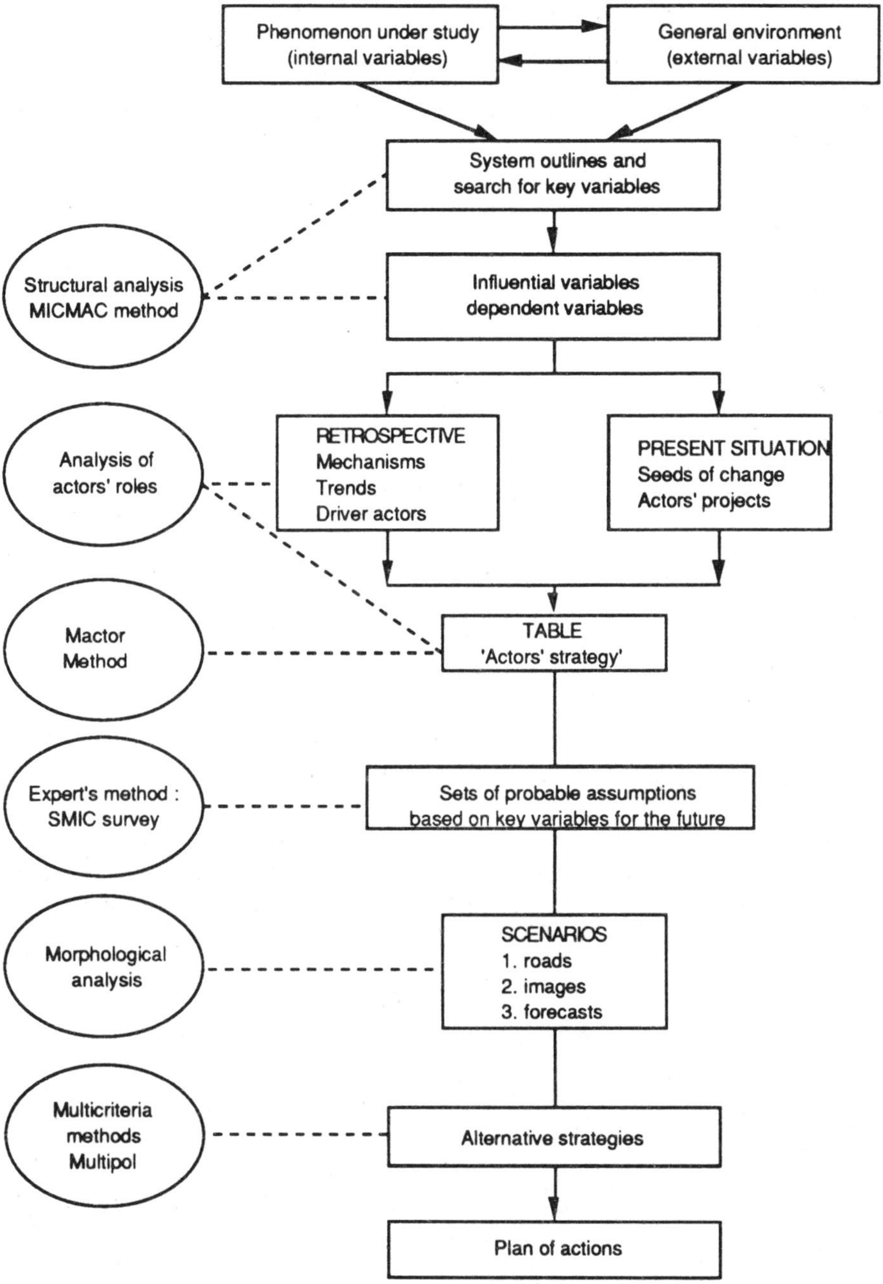

Figure III-3
The scenarios method

The base is constructed in three phases :

- the delimitation of the system studied and the general environment (political, economic, technological, etc.) ;
- identification of the key variables ;
- retrospective and actors' strategies.

Delimitation of the system studied. This forms a very important phase. Care should be taken not to exclude *a priori* from the field of study those technical, economic, and political elements that are now without influence on the phenomenon under study, but which might, in the longer term, begin to exercise significant influence on the development of the system. Conversely, one should avoid falling into the trap of carrying out a futures study for society at large, whatever the subject of the actual study.

When delimiting the system, one draws up as complete a list as possible of the variables that should be taken into consideration, whether quantifiable or not, thereby providing an overall vision of the system under study and its environment. In this way, we develop a reasonably accurate definition of the system. In order to achieve this result, a number of methods are used, *viz* interviews, seminars with specialists, brainstorming, checklist building etc.

One thus establishes the list of variables that apparently characterize the system, and one then divides them into two groups :

- *internal variables,* which characterize the phenomenon ;
- *external variables,* which characterize the general explanatory environment of the phenomenon as studied in its demographic, political, economic, industrial, technological and social etc, context.

The search for the principal determinants of the system and their parameters is implemented by an examination of the direct and indirect effects of general environmental variables (external variables) or the variables characterizing the phenomenon under study (internal variables).

The technique used in this research *-structural analysis-* is a commonly used, valuable tool. We will see that structural analysis demonstrates a hierarchy of variables (both driver power and dependence).

Highlighting certain variables confirms our initial intuition and raises questions about other variables that would not otherwise be asked. The typology of variables enables a better understanding of the system's structure.

The explanatory analysis is carried out across the groups of key variables as identified by structural analysis : it consists of a retrospective and current analysis of the actor's situation. The retrospective avoids overemphasis of the current situation, the result of which would be to bias the study with conjunctural factors. The aim is to identify the mechanisms and the leading actors which have influenced the development of the system in the past. It likewise aims to throw light on the invariant factors in the system and the major trends.

Analysing the contemporary situation also identifies the seeds of change within the movements of the key variables, as well as the strategies of the actors behind these movements. To that end, the analysis takes into consideration not only the quantified or quantifiable data, but also the qualitative parameters : economic, sociological, political and ecological, etc.

This analysis -at the end of the database stage- results in the identification of the 'actors' strategies'. This leads to a confrontation between the actors' intentions and to the resultant development of the balance of power between them which determines the future. This provides a synthesis (in table form) of the analysis of past developments and the current situation.

3.2. Building scenarios

Given the influential factors, the trends, the actors' strategy and the seeds of change that we have touched on in the preceding section, we can set in motion the scenarios method[9] by having the evolutionary mechanisms intervene and by confronting the actors' strategies (all possible convergences and divergences).

<table>
<tr><th colspan="4">Dimensions and configurations of the Interfuturs scenarios
J. Lesourne, D. Malkin (1979)</th></tr>
<tr><th>Dimensions</th><th colspan="3">Configurations envisaged</th></tr>
<tr><td>Relations between developed countries</td><td colspan="2">Collegiate management</td><td>Partial fragmentation between poles</td></tr>
<tr><td>Internal dynamics of developed societies</td><td>Consensus, favouring high growth</td><td>Rapidly changing values and moderate growth</td><td>Conflict between social groups and moderate growth</td></tr>
<tr><td>Evolution of relative productivity</td><td colspan="2">Convergence</td><td>Divergence</td></tr>
<tr><td>Relations between North and South and among developing countries</td><td>Large increase in North-South economic exchange</td><td>Increased North-South divide</td><td>Fragmentation of the South by region, in liaison with the developed countries</td></tr>
<tr><td colspan="4">A scenario associates a specific configuration with each dimension. Thus there are 36 possible combinations here. Interfuturs focused its analysis on some of these.</td></tr>
</table>

Table III-2

[9] A scenario is the set formed by the description of a future situation (or 'final image') and the consistent route which interconnects the present and final situations.

The choice of final images. If the developmental possibilities arising from the problem under consideration are characterised by *n* hypotheses, then there are 2^n possible final images[10].

The SMIC[11] method allows a hierarchy of the 2^n final possible images to be obtained from the probabilities assigned to the hypotheses ranked in order of decreasing probability. A choice is then made of the image corresponding to the most probable scenario, together with the images of the contrasting scenarios.

Allowing for the degree of uncertainty which governs the hypotheses, the method relies essentially on the consultation of experts. This consists of :

- Questioning the experts as to the probability of the hypotheses occurring or not : the simple probabilities of each hypothesis together with the conditional probabilities, since the probabilities can be interconnected. The experts (twenty or thirty) are consulted by questionnaire. They are chosen from different sectors in keeping with the field to be explored (government, entrepreneurial, international, university, etc.).
- Calculating the probabilities assigned by each expert to the various scenarios possible, ranking them by hierarchy.
- Carrying out a sensitivity analysis : while varying slightly the probability of a hypothesis, the variations induced in the other hypotheses are then observed.

These procedures then allow deduction of the inflential and dependent hypotheses.

The results provided by the various experts and the resulting hypotheses are then compared, allowing identification of :

- the final image on the one hand, of the reference scenario, which is the image most often quoted among those best 'placed' by the experts, and which corresponds to the most probable overall outcome ;
- the contrasted images selected, on the other hand, from among the images most often cited by the experts and having a significant mean probability of occurrence. The corresponding scenarios describe an environmental evolution which is typically very different from that of the reference scenario. Often images that are pessimistic or optimistic (from a desired point of view) are selected.

Developments and 'pathways'. At this stage the scenarios are still embryonic, since each is limited to the outcome of hypotheses. The main problem is now to describe the 'pathway' from the present situation to the final images selected for the reference scenario and the contrasted scenarios.

---

[10] If $n = 2$, there are two hypotheses *H*(1) and *H*(2), and four possible final images :
H(1) and *H*(2) occur ;
H(1) occurs, *H*(2) does not occur, and *vice versa* ; neither *H*(1) nor *H*(2) occurs.

[11] SMIC (System and Matrix of Cross Impacts), presented in Chapter V on expert consensus methods.

The elaboration of a scenario usually calls for a division of the period under study into successive sub-periods with intermediate images. Naturally the number of these sub-periods depends on the natural cycles present in the system.

To ensure coherence of the 'pathways' between the different images (present situation, intermediate and final images), the basic hypotheses are worked through thoroughly. They result either from the conclusions developed progressively (using information gathered from the base, particularly the table of actors' strategies) or by induction from the fundamental hypotheses.

Thus the scenarios method consists of coherently describing the developments as and when they arise, between the present situation and the chosen horizon, by bringing to bear the evolutionary mechanisms compatible with the hypotheses, while following the trends of the main variables for the phenomena as revealed by structural analysis. The scenario is completed by a detailed description of the final image (and the intermediate images if necessary).

The scenarios method, as described here, represents a path, the logic of which (delimitation of the system, retrospective analysis, actors' strategy, working out of scenarios) has been confirmed by numerous futures studies (see Figures III-4 and III-5).

However, this logic proves to be an inadequate tool when it comes to undertaking analysis, understanding and explanation of increasingly complex systems, hence the necessity of using the more formal tools of systems analysis as defined by Y. Barel (1971) as follows :

In most cases, systems analysis consists of emphasizing the fact that the objective under investigation must be placed in a wider context than the original system. The term 'systems analysis' underlines the fact that it is useful to break down complex problems into their elementary components.

In the chapters which follow we present some of these formal tools, which may be needed at various stages of the scenarios method.

- *Structural analysis and the MICMAC method*, particularly useful for delimiting the system and determining the key variables, are set out in Chapter IV.
- *The analysis of the actors* is the main topic of Chapter V.
- *Expert methods* (*Delphi and cross-impact*) allow probabilities to be assigned to the hypotheses for the key variables of the future probabilities. Chapter VI describes one of them : the SMIC method.
- The methods allowing *decisions* to be taken in the presence of *multiple criteria* and in an uncertain future are essential to move from *prospective* to strategy. To the extent that multicriteria methods are decision-aids, useful in both *prospective* and strategic management, they receive specific attentive in chapter VII.

Through presenting these different methodological tools, at the same time we gain better insight into how to put the scenarios method into operation. However, although the path is logical, it is not absolutely necessary to follow it from A to Z : everything depends on the level of knowledge one has of the system being investigated and of the objectives being pursued. The scenarios method is a modular approach : one can limit the study to this or that module, as required, eg :

- structural analysis and the search for key variables ;
- analysis of the strategy of the actors ;
- expert enquiry on key hypotheses for the future.

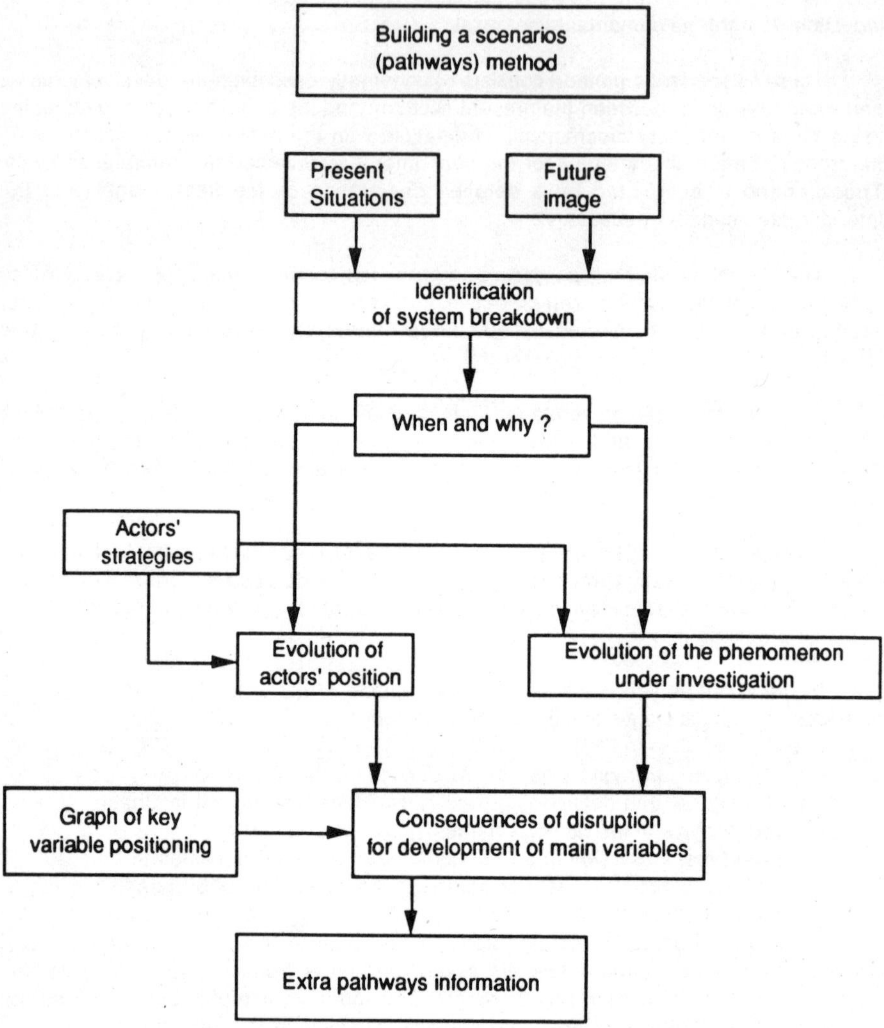

Figure III-4

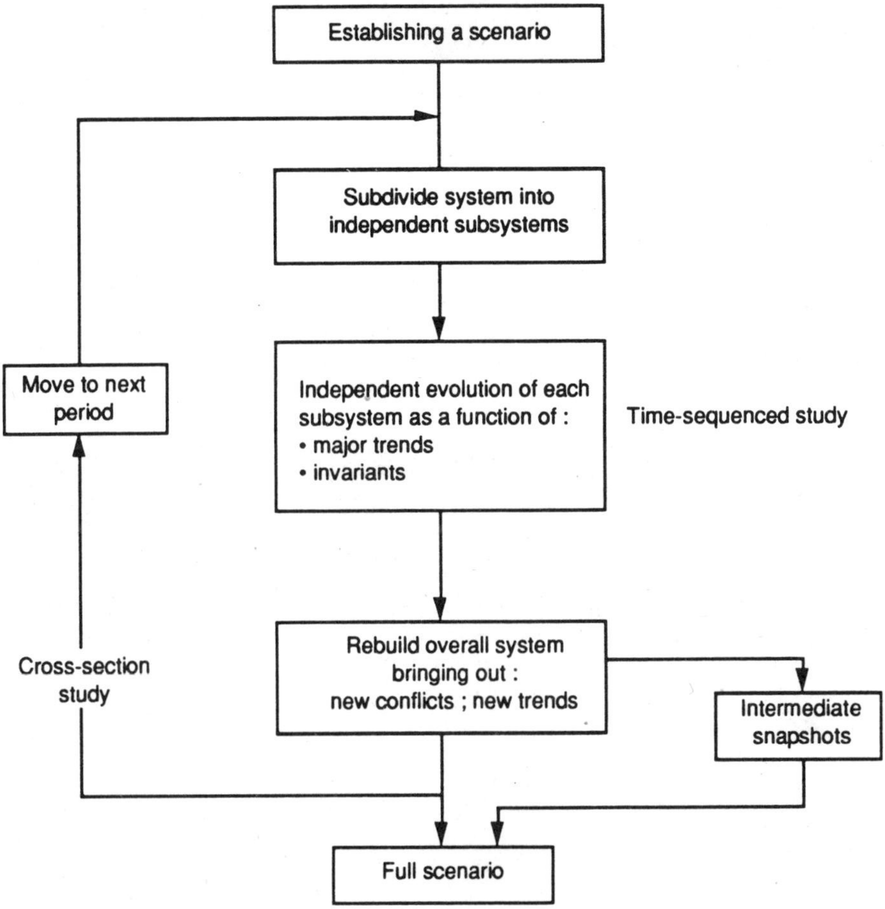
Establishing a scenario
Subdivide system into independent subsystems
Independent evolution of each subsystem as a function of :
• major trends
• invariants
Time-sequenced study
Move to next period
Cross-section study
Rebuild overall system bringing out :
new conflicts ; new trends
Intermediate snapshots
Full scenario

Figure III-5

One of the main constraints on the scenarios method is time : it generally takes 12-18 months to follow the whole path through, and at least half of this is taken up with constructing the base. If there are only three to six months available for the study, it is preferable to concentrate on the module which seems to be the most important.

The full scenarios method has been applied in under half of the cases quoted in exhibit III-1 which follows. To illustrate the modular nature of the tools of *prospective*, we present them in a number of case studies. For reasons of confidentiality, it is not possible to present a complete and detailed case in all its phases.

The logical pathway which must lead to the presentation of a plan of action consists of constructing a basis for thought, the working out of scenarios, and the evaluation of alternative strategies. Although the method does not aspire to universality of application and is no sort of panacea, it at least has the merit of being the fruit of experience ; over nearly ten years, more than 30 *prospective* studies have been successfully concluded on similar bases.

We must not expect from a *prospective* method that which it cannot provide, however sophisticated it might be : *viz*, that it should tell us what the future *really* holds for us. No-one can do that, because the future is composed not only of the interplay of determinate factors but also of individuals' freedom.

However, the scenarios method can provide simple help towards thinking constructively about the future. It can help (and this is a strong point in its favour) to choose the strategy which, in the midst of all kinds of constraints, will prove the most likely to bring our plans to fruition while retaining a maximum set of possible advantages.

Example of a Scenario ; Doubling life expectancy

We could live, on average, to an age of 140 for men, and 150 for women. If we suppose the age for marriage does not vary much, there would be an average of at least four or five generations alive at the same time in each family. What would the retirement age be ? If it were 65, the number (proportion) of old-age pensioners would become intolerable for society. As this would be impossible, the retirement age would be postponed. Thus strong expansion would be required in order to create full employment, and we would work to 100 or more. But, to work for 100 years implies keeping abreast of progress : general retraining would become a lifelong commitment. Since one cannot envisage learning sciences that would still be useful 100 or 200 years hence, a change of objective for primary and secondary education would be needed. It would have to provide the basic tools and prepare the intelligence to adapt itself to change by exercises in mental gymnastics (mathematics and Latin, for example, as well as exercises in creativity). There would be an imbalance between generations and conflicts (short of a radical change in education). Extra accommodation would be required, since the population itself would double, even though the birth rate might remain stable. There would be profound changes in inheritance : we would not inherit goods or power until nearly 100 years of age. Power would tend to remain in the hands of the over-100's. But that would be unacceptable and the younger generations would claim their autonomy. They would be treated as minors until they are nearly 50. Thanks to contraception -accepted by all under the absolute necessity of restraining population growth- women would be free of maternity around 35. They would then have around 115 years' life left. Because their services would be needed to support the aged they would all take up employment. Their salaries would no longer be considered as incidental and they would have access to all positions.

A number of female geniuses would be revealed, all those who had not hitherto been able to break out of the stifling sociological web which had up to then been the binding rule. Public opinion would accept them. All those men and women who had neither passion nor creativity nor adequate spirit or soul would find life too long and would commit suicide. The troublemakers would last for a long time, with a concomitant growth of criminality. Moral independence would be sought by other means : psychiatry would be revolutionized, etc.

Source lost in the mists of time

Exhibit III-1

4. Illustrations

Selecting illustrations is problematic. On one hand, many interesting examples of corporate scenarios cannot be published for reasons of confidentiality. On the other hand, most scenarios published by public administrations or international organizations have had no impact on their strategy.

4.1. Scenarios as tools of strategy and/or management

As regards companies, we need to draw a distinction between those that are carrying out highly confidential prospective studies for the sole use of the directors making strategic decisions (Lafarge, Pechiney, Mercedes or Nestle come to mind), and those which are rather using prospective as a tool for collective thought and mobilization of minds (such as Renault, RATP or the Ministère de l'Equipement with the DDE) and which make communication compulsory.

In the first case -prospective as a strategic tool- the Lafarge group represents one of the best examples of 'cold' prospective thought which has had an impact on strategy : by the mid-1970s this group had anticipated the decline of cement (-1 % annually between now and the end of the century), and had decided to invest in a leading-edge field (biotechnology, with the take-over of the Coppee group) whose sole characteristic in common with cement was its low manpower requirements. Companies of this type are always in step with the future, and have already anticipated the consequences of the creation of Europe and the opening-up of Eastern Europe.

In the second case -prospective as a tool for mobilization and management- the process of involving staff, which these prospective exercises facilitate, allows the company to be better informed as it faces change. The restructuring carried out at Renault (a one-third reduction in manpower between 1985 and 1989) was probably facilitated by the new awareness which emerged from the collective consideration of company change carried out between 1982 and 1984 -Operation IESC (Industrial, Economic and Social Change)- in which several thousand middle management and supervisors participated. In this case, transparency is mandatory, and just as there was an IESC notebook, so there are prospective and management notebooks at the Ministry of Equipment. These notebooks act as sound-boxes for the circulation and amplification of ideas.

Between these two extremes lie one point in common and several intermediate positions. The common point is the permanent but cyclical nature of prospective, marked by strong upbeats every four, five or seven years. The long-term backcloth must be of sufficiently good quality to last for several years. It is a little like driving a car -by switching on to full beam a few times, we are able to drive even better with dipped headlights.

As examples of intermediate cases of prospective, where it is both a strategic tool and a directors' tool for mobilization, we can cite the big oil groups Shell and Elf. Both have used scenarios for over 20 years and would even go so far as to advertise this practice as one of the key elements of their strategic management.

We shall not dwell here on the experience of Shell. We merely note that they use a fairly rudimentary method of scenario construction. Scenarios have primarily acted as a way of uniting and encouraging strategic activity and of creating a shared basis for thought for the directors of a highly decentralized group. The success of the scenario method has been greatly enhanced by the oil shocks which were already foreseen in 1971-1972.

Our impression, after several accounts by Shell management, is that they are concerned above all to stimulate the imagination of their strategists and to make them think together, for example by constructing scenarios of a technological society where information would universally replace energy... Yet it is not for this reason that the Shell group has moved out of the energy field somewhat and into telematics. Although the scenarios have a high level of internal transparency (a tool for communication between directors) and a good degree of coherence (intellectual logic) they seem to be much weaker when it comes to examining the relevance of questions and their probability.

At the methodological level, this work was inspired by a Frenchman, Pierre Wack (1985), whose own inspirational sources came from the founders of the Ecole Française de Prospective, who are not well known in Europe and even less in the USA. Pierre Wack has a number of spiritual successors such as Peter Schwartz, who in 1984 took over from Wack within Shell's prospective group, and who left for the USA in 1986 to set up the Global Business Network (GBN), a network of prospective practitioners serving an international club of companies.

Today Peter Schwartz is popularizing scenarios in the English-speaking world, and has even managed to win over his well-known friend, Michael Porter, who has incorporated the notion of scenarios in his most recent works. In this way French scenarios will soon be rediscovered and imported into Europe under the 'made in the US' label.

Planning at Shell, 1945-1980

The chronological list below illustrates how Shell moved from linear, highly quantified forecasts to the acceptance of uncertainty and the description of possible futures based on scenario analysis.

1945-1955 Physical planning
1955-1965 Planning by project and selectivity
1965-1972 Unified Planning Machinery (UPM) system
1967 Start of the Horizon 2000 study
1969-1970 Horizon Year Planning Exercise (with a 15-year horizon)
1971 Experimenting with scenarios at the company's registered offices in London
1972-1973 Introduction of planning by scenarios
1975 Introduction of medium-term cyclical scenarios
1976-1977 More thorough study of 'societal analysis' in planning
1978-1979 Deeper analysis of geopolitical and political risk
1979-1980 New examination of the very long term,+ development of planning capacity within the Group.

The method described by Pierre Wack is now well adapted. Group planners have accumulated a great deal of experience in analysing the crucial factors intervening in their field of activity, in identifying the relationships which develop between the various actors present, and in describing the process of evolution of these balances of power. All these analyses are incorporated into the coherent diagrams put forward for consideration by the decision makers.

The task of constructing global scenarios is carried out as a service by part of the Shell Group, which acts as a global environmental observatory. It produces global scenarios of developments in the economic environment, the energy environment, the oil environment, and so on. In these scenarios there are analyses of, among other things, demographic phenomena, political developments, changes in values and lifestyles, technological and economic developments, monetary problems, energy demand as a function of these factors, energy supply, the specific position of oil, the possible evolution of relations between the producer and consumer nations, the formation of crude oil price structures and the hypothetical evolution of these prices, etc.

Starting with scenarios of the global environment presented by the Group, the subsidiary companies construct their own scenarios, by studying those aspects which are more specific to their national environment and which have an impact on their activities.

Conceived as tools to aid strategic thought, the national scenarios must be multiple and yet not too numerous ; they must be the result of thorough and rigorous analysis, yet remain simple and easy to use ; and they must cover a broad spectrum of possibilities, while remaining in the realm of the probable. In 1981 all the oil companies, fearing the consequences of the conflict which had just broken out between Iraq and Iran, built up reserves of oil. Shell, thanks to the method described above, got rid of its surpluses before the market became overcrowded and prices collapsed.

4.2. Successful utilization of scenarios - the case of Elf

Here we wave the French flag with the case of the Elf Group, which carried out three prospective exercises in 15 years ; the first in 1969 looking ahead to the horizon of 1985, the second in 1978 with the horizon of 1990, and the third in 1985-1987 with the horizon of 1995. We were fortunate to be associated with the last of these, and reasons of confidentiality force us to limit our comments to the methodological aspects and to what François Didier was able to say (1989) and Paul Alba to publish (1989).

First exercise in 1969 : Elf up to 1985

A small team, reporting to the Research Director (Bernard Delapalme), made up of several internal and external consultants, was set up and produced a report. With hindsight it is interesting to note that although the oil shocks were not foreseen, nevertheless the vulnerability of the Group's situation in oil and in Algeria was perceived. Hence the recommendation that the Group should diversify, both geographically (into the North Sea) and sectorally (into chemicals, pharmaceuticals), which was acted upon effectively. In the field of technology, developments in batteries for fuel (electric) vehicles and artificial proteins were generally overestimated : two or three years later the group halted its research in this field. The arrival of telematics and the growing importance of environmental problems were foreseen, with the creation of a centre for information and research on the harmful effects. Overall, the sucess rate of this first exercise is largely positive. It recommended that the Group should double its size in relation to its competitors between 1969 and 1985. This objective was achieved.

Second exercise in 1978-1979 : Elf up to 1990

This study, under the responsibility of the Director of Strategy, François Didier, engaged the equivalent of eight full-time staff. The main goal was to define strategies in the face of three identified scenarios of global development (dark, grey and pink). As in the preceding exercise, developments in the energy field were wrongly perceived : it was at the height of the second oil shock, yet the price of oil in constant dollars fell. On the other hand, the study was very prudent as regards technological change. This did not prevent it from emphasizing innovation in the technical field, as well as in the economic and socio-organizational fields, and reorganizing its chemical activities while developing biotechnologies with Sanofi. Also to the credit of this study is a recommendation which was effectively acted upon : the setting up of Groups for Reflection and Study on Strategic Themes (GRETS). Around 20 of these were operating during the 1980s.

Third exercise in 1985-1987 : Elf up to 1995

Still under the responsibility of François Didier, the study took 18 months and involved several dozen people in the group. It was carried out in two phases : an exploratory phase, in order to construct environmental scenarios ; and a normative phase, in order to define strategies in the face of these scenarios. During the exploratory phase about 10 working groups were formed according to branch of activity and theme (environment, research, geopolitics). During the normative phase, three sample strategies were studied : 'Natural resource', 'Commodities', 'High tech, high growth'.

This exercise, like the earlier ones, was undertaken without a particular methodology, but with a high level of professionalism in activating the groups and respecting deadlines. The collective mobilization was undertaken in an upbeat manner : meetings with the president, branch directors, etc.

I had the opportunity to follow this exercise closely in my role as external consultant to the pilot committee -an exciting and, at times, difficult rôle of observer ; I was required to remain silent for hours and to react, if possible in a critical manner, to what had been said and put forward by different members of the group, some of whom were high-level managers.

The two external consultants were also used sensibly, as they were placed at the disposal of groups which felt the need for lively input, but were not imposed upon them. It is premature to assess the success record of this exercise. P. Alba (1988) merely notes as a conclusion : 'Once a company is important it cannot make leaps'. Elf Aquitaine has thus confined itself to basing its future development on its three industrial branches (oil, chemicals, health and hygiene) and on these alone.

The exercise to 1995 led to a memo from President Pecqueur on company direction, written on 17 July 1987 and distributed to all staff.

The Elf and Shell groups make good use of scenarios precisely because of the high degree of internal involvement that they have been able to develop. This does not prevent errors in forecasting and strategic diagnosis, and we therefore believe that these groups would be well advised to make a little more use of existing prospective tools in order to strengthen the relevance, coherence and probability of their analyses. As regards transparency, it would hardly be possible to do more for collective memory whilst observing necessary confidentiality.

Intelligent use of prospective and of scenarios (as a tool for strategy and management) has also long been evident in companies such as the Paris Public Transport System and for some years at EDF (French electricity board).

5. Anticipation and scenarios: myths and realities

The very use of the word 'scenario' can prove dangerous for future thinking : there is a risk of being swamped by media successes with little or no scientific grounding. Let us examine two preliminary questions :

- does using the term 'scenario' for any combination of hypotheses (for a given analysis), however attractive this may be, confer a degree of future respectability ?
- need one necessarily draw up full and detailed scenarios when undertaking future thinking ?

The answer is most assuredly : 'No !' on both counts. A scenario is not a future reality but a way of foreseeing the future, thereby throwing light on the present in terms of all possible and desirable futures. The test of reality, and a concern for efficiency , should be used to guide *prospective* thinking in order to gain a better mastery of history. A scenarios approach can only be credible and useful if it complies with four prerequisites : relevance, consistence, likelihood and transparency.

In other words, one must ask the right questions and clearly formulate the true hypotheses which are keys to the future. Without this procedure, there is a risk of leaving out some 80 % of all possible futures. With modern probability tools, such as the micro-computer package SMIC - Prob-Expert, it takes only a few minutes to provide results for a group study. Curiously, certain proponents of the *prospective* approach refuse to submit their own thoughts on an issue to a system which is akin to a lie-detector, or which would at least reveal contradictions in their reasoning.

The last prerequisite mentioned above (transparency from A to Z) implies that: '*a clear concept can always be stated clearly*'. This should apply to any problem, the methods used to solve it, the reasoning behind it, the results and the conclusions in regard to the scenarios envisaged. Far too often, unfortunately, either the simple reading of the scenarios proves laborious and the reader must invest considerable effort in ascertaining the prerequisite conditions (relevance, consistence), or the literary quality is so low that the reader finds it indigestible and sets it aside. Thus, due to a lack of close and critical review, a number of scenarios remain credible, i.e., they are given the benefit of the doubt and the reader is left feeling somewhat guilty that he has not read the text through to a logical end.

Without transparency, results will be unadaptable and will not enable implication of the actors (the public) that we wish to involve through the scenarios. Naturally the transparency and attractiveness of scenarios do not preclude quality of content ; scenarios with catchy titles, or which are presented in an emotion-ridden, pleasurable or doomsday style -such as '*Future Shock*'- can be convincing. Such works are fiction, i.e., a literary genre which *per se* is quite honourable and often makes for superb reading. A famous example is George Orwell's '*Nineteen Eighty-Four*'. However, they rarely contain relevant, coherent or even likely scenarios.

By replying negatively to the second question above, we want to make it clear that *anticipation and scenarios are not synonymous*. Too many studies in *prospective* have become bogged down over time because a group decided to launch into '*The scenarios method*'. But why, we may ask, did they do so ? A scenario is not an end in itself ; it only becomes meaningful when its results and implications are embodied in real action. Undertaking a scenarios approach is time-consuming (12 to 18 months is not uncommon) and there must be several persons involved in order to establish a team context and make the process viable. After three years the leaders of the OECD Interfuturs team (1976-1979) announced that they had insufficient time usefully to exploit all the results ! cf. J. Lesourne and D. Malkin (1979). We can safely add an extra year for circulating and publicizing results.

In most corporate and administrative organizations, such teams will be required to report within the year. In extreme cases, policy-makers may launch a *prospective* study that they wish to see finished in a matter of a few weeks. Thus the prevailing conditions are rarely ideal and it is better to throw a little light (rather than no light at all) on the impending decisions. Sheer common sense dictates the simple questions that one should raise at the outstart : what can be done in the given time, using the means available ? How can it be done in such as way as to be both credible and useful to the decision-makers ?

From this point of view, it will often be advisable to limit the scenarios to several key hypotheses, say four, five or six. Beyond such numbers, the sheer magnitude of possible combinations is such that the human mind simply gives up. Such straightforward scenarios are used as backgrounds for strategic options such as '*what if...?*' or '*what for...?*'. Short-cuts in a scenarios approach make it all the more crucial to do some preliminary thinking about the key variables, the trends and the actors' strategies.

One final difficulty that arises when building scenarios and selecting methodology relates to lead-times. Even if one had months, or even years, to finish the assignment, there is a risk inherent in the start-up phase because team members or even the team leader may change as the study progresses. A futures study rarely survives after the departure of the initiator. In major organizations -given existing staff mobility factors- it is preferable to limit the length of the project to one year and to plan for interim status reports. It is also advisable to identify a preliminary exploratory phase, during which the elements at stake are identified, and a regulatory phase during which the various strategic policy choices are defined, in terms of items identified in the preceding phase.

Here we end our general presentation of the scenarios method. In the following chapter we shall return to each of the stages involved (Cf. the general diagram of this chapter) and present the problems that arise, as well as the tools available to overcome them.

This will involve, in turn, identifying the key variables for the structural analysis (Chapter IV), analysing actors' games with the Mactor method (Chapter V), surveying the field of possibilities with morphological analysis (Chapter VI), and reducing uncertainty by the use of expert methods (Chapter VI).

CHAPTER IV

IDENTIFYING THE KEY VARIABLES : STRUCTURAL ANALYSIS

1. Origins and objectives of structural analysis

2. Listing all variables

3. Location of relationships within the structural analysis matrix

4. Search for the key variables with the MICMAC method

- 4.1. Direct and indirect classification (MICMAC)
- 4.2. The MICMAC principles : the raising of matrix to the power
- 4.3. Comparison between direct, indirect and potential classifications
- 4.4. The influence - dependence chart

5. Value and limitations of structural analysis

1. Origins and objectives of structural analysis

A system consists of a set of interrelated elements. The system structure, ie the network of relationships between these elements, is essential to an understanding of its evolution, because this structure maintains a certain permanence. The aim of structural analysis is to highlight the structure of the relationships between the qualitative variables, whether they are quantifiable or not, which characterize the system under study (eg a company and its strategic environment).

Structural analysis enables a system to be described by using a matrix which interconnects all the system components. This method enables analysis of these relationships and identification of the main variables.

With regard to the techniques used, as J. Barrand and C. Guigou (1984) noted, 'Structural analysis is based on Leontiev's input-output matrices, on the theory of graphs and the simulation exercises of operational research carried out soon after the last war in the USA, and in particular by the Rand Corporation to fulfil American army requirements'. Some systems analysis and technological forecasting methods have their origins in defence research. This was the case in France for the method of 'relevance trees' developed by the Centre de Prospective et d'Evaluation (CPE) (Centre for Prospective and Evaluation) of the French Ministry of Defence. This was not the case with structural analysis, however which seems to have been introduced into France by Professor Wanty, who worked for the Belgian subsidiary of the METRA International Group and who taught at the University of Paris Dauphine in 1969 and 1970. Since then structural analysis has become more widespread through, in particular, the work of Professors R. Saint-Paul and P. F. Tenière-Buchot (1974), and our own work at SEMA.

Structural analysis has two complementary objectives : first, during the initial phase to obtain as thorough a representation as possible of the system under study, in order, second, to reduce systemic complexity to its main variables. In his thesis on structural analysis and its developments, J. F. Lefebvre (1982) lists several of its applications :

- it can help in thinking about a system in order to build a more elaborate model such as, for instance, systems dynamics ;
- it can be used on its own in order, eg, to assess strategic choices ;
- it can form part of an overall approach such as the scenarios method ; and
- it can help group communications and discussions or group adherence to a specific objective.

In practice, structural analysis has been used in two main ways :

- in decision-making (research, identification of the variables on which to act to achieve the selected objectives) - the POPOLE model of P. F. Tenière-Buchot (l973) is a good example ; and

- in forecasting (research on the key variables which bear on the future dimension). This use was developed in the early 1970s and we were attracted, in particular by the development of the MICMAC method where the importance of a variable is measured less by its direct interrelationships but rather by many indirect interrelationships (J. C. Duperrin and M. Godet, 1973).

The next section deals mainly with the latter use of structural analysis in forecasting. This comprises several stages :

- listing all the variables ;
- location of interrelationships within the structural analysis matrix ; and
- search for the key variables by the MICMAC method.

2. Listing all variables

In order to develop as exhaustive a list as possible of the variables which define the system formed by the phenomenon under study and its environment, no research path is, *a priori*, excluded. All brainstorming and intuitive methods are useful here.

The process of listing all the variables should be assisted, preferably, by non-directed interviews with the representatives of the actors presumed to be involved in the system under study. The questions should be open, such as 'In your opinion, what are the factors which will condition the future evolution of such and such a phenomenon ?'

To identify these variables, several different political, economic, technological and social viewpoints should be adopted, in order to build up files and to organize several sessions of collective thinking. Following the accumulation of raw data, the actual listing of all variables is based on aggregating and refining the data so that a homogenous list is obtained. Also, given the nature of the phenomenon under study, it is often advisable to reclassify the variables by distinguishing between internal and external variables ; the internal variables characterize the sub-system under study whereas the external variables make up its environment.

Finally, detailed explanations of these variables are essential to identify the various interrelationships. Indeed, such an explanation can provide the detailed analysis of everything implied in the definition of a variable. Without the creation of this common base, the analysis and identification of interrelations could be rendered impossible or meaningless. These files, once completed, are kept open and they are updated as and when required. They thus form an information database which can systematically sort data.

Below, we describe the scale models built, under our supervision, by J. Barrand and C. Guigou (1984) as a case study of structural analysis. We concentrate on the determinants of employment and unemployment ; the analysis was reduced to the 41 variables shown in Table IV.1

3. Location of relationships within the structural analysis matrix

Within a systemic worldview, a variable can only exist because of its interrelationships ; intuitive recognition of the existence of certain interrelationships enabled us to pinpoint some variables when preparing the list.

Table IV.1
Determinants of employment and unemployment

Internal variables		1. Unemploymenl rate
		2. Unemployment rate for women
		3. Unemployment rate for young people
		4. Number of long-term unemployed
		5. Employment in services
		6. Employment in industry
		7. Employment in agriculture
Environmental variables (external)		
Economic and financial		8. Household income
		9. Rate of economic growth
		10. Household consumption
		11. Inflation
		12. Savings
	Internal	13. Financial situation of companies
		14. Interest rate (savings)
		13. Financial situation of companies
		15. Rates on the money market
		16. Money supply
		17. Budget deficit
		18. Constraints on the external balance of payments
		19. International context
	International	20. Degree of openness of the economy
		21. European harmonization
		22. Energy price and raw materials
Technological and industrial variables		23. Investment for rationalization
		24. Investment for expansion
		25. Operational productivity per hour
		26. Company competitiveness
		27. Technological and industrial evolution
Socio-demographic variables		28. Working population
		29. Employment rate among women
		30. Geographical concentration of unemployment
		31. Immigrant workers
		32. Parallel economy, moonlighting
		33. Social relationships

34. Uncertainties for the future
35. Evolution in ways of life

Institutional variables

36. Work legislation and regulations
37. Worksharing and income sharing
38. Distribution of mandatory wage deductions
39. Total value of mandatory wage deductions
40. Training
41. Work costs (average hourly wage)

Structural analysis attempts to interrelate the various variables in a dual input table (see Figure IV-1).

Before establishing whether there is a relationship between the two variables, the *prospective* group must systematically answer the following three questions :

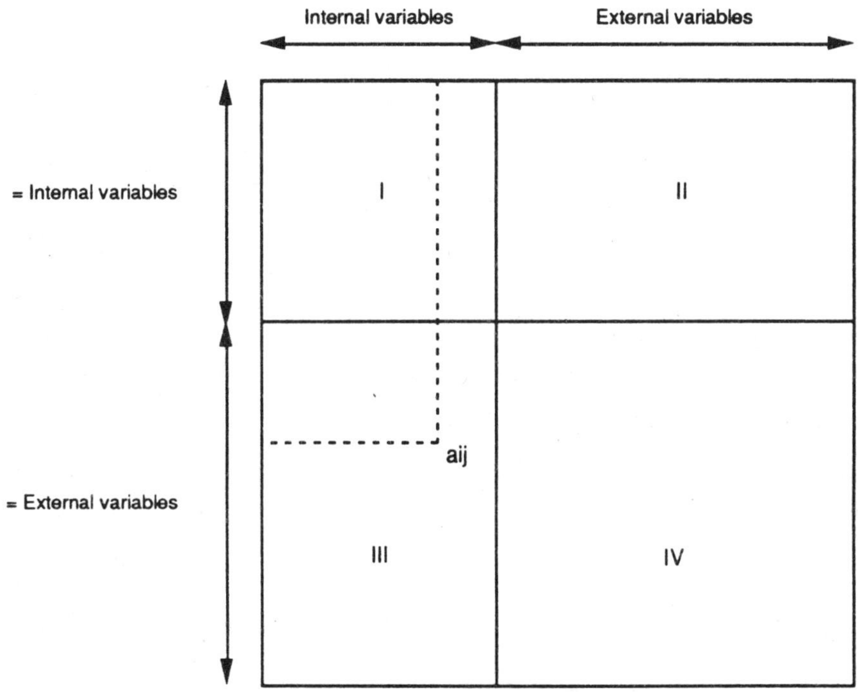

Figure IV-1
Structural analysis

(1) Does variable *i* causally affect variable *j*, or is this relationship the other way round, ie *j* to *i* (Figure IV-2(a)) ?

(2) Does *i* have an impact on *j*, or does some collinearity exist, ie, the third variable *k* has an impact on *i* and *j* ? (Figure IV-2(b)).

(3) Is the relationship between *i* and *j* direct, or does it operate through another listed variable ? (Figure IV-2(c)).

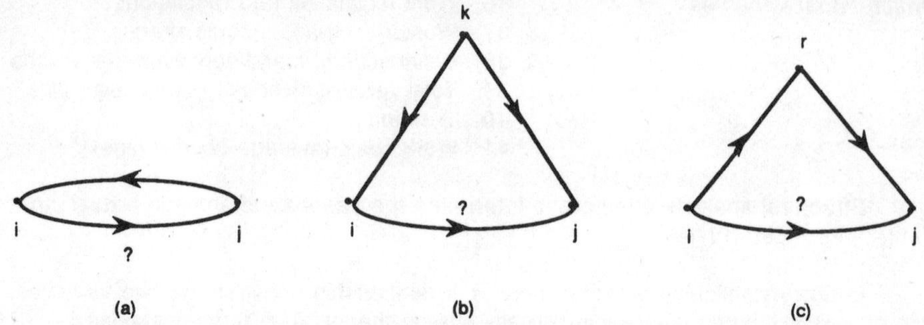

Figure IV-2
Three possible cases suggesting that *i* has a direct impact on *j*.

Many errors can be avoided by using this procedure when filling in the matrix.

At present some variables only have a weak influence. However, they could become much more important in a different context in the future ; this is the case, for example, with the 'new technologies for industry and agriculture' variables. Therefore, we should take into account *potential* relationships which, depending on the case, are to be added to the reference relationships, ie to those certainly in existence.

Normally, filling in the matrix is a *qualitative* exercise : we only state whether a relationship exists or not, although the strength of a particular relationship can also be specified. Thus, several direct relationship strengths can be distinguished: very strong (VS), strong (S), average (A), weak (W), very weak (VW) and potential (P). The term 'potential' refers to incipient relationships which still only have a weak influence but which could, in a future context, become very influential (for example the consequences of technical change). Thus, a certain dynamic can enter into the structural analysis, and the sensitivity of some results can be tested against the intensity of the relationships that are being taken into account. See Table IV-2 for matrix example.

One of two methods can be used to fill in the matrix:

- either in rows, by identifying the influence of each variable on all others ;
- or in columns, by recording which are the other variables influencing each variable.

Theoretically, it is useful to use both methods and to compare the results by superimposing the two completed matrices in order to identify differences and, consequently, the errors made. However, this practice often proves to be a time-consuming luxury the researcher can rarely afford. Indeed, most structural analyses completed thus far interrelate several dozens of variables, ie several thousand questions have to be asked, which takes several days of hard work.

Also, structural analysis is a systematic questioning procedure ; without the insights offered by the matrix, many of these questions would never be asked. Moreover, new variables are sometimes discovered that nobody had thought of when drawing up the original list of variables.

Filling in the matrix is a good technique for stimulating dialogue. Indeed, it stimulates exchanges of views and discussions to help create a common language within a *prospective group*. As it is, the structural analysis matrix remains qualitative. With more time available, with a more refined method, and, especially, if we are aiming at a different objective, we could develop a more quantitative matrix :

- *Giving a positive or negative value to direct relationships,* as in the first experiment of J. C. Duperrin and M. Godet (1973). This can be a profitable exercise and reveals positive (amplifying) and negative (regulating) feedback. To perform such an exercise without making an effort disproportionate to its anticipated usefulness, the exercise should deal only with a small number of variables (10 or 15). First, it is not always clear whether an impact is positive or negative ; second, the designation of a particular variable could be open to question because turning variables into their opposites (eg, increase and decrease) does not automatically alter the value of the row and column relationships. For example, there is the case of consumption as a function of income : as income increases, consumption increases ; when income decreases, consumption does not necessarily decrease.

- *Quantifying the strengths of variables.* The coefficients *aij* can for instance be considered as elasticities (the percentage variation in variable j following a relative variation in variable i). In this case, we assume that we can reasonably estimate such elasticities (ranging, a *priori,* somewhere between less than infinity and infinity).

This means that it is impractical or too costly to perform this exercise for a matrix with more than 10 or 15 variables. In any case, it is not very useful arbitrarily to attach a quantitative value between 0 and 10 and then perform calculations which will have little meaning since the accurate value of the starting coefficients is not known (H. Lesca, 1982).

Although such refinements may be interesting in principle, they are ill suited to the future use of structural analysis. The search for key variables requires an overall vision of the system under study and excludes restricting the analysis at the start to several variables since one is actually trying to identify the main variables from among several dozens of others.

Practical recommendations

Sufficiently considered preliminary thought usually leads us to characterize the system under study by a list of about 70 variables (less structured consideration can easily lead us to keep about 100 variables). This point is important in terms of the number of questions to ask : which can vary by a factor of two (5000 or 10000). We need to allow a minimum of three months to carry out a good structural analysis, including internal and external interviews.

Experience seems to show that a correctly filled in matrix should be between 15 % and 25 % full, depending on the size of the matrix. Higher levels (30 % to 35 %) are indicative of excessive filling in, with secondary relationship having wrongly been considered as direct.

Influence of	On internal variables	On external variables
Internal variables	20 %	10 %
External variables	15 %	25 %

(Example of normal density of direct relationships per section)

The influence of external variables on internal variables is much stronger than the other way round, which is not surprising. In the same way, the effects of the internal and external variables on themselves are greater, as one would expect.

The higher the rate of entry of direct relationships, the less relevant will be the consideration of indirect relationships by the MICMAC method. Thus, if the matrix were filled in 100 % the indirect relationships would merely be a similar multiplication of direct relationships.

To fill in a matrix of 70 variables will require about three days' work by a group of 5-10 people. During the first half-day, which is often laborious, the group will barely be able to examine more than four or five variables and their impacts on the whole of the system. In doing this a common language and a certain coherence in worldview are created, so that quite naturally the rest of the exercise proceeds much more quickly and easily (a rate of 1000 questions per half-day is common for the rest of the process). But the group must be open to debate, and should sometimes mark any doubts with question marks, so that they may come back to these afterwards.

Measuring intensity and taking into account potential relationships also represent acceptable compromise solutions to enable collective thought to proceed without causing excessive individual frustration.

4. Search for the key variables with the MICMAC method

Having developed an exhaustive list of the variables to be taken into account, we now have to reduce the complexity of the system and to identify which key variables should be studied first.

	Influence of : on	1	2	3	4	5	6	7	8	9	10	11	12	13	14	15	16	17	18	19	20	21	22	23	24	25	26	27	28	29	30	31	32	33	34	35	36	37	38	39	40	41
Internal variables	1 Unemployment rate		S	VS	VS				A									S														A	A	VS	VS	VS	A	P	VS	VS	A	P
	2 Unemployment rate for women	S		W					A																					A				A			P				A	
	3 Unemployment rate for young people	S	W		A				W																																	
	4 Number of long-term unemployed								S																								A	S	A	S	A		P		A	P
	5 Employment in services	VS	A	A			W		S															W						W						A						
	6 Employment in industry	VS	A	A		W			S					P										A			A	W				A				A						
Environmental variables	7 Employment in agriculture	A							S																											A						
(external)																																										
Economic and financial	8 Household income										VS		VS																	S			S	S		VS		S			VS	
	9 Rate of economic growth					S	A	W			VS		VS	S			A							A	S			S		A												
	10 Household consumption									A		A	VS	S					A		A				A																	
	11 Inflation								VS		S			S	VS	VS	P		VS								VS							VS	VS							VS
	12 Savings								W			VS				A																										
	13 Financial situation of companies					A	A	A																S	S		W	A						A								
	14 Interest rate (savings)								W			S	VS																													
	15 Rates on the money market											S	W	VS	S		S																									
	16 Money supply											VS				S																										
	17 Budget deficit									A		A					S		VS									A												S		A
	18 Constraints on the external balance of payments									S	P	S				S	A	S			P	A						S														
	19 International context									S		A		S	W	VS			S		S	A	VS				A	W				A			S		P					
	20 Degree of openness of the economy									A				W					S			W					S	S							W							
	21 European harmonization							S		W									A	P	S						S	S				S		P	W		P					
	22 Energy price and raw materials										S	S		S					VS	S				VS				S							VS	A			S			
Technological and	23 Investment for rationalization					VS	VS	VS						S												VS	VS				A			VS	W	S	S	S			S	S
industrial variables	24 Investment for expansion					VS	VS	VS						S													VS							VS	W	S					W	W
	25 Operational productivity per hour					S	S	S						VS													S	W						W	A		A	A				S
	26 Company competitiveness									VS				VS	VS				S		S							S						A							S	
	27 Technological and industrial evolution					A	S	A			VW													S	S		S				A	A		S			A	A			A	
Socio-demographic	28 Working population	S	S	S							A																												S	S		
variables	29 Employment rate among women	S	S	S					S																				S		A			A		S	A					A
	30 Geographical concentration of unemployment																											S		A				VS	S	S	S	A			A	A
	31 Immigrant workers	S		A																								S	S		W		W	S		A					A	A
	32 Parallel economy, moonlighting					S	S	S																										A			S					
	33 Social relationships					A	VS	A	A					S										A		S	S	S				S			VS	VS	S	S	S	S	VS	S
	34 Uncertainties for the future					S	VS	A				A	VS																	S						VS					A	
	35 Evolution in ways of life										VS		S																A	VS			S	S	A		A	A				
Institutional variables	36 Work legislation and regulations					S	S	S																S					S	A		VS	S	S				VS			A	VS
	37 Worksharing and income sharing					VS	VS	VS	VS																					A			A	S		VS					A	
	38 Distribution of mandatory wage deductions								VS									S									VS						S	S								
	39 Total value of mandatory wage deductions								VS									S									VS						S	S					S			A
	40 Training					W	W	W																		S		A					A	S		A						W
	41 Work costs (average hourly wage)					VS	S	VS	VS			S		S										S			VS	A				VS	VS	S								

When dealing with an internal sub-system, related to an external environment, there are two kinds of major variables : first, the external variables which are the most influential and the most useful in explanation (the system's main determinants) ; second, the internal variables which are the most sensitive to this environment. The environmental variables which do not seem to affect the system under study can be discarded.

MICMAC tries to pinpoint the independent and dependent variables (the key variables) by building a typology of these variables in both direct and indirect classifications.

4.1. Direct and indirect classification (MICMAC)

Straightforward examination of the matrix reveals which variables have the greatest direct impact[1] but is not enough to reveal the hidden variables which sometimes greatly influence the problem under study.

Indeed, in addition to the direct relationships, there are also indirect relationships between variables, through influence chains and reaction loops (feedbacks). A common matrix comprising several dozens of variables can include several million interactions in the form of chains and loops. The human mind cannot conceive and interpret such a network of relationships.

The MICMAC method[2], a system of multiplication of matrices applied to the structural matrix, is used to study the diffusion of impacts through reaction paths and loops ; thus, a hierarchy can be developed for the variables ;

- in order of their influence by taking into account the number of paths and loops of length 1, 2, ... n ... arising from each variable ; and

- in order of dependence, by taking into account the number of paths and loops of length 1, 2, ... n ... accruing to each variable.

---

[1] The first set of information can be obtained by first analysing the direct impacts : the sum of the first line represents the number of times that variable i has an impact on the system. This number is the independence factor of variable i. Similarly, the sum of the j column represents the number of times j was influenced by other variables and represents the dependence factor of variable j. Thus, for each variable, an independence factor and a dependence factor can be obtained, to classify variables according to these two criteria.

[2] MICMAC : Matrice d'Impacts Croisés - Multiplication Appliquée à un Classement (Cross impact matrix - multiplication applied to classification). This method was developed at the CEA between 1972 and 1974 by J. C. Duperrin and M. Godet (1973).

Let us examine the following example where the system of variables can be broken down into two sub-systems, S_1 and S_2 , which are not independent since they are interconnected through variables *a, b, c.*

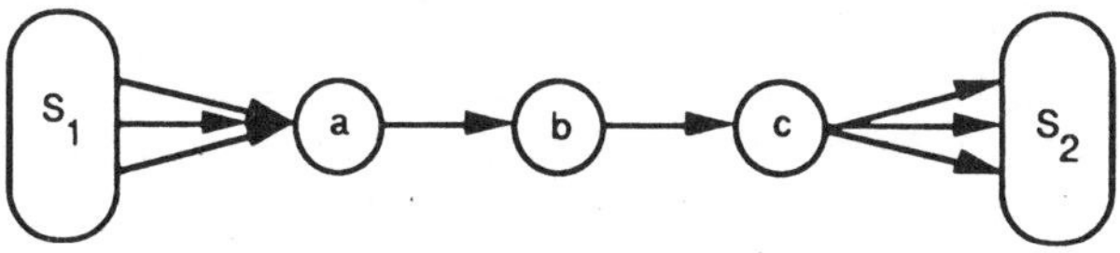

As regards the direct effects :

- *a* is strongly dependent on sub-system S_1 ;
- *c* dominates sub-system S_2.

When analysing the direct effects, variable *b* is neglected although it can represent an essential element of the system's structure since it is the relational cross-section point between both sub-systems S_1 and S_2.

4.2. The MICMAC principle : the raising of matrix to the power

The MICMAC principle is a simple one, and is based on the classical properties of Boolean matrices, which are summarized as follows.

If variable i directly influences variable k and if k directly influences variable j, we have the following :

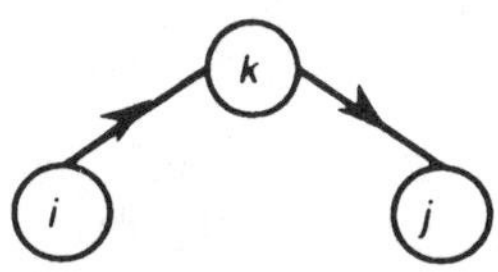

In this case, any change affecting variable i can have repercussions on variable j. There is an indirect connection between i and j.

Numerous indirect relationships of the  type which exist in the structural analysis matrix cannot be taken into account in a direct classification. When the matrix is squared, second-order relationships are revealed, such as 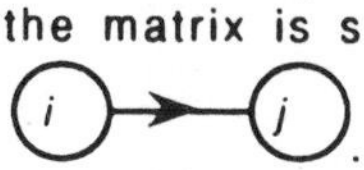.

Indeed, $A^2 = A \times A = \{a^2ij\}$

where

$$a^2_{ij} = \sum_k a^1_{ik} \cdot a^1_{kj}$$

When a^2_{ij}, does not equal 0, there is at least one k where $a^1_{ik}.a^1_{kj} = 1$, ie there is at least one intermediate variable k where variable k where variable i has an impact on $k(a^1_{ik} = 1)$ and where variable k has an impact on variable $j(a^1_{kj} = 1)$.

We can say that a second-order path goes from i to j ; if $a^2_{ij} = N$, there are N paths of second-order length going from i to j via N intermediate variables. In particular, when $a^2_{ij} = N$, there are N circuits (or influence loops) of second-order length going through variable i.

Similarly, by calculating A^3, A^4, ..., A^n, the number of influence paths (or influence loops), of the 3rd, 4th, ..., nth order, interconnecting the variables, can be found.

Each time this process is repeated, a new hierarchy of variables can be deduced. Their classification is based on the number of indirect actions (influences) they have on the other variables. When raised to a certain power (usually the power of 7 or 8), this hierarchy proves to be stable. This hierarchy is the MICMAC classification.

When the linear sum $i\ a^n_{ij}$ is raised to a power for variable $i(a^n_{ij})$ being one element of the matrix raised to the power of n), this means that there are a large number of paths of length n rising from variable i, and that variable i subjects the other system (or sub-system, when dealing with a block) variables to a large number of influences.

Hence the MICMAC classification can classify the variables according to the influence that they have (or that they are subjected to), by taking into account the whole network of interrelationships described by the structural analysis matrix.

To make this less abstract, let us take the following example from J. F. Lefebvre's thesis (1982) : a system is identified by three variables : A, B, C, which interact in the following way :

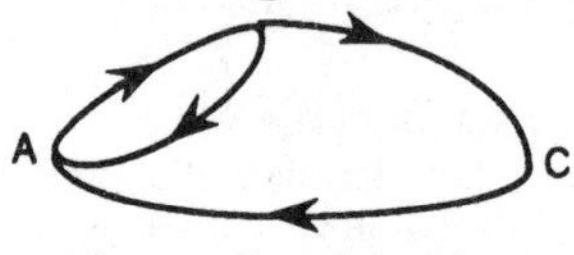

The structural analysis matrix can thus be written as follows :

$$
M = \begin{array}{c} \\ A \\ B \\ C \end{array}
\begin{array}{c} \begin{array}{ccc} A & B & C \end{array} \\ \begin{pmatrix} 0 & 1 & 0 \\ 1 & 0 & 1 \\ 1 & 0 & 0 \end{pmatrix} \end{array}
\quad \boxed{\begin{array}{c} 1 \\ 2 \\ 1 \end{array}}
$$

Sum of the elements in each row

$$\boxed{2 \quad 1 \quad 1}$$

Sum of the elements in each column

In this first matrix, the diagonal elements are always set at zero : this means that the influence one variable has on itself is not taken into account whereas in the indirect effects (updated by squaring the matrix) this influence is taken into account (these effects always occur through another variable).

$$M^2 = \begin{pmatrix} 1 & 0 & 1 \\ 1 & 1 & 0 \\ 0 & 1 & 0 \end{pmatrix} \quad \boxed{\begin{matrix} 2 \\ 2 \\ 1 \end{matrix}}$$

$$\boxed{2 \quad 2 \quad 1}$$

The digit 1 in the first row, first column, means that there is a circuit of length 2 going from A to A.

Indeed:

The digit 1 in the second row, first column, means that there is a path of length 2 going from *B* to *A*.

Indeed:

$$M^3 = \begin{pmatrix} 1 & 1 & 0 \\ 1 & 1 & 1 \\ 1 & 0 & 1 \end{pmatrix} \quad \boxed{\begin{matrix} 2 \\ 3 \\ 1 \end{matrix}}$$

$$\boxed{3 \quad 2 \quad 2}$$

It is clear that all elements of a matrix raised to the power of 3 show that the paths and loops of length 3 go from one variable to the other. It should be noted, and this has already been underlined, that the row and column classification becomes stable when the elements are raised to a certain power. But, the classifications of this matrix raised to a certain power emphasize clearly the importance of certain variables by the indirect effects (feedback) that they have.

$$M^4 = \begin{pmatrix} 1 & 1 & 1 \\ 2 & 1 & 1 \\ 1 & 1 & 0 \end{pmatrix} \boxed{\begin{matrix} 3 \\ 4 \\ 2 \end{matrix}} \quad M^5 = \begin{pmatrix} 2 & 1 & 1 \\ 2 & 2 & 1 \\ 1 & 1 & 1 \end{pmatrix} \boxed{\begin{matrix} 4 \\ 5 \\ 3 \end{matrix}} \quad M^6 = \begin{pmatrix} 2 & 2 & 1 \\ 3 & 2 & 2 \\ 2 & 1 & 1 \end{pmatrix} \boxed{\begin{matrix} 5 \\ 7 \\ 4 \end{matrix}}$$

$$\boxed{4 \quad 3 \quad 2} \qquad\qquad \boxed{5 \quad 4 \quad 3} \qquad\qquad \boxed{7 \quad 5 \quad 4}$$

Here, the row and column classifications become stable from the power of 4.

We obtain the same stability, after several repetitions, with a starting matrix filled in using 1, 2 and 3, depending on the intensity of relationships. Taking immediate account of the relationships in this way is understandable in so far as we can consider a relationship between two variables of intensity-level '2' to be the equivalent of two direct relationships of intensity level '1' between these variables.

4.3. Comparison between direct, indirect and potential classifications

Our concern is to pinpoint the most influential and the most dependent variables. It is understood that the influential variables are those whose evolution will have the greatest effect on the system, while the dependent variables are those that are most sensitive to the evolution of the system.

In addition to a simple examination of the matrix, which allows us to discern which variables have the highest number of direct connections with the system, it is a good idea to pick out the 'hidden' variables, ie those which, taking account of indirect relationships and feedback loops, also appear to be very important.

Variables are thus classifed according to the number and intensity of relationships in which they are involved, either in an influential or a dependent capacity. There are three classifications : direct, indirect, and potential, according to the nature of the relationships taken into consideration.

Comparison of direct, indirect and potential classifications is all the more interesting in that we can associate an approximate time horizon with each of these different classifications :

- direct classification results from the short- to medium-term interplay of relationships ; its horizon often corresponds to less than a decade ;
- indirect classification integrates chain reactions which necessarily take longer and the time horizon recedes to the medium- to long-term (10-15 years) ;
- potential classification goes further than the indirect classification, as it integrates relationships which will not emerge until much later and which will only have repercussions on the system in the very long term.

Obviously the comparison between the classifications (direct and MICMAC) can confirm the importance of certain variables and also reveal other variables which were previously thought to be unimportant but which play a leading role because of indirect actions. It would be wrong to neglect them during the explanatory analysis. The example given here explains how a hidden variable linked to the development of nuclear power in France was revealed (Exhibit IV-1). Every structural analysis using the MICMAC method revealed two general points :

- (at least) four-fifths of the results confirmed initial expectations, and for many variables the indirect classification does not differ from the direct classification. Therefore, the highest ranked variables can be selected without too much hesitation, whereas those which seem in all cases to be secondary can be rejected ;
- between 10% and 20% of the results seem counter-intuitive since, in the different hierarchies, certain variables move quite noticeably up or down the order.

This analysis stimulates discussion within the prospective group and new questions arise. Some of these question preconceived ideas, other questions arise because of the ideas themselves.

We can still remember the shocked reaction of the management of the French post office in 1978 to the classification of the positions of these variables with respect to their dependency *vis-à-vis* the general environment. The direct classification seemed the logical one, the mail traffic variables being the most dependent, whereas the workforce policy variables (manpower levels, wages) or the quality of service were considered as internal control variables. The MICMAC classification turned this hierarchy upside down. After long discussions, this *a priori* counter-intuitive result became self-evident : on the one hand, mail traffic since 1973 had been recording quasi-autonomous development, almost independent from variations in economic growth to which it had been closely correlated in the 1960s. On the other hand, one had to admit that the workforce policy of a public service has practically nothing to do with what its general management wants, but is closely linked to overall government policies for the public sector, the latter also being connected to the political situation. The policy of upgrading the lower salaries and of creating more jobs in the civil service after May 1981 had strong repercussions on the French postal services : over 50 % of the workforce belonged to the lowest categories C and D of the public sector.

Uncovering hidden variables

The following example is based on a prospective survey of French nuclear power. This survey was carried out in 1972 by the CEA (French atomic energy commission.

By adopting several viewpoints (political, economic, technological, etc) the think-tank for this survey prepared a list of 51 variables which should be taken into account.

The results obtained are as follows :

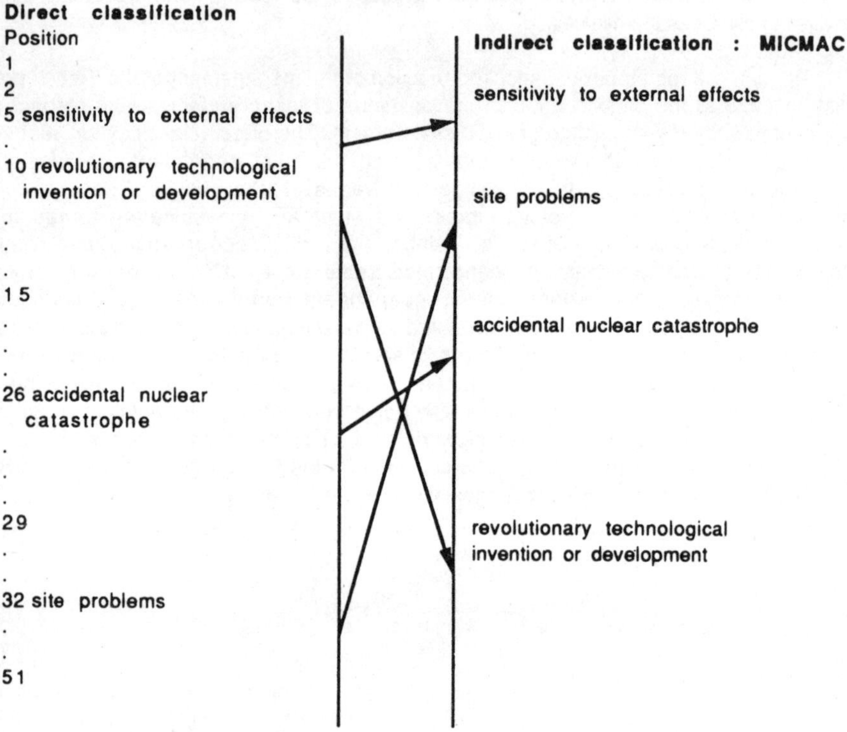

The variable 'sensitivity to external effects' moved up from 5th to 1st position. Thus, since 1972 structural analysis has enabled us to foresee how important collective psychology and public opinion reactions would be for the development of nuclear energy.

This evolution is even more striking in the case of the variable *'location problems for the siting of nuclear plants'* which moved up from 32nd position in the first classification to 10th in the second. Thus, *the kind of problems that EDF (French central electricity generating board) had to face at Plogoff had been identified almost ten years before they became a reality.*

4.4. The influence - dependence chart

Each variable is associated with an influential indicator and a direct dependence indicator across the whole system. The sum of variables can then be positioned on a influence-dependent chart.

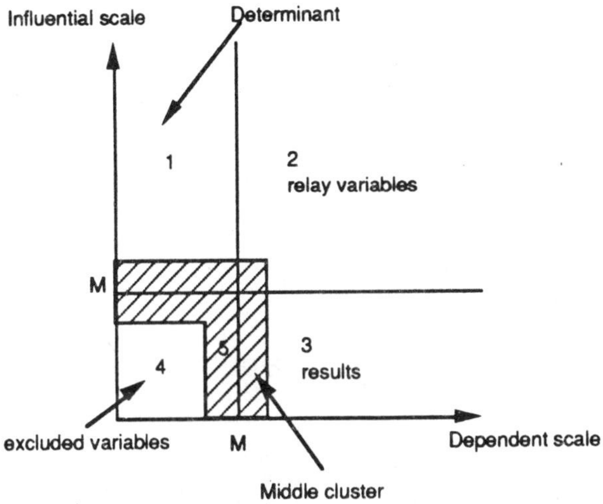

This chart can be divided into five sectors :

Sector 1 : Influential variables. These high influential, low dependent variables are the explanatory variables which condition the rest of the system.

Sector 2 : Relay variables. These variables, which are both highly influential and highly dependent, are unstable by nature. Any action on these variables will have repercussions on other variables ; this will feed back to the relay variables, amplifying or defusing the initial impulse.

Sector 3 : Resultant variables. Low influential and high dependent variables. These results variables are influenced by the determinants (sector 1) and the relay variables (sector 2).

Sector 4 : Low influential, low dependent variables (near the zero point). These variables constitute marked trends or factors which are relatively unconnected to the system, having only a few relationships with it. Because of their relatively autonomous development, they are not determinants of the future of the system and we can therefore exclude them from the analysis without too many scruples.

Sector 5 : Averagely influential and/or dependent variables. We can say nothing *a priori* about these 'middle clusters' of variables.

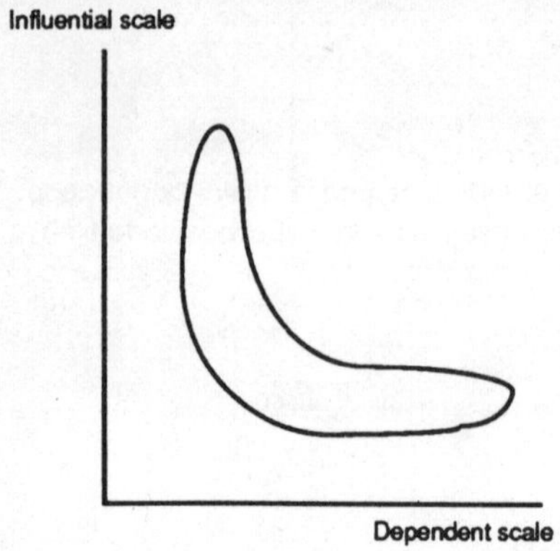

1. Relatively stable system

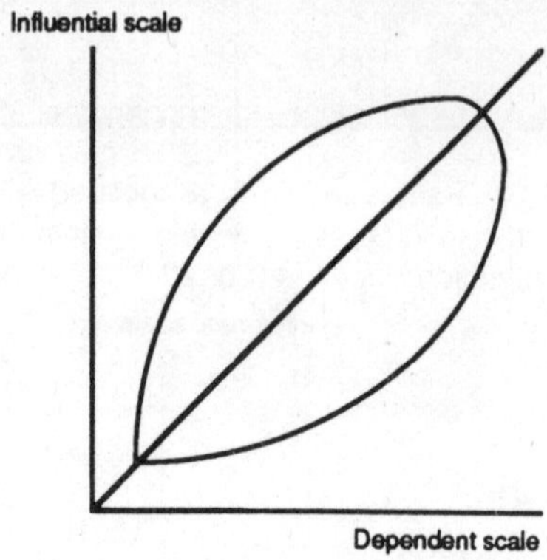

2. Unstable system

...regarding the system's stability or instability

A low number of relay variables confers relative stability on the system. In fact, in an unstable system (cluster of points around the main diagonal), each variable is both influential and dependent, and any action on one variable has repercussions on all the others and in turn on the original variable. The advantage of a stable system is that it introduces a dichotomy between the influential variables, on which one can or cannot act, and the results variables which depend on them.

A major benefit of constructing the influence-dependence chart is that it can check whether what is being explained is related to what is assumed *a priori* to be an explanatory factor and which should normally be considered to be influential. This chart often provides surprising results.

The relay variables of the north-east section are, *a priori*, the key variables at stake in the system - those over which the actors will fight, because of their unstable character.

Frequently, among these key variables, we find taboo subjects that nobody speaks about, precisely because they are important. On the other hand, many topics which figure among the declared priorities of the company or organization are often situated in the zone of excluded variables, because they are neither influential nor dependent.

In addition to the scenario exercise, a structural analysis should be carried out as a preliminary to the construction of any econometric forecasting model.

This analysis could be usefully completed by the method which breaks down the various parameters into carefully related components so as to reveal related (hierarchical) or unrelated sub-systems, and to display the key role played by certain relay variables, as suggested by J. F. Lefebvre (1982).

I - International variables
M - Monetary variables
R - Technical and economic relay variables
G - Global economci variables
B - Business variables
SW - Social and work variables

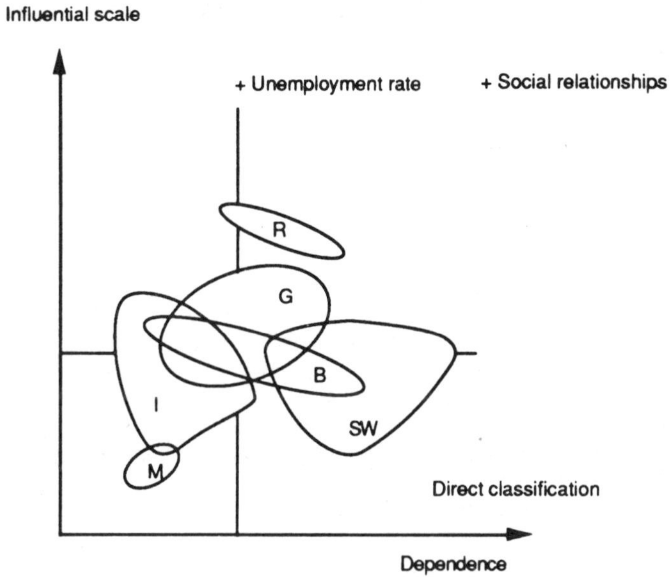

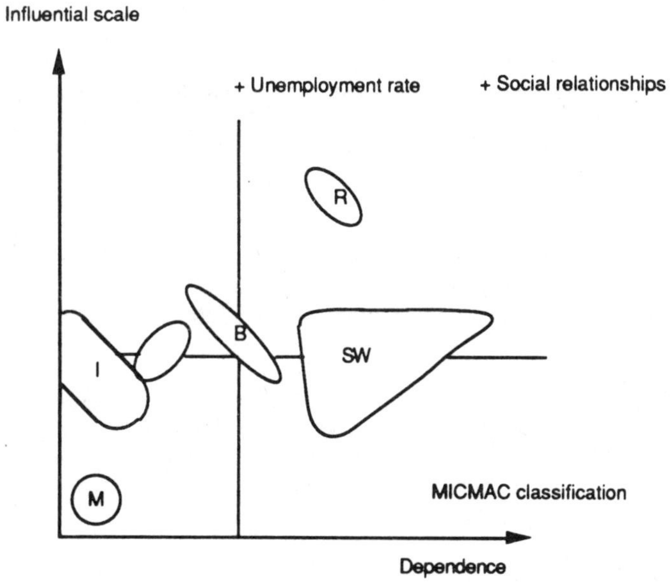

There is no single, official, scientific interpretation of the MICMAC results. The think-tank has to ask the right questions and propose explanations. Thus, for instance, in our example we might have wondered why the unemployment rate -the parameter which is influential and has a high level of dependence- seems likely to be able to explain unemployment through the biasing of social relationships. It might mean that unemployment is not only a resultant (the consequence of rigidities) but also a change factor which, when raised to a certain level, affects the social climate and imposes politically motivated measures of flexibility to create jobs and job-sharing schemes.

All these questions have to be answered. This is the aim of the next step in the scenario method. This step essentially deals with the key variables identified by structural analysis, locates which actors are involved with these variables and for whom the past, present and future roles have to be carefully studied. Prior to initiating this analysis on the rôle of actors, we offer here a (provisional) conclusion on the value and limitations of structural analysis.

5. Value and limitations of structural analysis

The analytical method described above attempts to identify the key variables (whether hidden or not), to ask the right questions or to analyse counter-intuitive aspects of the system's behaviour. The method should help, but not replace, the decision-maker. It does not try to describe accurately how the system works, but rather its aim is to pinpoint the main elements of the system's organization.

The results should be used while bearing in mind the limitations of the analysis :

• The first limitation derives from the subjective character of the list of variables. The precautions taken offer some guarantee of objectivity, but for practical reasons the number of variables should not exceed a few dozen. Therefore, some sub-variables related to one of the problem's dimensions have to be regrouped, more or less arbitrarily. For this method, this is a disadvantage as well as an advantage because any model arbitrarily favouring the quantitative elements to the detriment of the qualitative elements is rejected.

• The choice of a typology of relationships conditions the results. Usually, two types of relationship are taken into account :

(a) the so-called reference relationship (known relationships which are true today and should remain so in the future) ; and

(b) the potential relationships (possible relationships which have not yet appeared, but whose development is incipient).

On the plus side, this typology is simple. On the minus side it considers as potential, not only what is incipient, but also what is doubtful or disputed. A more extensive study, having more time and means at its disposal, would classify the relationships and their nature (conditional, causal, technical, institutional, psycho-sociological, etc).

• Processing the structural analysis matrix only determines the existence or non-existence of various relationships. However, this matrix includes relationships with widely varying intensity. Its characteristics should be borne in mind when interpreting the results. That is why the intensity of these relationships should be determined, even if only on a qualitative view, in order to carry out sensitivity analyses. However, we should not walk into the trap of excessively quantifying the relationship in order to obtain a semblance of accuracy.

While keeping in mind the above limitations of *structural analysis* the results obtained and their essential value should be recalled. This method, first of all, is a tool which should be used to classify ideas and to tackle a problem systematically. Since several thousands of questions have to be asked, certain questions have to be asked to uncover variables which would never have been thought of otherwise.

First, the structural analysis matrix acts as a matrix of discovery and helps to create a common language within a think-tank on the prospective exercise.

Second, since a certain number of feedback effects involving each variable have to be taken into account, a hierarchy based on the influence and the dependence of the variables should be prepared for such variables. Thus, the main influential of the phenomenon under study can be revealed. The control variables and the resultant variables thus uncovered help better to understand the organization and the structure of the system under study.

One can scoff at the fact that 80 % fo the results obtained confirm initial intuition and are obvious. It should first be noted that obvious points are easy to prove with hindsight, but it is more difficult to forecast accurately what, in the quagmire of preconceived ideas, is undeniably certain and obvious. Furthermore, *80 % of the obvious results show that this approach is logical and common-sensical. This requirement is essential to give some credit to the 20 % of 'counter-intuitive' results.*

CHAPTER V

UNDERSTANDING THE ACTORS' STRATEGIES : THE MACTOR METHOD

1. Constructing the actors' strategy table

2. Identifying the strategic issues and associated objectives

3. Positioning each actor in relation to the strategic objectives (signed position matrix)

4. Ranking the objectives for each actor's (valued position matrix) and assessing the range of possible convergences and divergences

5. Evaluating the balance of power and formulating strategic recommendations (weighted valued position matrix)

6. Key questions for the future

This stage is essential. Proper *prospective* thinking cannot be carried out unless there is an in-depth retrospective study. Notably, this means considering all the key variables and questions identified earlier, and building up a database (both quantitative and qualitative) which should be as extensive as possible. All sources of statistical information should be drawn upon to identify the major evolutionary trends, to analyse past discontinuities, the conditions under which these came about, and the rôle played by the main actors of this evolution.

As in the case of structural analysis, the above information should be supplemented by qualitative interviews with the actors themselves ; this approach enables one to identify the main events which point the way to the future, to gain a better overview of the interplay of events and a better comprehension of the relationships between the actors. It is only when a solid database is available and there is a thorough knowledge of future challenges that the MACTOR method can be usefully implemented.

The future is never totally predetermined - however influential past trends may be, the future remains open to several possible scenarios. The actors in the system under examination possess various degrees of freedom which they will be able to exercise, through strategic action, in order to arrive at the goals they have set themselves, and thus successfully to carry out their project.

From this, it follows that analysis of these actors' moves, confronting their plans, examining the balance of power between them (in terms of constraints and means of action) is essential in order to throw light on the strategic issues and the key questions for the future (which are the outcomes and consequences of foreseeable battles).

If we focus our attention on energy, for example, these key questions will be concerned mainly with the price of oil, the demand for energy, the maintenance or collapse of solidarity among OPEC member countries, and so on. To take another example, in a 1976 futures study of cosmetics consumption up to 1990, analysis of actors' strategies showed that the existence of companies with specialized distribution was threatened by the moves of other actors (such as mass distributors, consumer movements, and trendsetters).

In the field of prospective there is general consensus on two points regarding analysis of actors' moves.

On one hand, everyone concurs in recognizing it as a crucial -and perhaps the most important- step in constructing a basis for thought which will enable scenarios to be built. Without careful analysis of actors' moves, scenarios will lack relevance and coherence.

On the other hand, the same people lament the notable lack of a systematic tool for analysing actors' behaviour. This lack is all the more remarkable in that analysis of actors' behaviour is so often preceded by a rather clumsy structural analysis, using tools (the MICMAC method) to help identify the key variables and ask the right questions - in other words, to improve the pertinence of the thought process.

We recall that this is a matter of focusing on those actors who directly or indirectly control the key variables identified by the structural analysis. We then construct an 'actors' strategies' table, presented in the form of a square matrix (actors x actors) in which :

- each diagonal cell contains the aims and objectives of each actor, insofar as these can be identified ;
- the other cells contain the means of action which each actor may use against the others in order to achieve its aims.

Filling in this table is a group discussion activity, sharing the information gathered on each actor and its relationships with the others. This information on actors' behaviour can be collected or complemented by conversations with experts who are representative of each group of actors. Given that it is generally difficult to ask an actor to reveal his own strategy and his own strengths and weaknesses, it is much easier to get him to talk about the other actors. By sifting through sets of partially true information, a more or less coherent picture of the whole situation emerges.

It is often said that it would be good to take advantage of information derived from game theory, in order to make intelligent use of the near-complete data collected in the actors' strategy tables. We support this view, and have no doubt that one day young researchers will propose significant ways forward. In the meantime, to our knowledge, the available tools have hardly developed at all over the past few years.

In 1985, however, we outlined a path which seemed to us promising, and by taking up this idea once again we have now created and developed the MACTOR method (Matrix of Alliances and Conflicts : Tactics, Objectives and Recommendations). Our aim is to create an analytical tool which will allow us to make better use of the informational added value contained in actors' strategies tables. Although the 'game theory' path still appears to be of interest, we did not pursue it rigorously in creating MACTOR. Others will certainly do so, but we would suggest that they bear in mind the following recommendation : develop tools that are sufficiently simple to be appropriable (understandable) by the users and which lend themselves easily to multiple and varied applications.

Analysis of actors' moves, as we propose with MACTOR®, proceeds in the following six stages :

1. Note down each actor's plans, motivations, constraints and means of action (construct the 'actors' strategy' table).

2. Identify the strategic issues and objectives associated with these battlefields.

3. Position each actor on each battlefield and note the convergences and divergences.

4. Rank the objectives for each actor and assess possible tactics (interaction of

possible convergences and divergences) in terms of their objective priorities.

5. Evaluate the relationships of power and formulate strategic recommendations for each actor, in keeping with the actor's objective priorities and available resources.

6. Raise key questions about the future - ie formulate hypotheses regarding the trends, events and discontinuities which will characterize the evolution of the balance of power between actors. It is around these key questions, and hypotheses as to their answers, that the scenarios will be constructed.

The added value created by the MACTOR method derives primarily from stages 3 (positioning actors in relation to their objectives) ; 4 (tactics for possible alliances and conflicts) ; and 5 (strategic recommendations). In future, more attention will be devoted to these stages, for until now we have too often passed rather quickly from stages 1 (constructing actors' strategy tables) and 2 (strategic issues) to stage 6 (key questions for the future).

How do we conduct this analysis of actors' behaviour in six stages ? What exactly does the MACTOR method consist of ?

To answer these questions, we have once again chosen to illustrate the method with an example which relies on material collected while carrying out several prospective studies in the field of air transportation. Most of these studies were carried out in the 1970s (at the time when we ran SEMA prospective), for Aerospatiale, for the Directorate General Civil Aviation (DGCA) in France, and especially for the Paris Airport Authority.

Mactor method : sequence of stages

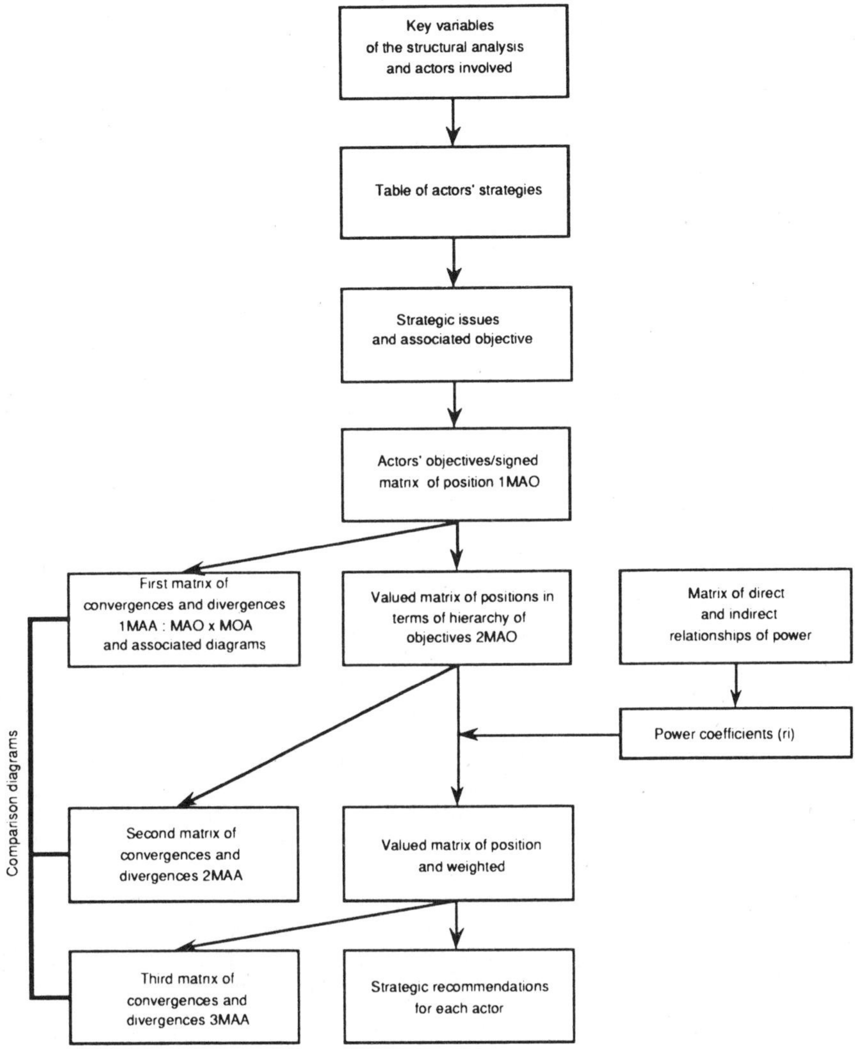

Figure V-1

An example like this has not dated - it is now that it is most valuable, for we can check whether or not the conjectures made about the future (which is now the present) were well founded. Moreover, more recent analyses of actors' moves, relating to futures yet to arrive, are almost systematically confidential. The example of air transportation is currently one of the only ones that can be made public. Other examples, relating to the Post Office or other firms, may perhaps emerge from their wraps of confidentiality after a longer prescribed period. The directors of Paris Airport Plan have confirmed to us that this example of 'retrofutures' retains a certain topicality. Furthermore, a new study of actors' moves in air transportation up to 2010, using the MACTOR method, has been set up - naturally its results cannot be published, whether they are relevant or not. If an actor reveals to others the nature of the questions he is asking himself, and the way in which he is formulating them, he has already said too much about his strategy... unless of course part of his strategy is to use the effect of declaring his hand, as in poker.

1. Constructing the actors' strategy table

We are focusing, then, on the behaviour of actors in air transportation in the Paris region up to 1990, as analysed in 1978. The first question concerns the number of actors to take into account. Should we consider the airline companies as a single actor, or should we subdivide them according to a particular characteristic (size, legal status, nationality...) ?

Similarly, the state is generally a polymorphous actor - there is the DGCA, but also the Ministry of Finance, the government, and so on. These actors, which together make up the state, differ in their objectives, their behaviour, and their criteria for decision-making. A complete analysis would have to integrate other actors such as the trade associations, the European institutions, and the international air transportation organizations. One could thus multiply the number of actors at will, and almost inevitably run the risk of making analysis of the system impossible. Experience shows that a total of 10 to 20 actors constitutes a realistic and operational compromise.

The actors' strategy table is constructed in a square matrix (actors x actors), similar to the following table, which we have redrawn from memory. The cells on the main diagonal are generally the fullest, for in these cells we are setting down in black and white each actor's identity card. In contrast, many of the other cells (actions of one actor towards another) are almost or totally empty.

In order to simplify this account of MACTOR, we shall consider only six actors : aircraft manufacturers (A1), scheduled airlines (A2), charter airline companies (A3), the state (A4), Paris Airport Authority (A5), and the local residents' associations (A6). In the case analysed on behalf of Paris Airport in 1990, 12 actors were considered, as well as seven strategic issues and over 30 associated objectives.

Action of	Action on manufacturers	Airlines	State
Manufacturers	Objective : to survive and avoid crisis Problems : Plan for higher • performance aircraft • specific noise and fuel consumption standards to meet Means : Association between constructors Military orders Diversification of activities	Pressure on airlines to purchase new aircraft Diversification of needs and aircraft Standardization of the fleet for each constructor Availability of entire range No significant technological progress	Exercise "blackmail" in regard to jobs Demand finance for new projects
Airlines	Demand aircraft better suited to their needs Dominant criterion : Cost per passenger mile per ton effectively transported Reluctance to use large aircraft	Objective : To maintain market share Problems : Financial investment and salaries To maintain high frequency and occupancy Means : Cooperation between airlines (ATLAS) Increased use of branches Standardization and operating flexibility of the fleet Development of freight Concentration at the tertiary level (feeder lines)	Seek protection from competition in the form of discriminatory rights in relation to long-haul traffic
State	To protect the national aeronautical industry Military and civil aircraft order Finance for new projects Export credits Approaches to foreign governments Appeal to private finance	Protectionism Pressure on airlines to purchase Mercury Airbus with financial aid State protects airlines provided they develop and improve their section	Objective : Prestige and a French presence in the world Problems : Unemployment Inflation Means : Sustained growth

Source : M. GODET (1979)

2. Identifying the strategic issues and associated objectives

Through group reading and discussion of the actors' strategy table, the strategic issues -ie, the battlefields on which the actors will confront each other- are brought to light fairly easily. Here we concentrate on five strategic issues regarding which the six actors have converging or divergent objectives (convergences or divergences). These five issues concern the following :

E1 : *Definition of aircraft.* The aircraft manufacturers want to impose their own new aircraft designs on airline companies and on Paris Airport. For example, Boeing 747s were developed at a time when the existing runways were too short for them.

E2 : *Aircraft market.* National aircraft manufacturers rely on the state to develop their share of the national and international market. The other actors under consideration are not concerned with this objective.

E3 : *Allocation of traffic rights.* Here the scheduled airlines rely on the state to curb the aspirations of the charter companies, who favour deregulation. For its part, Paris Airport supports the opening of new lines which would allow an increase in the number of flights to Paris.

E4 : *Market for 'organized' flights.* The interests of charter companies regarding the 'organized' flights market are opposed to those of the scheduled airlines. The main concern of Paris Airport is to avoid having to turn traffic away, and from this point of view it is an objective ally of the charter companies.

E5 : *Noise pollution and disturbance near airports.* This issue is at the crossroads of actors' strategies, for it involves all of them. Residents demand less noisy aircraft, are opposed to the authorization of night flights, and their concerns are naturally echoed by the state (residents are also voters). Aircraft manufacturers represent an objective ally of the residents, in that more restrictive noise-control standards could lead to the abandonment of old aircraft in favour of new, less noisy craft. Scheduled or charter airlines and Paris Airport are naturally opposed to anything which could curb traffic.

Each of these strategic issues (battlefields) can be presented in the form of one or more precise objectives over which actors are in convergence, in divergence, or neutral.

For ease of exposition, we shall limit our analysis to the battlefields (01, 02, 03, 04, 05), which constitute only part of the objectives associated with issues E1-E5. A complete analysis of actors' strategies would have to take all objectives into account.

ISSUES (BATTLEFIELDS)	ASSOCIATED OBJECTIVES
E1 Definition of aircraft	01 - Impose aircraft specifications (size, performance) - Define aircraft specifications together
E2 Market for aircraft	02 - Defend and increase the national manufacturers' market share
E3 Allocation of traffic rights	03 - Maintain allocation of traffic rights - Partial deregulation - Total deregulation (free opening of new lines)
E4 'Organized flights' market	04 - Develop 'organized flights' - Control 'organized flights' - Avoid turning traffic away
E5 Noise pollution and disturbance near airports	05 - Regulate and reinforce noise standards

3. Positioning each actor in relation to the strategic objectives (signed position matrix)

The relationships between the actors on each battlefield can be represented in the form of a diagram of possible convergences and divergences. Of course, in order to understand the strategic situation as a whole, it is necessary to construct all the diagrams of possible convergences and divergences associated with each strategic objective, as well as diagrams of corresponding resources.

We soon see that strategies of convergence and divergence between actors vary from one objective to another. In order to maintain coherence, there can be no question of fighting against a certain actor on one battlefield while counting on his support for another, and vice versa.

For any given actor, the question is therefore to identify and evaluate possible strategic options and a coherent selection of objectives and alliances. Visual comparison of the diagrams of convergences and divergences is not easy ; however, a matrix representation (MAO - Matrix of Actors and Objectives) enables all these diagrams to be summarized in a single table. Below we see the positioning of actors towards the objective of regulating and reinforcing noise control standards.

Objective : regulate and reinforce noise control standards

+ = in favour of objective
- = opposed to objective

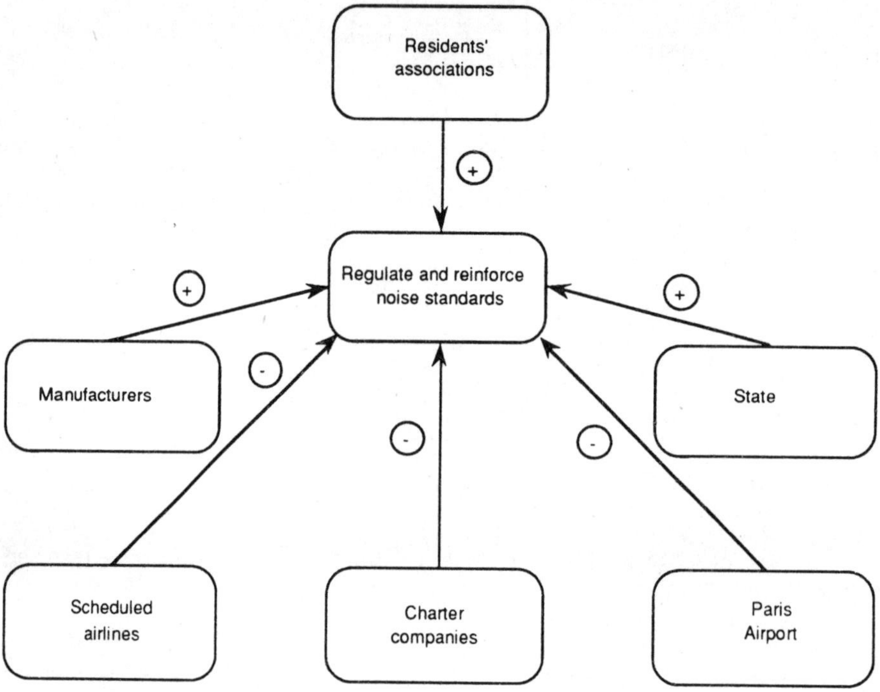

MAO : signed matrix of positions (actors x objectives)

		MAO						
		01	02	03	04	05	Total +	Total -
Manufacturers	A1	+1	+1	0	0	+1	+3	0
Scheduled airlines	A2	-1	0	+1	-1	-1	+1	-3
Charter companies	A3	-1	0	-1	+1	-1	+1	-3
State	A4	0	+1	+1	0	+1	+3	0
Paris Airport	A5	-1	0	-1	+1	-1	+1	-3
Residents' associations	A6	0	0	0	0	+1	+1	0
Total +		+1	+2	+2	+2	+3		
Total -		-3	0	-2	-1	-3		

01 - Impose aircraft specifications
02 - Defend and increase national manufacturers' market share
03 - Maintain allocation of traffic rights
04 - Develop 'organized flights'
05 - Regulate and reinforce noise control standards

The MAO matrix (actors x objectives) is filled in as follows :

(+1) Actor i in favour of objective j
(-1) Actor i opposed to objective j
(0) Actor i neutral in relation to objective j

So, for example, we find the fifth column represents the diagram associated with objective 05 : regulating and reinforcing noise control standards.

Commentary :

Simply examining the positive and negative totals of the lines and columns of the MAO matrix provides a wealth of information. Thus we see, on one hand, that the residents' associations (A6) are only concerned with one objective (noise, A5), while all the other actors are involved in four out of five battlefields. On the other hand, objective 05, noise pollution and disturbance near airports, is the one which most divides the actors and involves them all. Defining aircraft specifications (01), allocation of traffic rights (03), and to a lesser extent the development of the 'organized" flights market (04), are also highly contentious objectives.

4. Ranking the objectives for each actor (valued position matrix) and assessing the range of possible convergences and divergences

For each pair of actors it is interesting to note the number of objectives over which they are in convergence or divergence. This can almost be picked out visually from the MAO matrix. But for larger tables incorporating about 10 actors and 20 or so objectives, we must make use of a classic property of binary matrix calculation : by multiplying a matrix by its transposition we obtain the number of factors in common for each pair or lines in the original matrix (to transpose a matrix all we have to do is to place in columns the factors which were previously in lines). The transposed form of MAO (actors x objectives) is called MOA (objectives x actors). The product of matrices MAO x MOA, respectively (6,5) and (5,6) in format, gives matrix MAA (actors x actors) (6,6) in format.

In order to be able to distinguish which of the factors common to two actors (two lines of the MAO matrix) correspond to motions in favour of certain objectives (indicated by +1) or opposed to others (indicated by -1), we carry out the matrix calculation MAO x MOA, applying the following conventions :

- n Cij is obtained by the matrix product which retains only positive scalar products. This is also the number of objectives towards which actors i and j have a common attitude, either favourable or unfavourable (number of convergences).

- n Dij is obtained by the matrix product which retains only negative scalar products. This is also number of objectives towards which actors i and j have a divergent attitude (number of divergences).

The matrix MAA (actors x actors) is therefore made up of all pairs nCij, nDij. For example, MAA23 = +2, -2 means that scheduled airlines (A2) and charter companies (A3) take up the same position on two objectives (in this instance 01 and 05), and are in opposition on two other objectives (03 and 04) (cf. in the MAO matrix, lines 2 and 3).

Matrix of convergences and divergences (Actor x actor)

		A1	A2	A3	A4	A5	A6
Manufacturers	A1		0 / -2	0 / -2	+2 / 0	0 / -2	+1 / 0
Scheduled airlines	A2	0 / -2		+2 / -2	+1 / -1	2 / -2	0 / -1
Charter companies	A3	0 / -2	+2 / -2		0 / -2	4 / 0	0 / -1
State	A4	2 / 0	+1 / -1	0 / -2		0 / -2	+1 / 0
Paris Airport	A5	0 / -2	+2 / -2	4 / 0	0 / -2		0 / -1
Residents' associations	A6	+1 / 0	0 / -1	0 / -1	+1 / 0	0 / -1	

Matrix MAA therefore indicates for each pair of actors the number of objectives on which they are in convergence (NCij) or in divergence (NDij) ; matrix MAA allows us to obtain two complete diagrams of convergences and divergences. These diagrams are shown below ; the thickness of the lines is proportionate to the number of objectives concerned.

First complete diagram of convergences and divergences

The most striking thing is the strong convergence of interest between Paris Airport Authority and the charter companies, and to a lesser extent the scheduled airlines. We also note the lack of common objectives between Paris Airport Authorities (A5) and the state (A4) (at least for the objectives under consideration).

First complete diagram of convergences overs objectives (nCij)

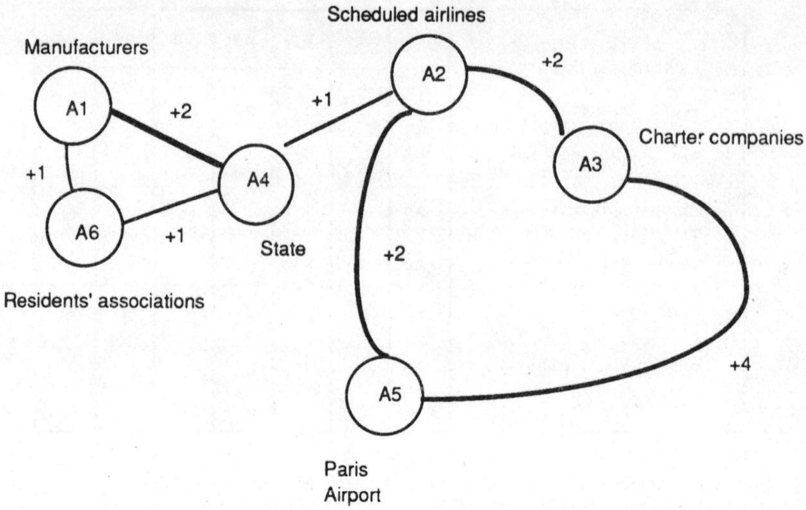

First complete diagram of divergences over objectives (nDij)

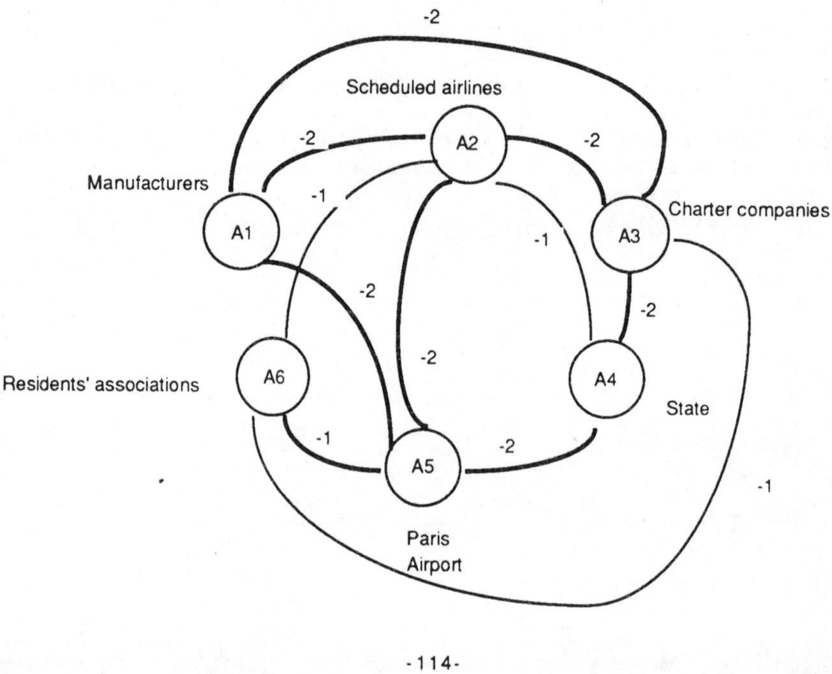

For their part, the aircraft manufacturers, the state and the local residents' associations constitute another group of allies on several objectives.

Complete diagram of divergences

Some actors are in potential conflict with almost all the others over two or three objectives. This is the case for Paris Airport (A5), the scheduled airlines (A2) (the actor most at risk), aircraft manufacturers (A1), and the state (A4).

These first completed diagrams remain rather elementary because they only take into account the number of convergences and divergences over objectives. To bring the model closer to reality, it is advisable to introduce two dimensions which have so far been omitted :

1) hierarchy of objectives, which varies from actor to actor ;
2) relationship of power between actors.

These dimensions also affect the interplay of possible convergences and divergences. Before looking at how to integrate the second of these two dimensions, we shall examine the first.

In order to take into account each actor's specific hierarchy of objectives, it is sufficient, for example, to note the positioning of actors in relation to objectives on a scale from -3 to +3, according to whether the level of opposition or agreement is high, medium or low. The more the actor feels concerned with an objective which is important for him, the higher the absolute value recorded.

We thus obtain a second valued position matrix of the MAO type, which we shall call 2MAO ; by multiplying it by its transposed form we obtain a second MAA-type matrix, called 2MAA.

Valued positions matrix (actors x objectives) 2MAO

Actors		01	02	03	04	05
Manufacturers	A1	2.0	3.0	0.0	0.0	1.0
Scheduled airlines	A2	-2.0	0.0	3.0	-1.0	-3.0
Charter companies	A3	-1.0	0.0	-3.0	3.0	-2.0
State	A4	0.0	3.0	2.0	0.0	1.0
Paris Airport	A5	-1.0	0.0	-2.0	2.0	-2.0
Residents' Associations	A6	0.0	0.0	0.0	0.0	3.0

2MAA : Valued matrix of convergences and divergences (actors x actors)

		A1	A2	A3	A4	A5	A6
Manufacturers	A1		0	0	+4	0	+2
			-4	-3	0	-3	0
Scheduled airlines	A2			+4	+2,5	+4	0
				-5	-2	-4	-3
Charter companies	A3		+4		0	+8	0
			-5		-4	0	-2,5
State	A4		+2,5	0		0	+2
		0	-2	-4		-3,5	0
Paris Airport	A5	-4	+4	+8	0		0
		0	-4	0	0		-2,5
Residents' associations	A6	-3	0	0	+2	0	
		+4	-3	-2,5	0	-2,5	

The matrix 2MAA is made up of all pairs of valued convergences (2 C_{ij}) and divergences (2 D_{ij}). Each element is obtained as the average intensity (in absolute values) of respectively convergences and divergences on objectives. Example :

valued convergence between A2 and A3

$$2\,C_{23} = \frac{|-2| + |-1|}{2} + \frac{|-3| + |-2|}{2} = 4$$

valued divergence between A2 and A3.

$$2\,D_{23} = \frac{|3| + |-3|}{2} + \frac{|-1| + |+3|}{2} = 5$$

by definition convergences are noted with the positive sign and divergences with the negative sign.

We can thus construct a second version of the complete diagrams of possible convergences and divergences, which in the event does not differ noticeably from the first (which is why these second diagrams are not presented here), except on one point. Between the first and second diagram of conflicts we note an increased degree of antagonism between the scheduled airlines and the charter companies. This derives from the total opposition of these two actors over allocation of traffic rights. Of course if we had chosen a different scale for measuring the importance of objectives the results would perhaps have developed more noticeably from one diagram to the other.

The interplay of possible convergences and divergences does not depend solely on each actor's hierarchy of objectives, but also on the ability of an actor to impose its priorities on others - ie, on relationships of power.

5. Evaluating the balance of power and formulating strategic recommendations (weighted valued position matrix)

If we place ourselves in the position of an actor, for example Paris Airport, we see that this actor is in potential divergence with almost all the others over a given objective, while at the same time it may form convergences over other objectives. A coherent strategy of objectives will therefore have to impose certain objective priorities. Conversely, defining objective priorities obliges one to formulate convergence policies.

Let us develop the example. Paris Airport has every interest in joining forces with the charter companies (A3) and the scheduled airlines (A2) if it wishes to fight for aircraft specifications which respond more closely to its constraints (02), and to oppose new standards and regulations on noise pollution and distrubance near airports (05). This being the case, Paris Airport, out of concern for coherence, should place on the back burner those issues in which its own interests diverge from those of the scheduled airlines, ie, traffic rights allocation (03), and the development of the organized flights market (04). This is particularly important as it is precisely over these two objectives (03) and (04) that the scheduled airlines' interests are opposed to those of the charter companies. For Paris Airport this tactic can only be put into practice if its potential allies, the airline companies, also pursue the same tactic.

In reality, everything depends on how objectives are ranked, which differs from actor to actor, and we should probably expect open conflict between the scheduled and charter airline companies over traffic rights and the 'organized' flights market. These objectives are also very important for Paris Airport, which in principle should first make a bid for convergence with the charter companies.

However, merely being in divergence with an actor is not sufficient actively to oppose it - also required are the direct or indirect means to oppose it. The tactical selection of convergences and divergences is necessarily dependent on these means. Sometimes it is even the existence of a favourable balance of power which sparks off conflict.

It is therefore useful to guide one's tactical choice by analysing relationships of power through two matrices - the matrix of means of direct action (MDA) and the matrix of means of indirect action (MIA). The first matrix, MDA, is simply a table (actors x actors) in which the potential influence of one actor over another is recorded on a scale from 0 to 3 (none, weak, average, strong) - one could use other categories. This first table already reveals relationships of power ; simply reading the totals for each line and each column reveals that the state is by far the most influential actor in the system, while at the same time it is one of the most susceptible to the influence of others. In contrast, the charter companies are the least well equipped to achieve their objectives, and are also among those actors most subject to pressure from others.

Apparent relationship of power : matrix of means of direct action

Total influence

		A1	A2	A3	A4	A5	A6	S
Manufacturers	A1	0	1	1	3	0	2	7
Scheduled airlines	A2	2	0	3	2	1	1	9
Charter companies	A3	1	2	0	1	1	0	5
State	A4	2	3	3	0	3	2	13
Paris Airport	A5	0	2	3	1	0	2	8
Residents' associations	A5	0	1	1	3	2	0	7
Total dependence		S	5	9	11	10	7	7

Real relationships of power : matrix of means of indirect action

MIA = MDA X MDA

Total indirect influence

		A1	A2	A3	A4	A5	A6	S
Manufacturers	A1	9	13	14	9	15	7	58
Scheduled airlines	A2	7	17	12	13	11	10	53
Charter companies	A3	6	6	13	8	5	8	33
State	A4	9	16	22	24	10	13	70
Paris Airport	A5	9	11	11	13	12	4	48
Residents' associations	A6	9	15	18	5	11	11	58
Total indirect dependence Di		40	61	77	48	52	42	

But in looking at relationships of power, we cannot restrict ourselves simply to means of direct action : an actor can influence another via the intermediary of a third actor. It is therefore useful to examine matrix MIA - means of indirect (second order)

action - obtained simply by multiplying matrix MDA by itself (MIA = MDA x MDA) (according to the principle of the MICMAC method).

By doing this, we discover that the local residents' associations are in a stronger position of power than one would have thought a priori (ranked second in terms of total indirect influence over actors' moves). This is thanks to their direct influence on the state, the most powerful actor in the system. The charter companies' position of power seems even less favourable than before (they have very weak influence, and are highly sensitive to pressure, particularly from the state and the scheduled airlines).

As for the Paris Airport Authority, it is in an average position of power in relation to the system as a whole. Its capacity for indirect action over the local residents' assications is much weaker than its potential for direct action. On the other hand, Paris Airport has significant leverage for exerting indirect pressure over the state while almost totally lacking means of direct action. We also observe that the airline manufacturers can if necessary exert strong indirect pressure over Paris Airport, probably via the intermediary of the state.

As we can see, reading the MDA and MIA matrices is a fruitful exercise. Looking at 1978 from the standpoint of 1990, in the final analysis Paris Airport Authority had practically no interest in allying itself too openly with the charter airlines, because these were the weakest link in the overall balance of power. So it should come as no surprise that in 1990, at the height of a euphoric growth in air transportation worldwide, the European charter companies were 'on their last legs', to quote Aviation Internationale magazine, No. 996, 15 December 1989. What they should do is to air their common interests with the scheduled airlines, while putting pressure on the state for a degree of liberalization of traffic rights.

Naturally, our example is oversimplified, and it would be unreasonable to expect to make any definitive strategic recommendations based on it. We should also recall that everything depends on how each actor prioritizes its own objectives in terms of the balance of power.

We have seen that it was possible to take account of each actor's hierarchy of objectives through the matrix of positions (2MAO). To say that one actor is twice as influential as another in the overall balance of power is implicitly to ascribe twice the power to this actor's influence over objectives. Its relationships of power between actors are characterized by ri coefficients, it is then sufficient to weight the lines of the valued position matrix by these coefficients. Thus we pass from matrix 2MAO to matrix 3MAO, the valued position matrix, weighted by relationships of power. By multiplying 3MAO by its transposed form we obtain a third matrix of convergences and divergences.

How should we define these ri indicators of relationships of power ? The first idea that comes to mind is to consider the Mi indirect influences in the matrix of real relationship of power. The measure of relative indirect influence (MI/ΣMi) gives a good indicator of the power of one actor over the others.

However, with identical relative influence, one actor will be in a better position of power than another if its overall dependence is lower. So we must balance the preceding coefficient Mi/ΣMi with an inverse function of dependence Mi/(Mi+Di).

$$\text{With } ri = \frac{Mi}{\Sigma Mi} \times \frac{Mi}{Mi + Di}$$

if Di dependence is zero, ri = Mi/ΣMi ; if Di dependence is strong in relation to influence, then the ri relationship of power will be much weaker than the simple relationship Mi/ΣMi.

Moreover, in order to facilitate understanding and calculation, we suggest

$$ri^* = \frac{ri}{\bar{ri}} = \frac{n\,ri}{\Sigma\, ri}$$

considering . Starting with the matrix of real relationships of power, in our example, we obtain the balance of power coefficient for each actor :

$$r_1^* = 1{,}23,\ r_2^* = 0{,}88,\ r_3^* = 0{,}36,\ r_4^* = 1{,}49,\ r_5^* = 0{,}83,\ r_6^* = 1{,}21$$

The sum of these coefficients is equal to six. If all the actors had the same relationship of power, all the ri would be equal to one.

In this example the hierarchy of power relations coefficients is exactly the same as that of overall influence. It is the state (A4) which has the most favourable position of power, followed by the manufacturers (A1) and the residents (A6)... at the other end of the spectrum the charter companies (A3) represent the weakest link in the game.

We pass from the valued matrix of position 2MAO to the matrix of valued positions balanced by relationships of power 3MAO by multiplying each line of 2MAO by the ri coefficient.

3MAO

	01	02	03	04	05
A1	2.5	3.7	0.0	0.0	1.2
A2	-1.8	0.0	2.7	-0.9	-2.7
A3	-0.4	0.0	-1.1	1.1	-0.7
A4	0.0	4.5	3.0	0.0	1.5
A5	-0.8	0.0	-1.7	1.7	-1.7
A6	0.0	0.0	0.0	0.0	3.6

We thus obtain a third matrix of convergences and divergences (3MAA) balanced by relations of power.

		A1	A2	A3	A4	A5	A6
Manufacturers	A1		0	0	5,4	0	2,4
			-4,1	-2,4	0	-3,1	0
Scheduled airlines	A2			2,7	2,8	3,5	0
				-2,8	-2,1	-3,4	-3,1
Charter companies	A3		2,7		0	4,5	0
			-2,8		-3,1	0	-2,2
State	A4		2,3	0		0	+2,6
		0	-2,1	-3,1		-3,3	0
Paris Airport	A5	-4,1	3,5	4,5	0		0
		0	-3,4	0	-3,9		-2,6
Residents' associations	A6	-2,4	0	0	2,6	0	
		+5,4	-3,1	-2,2	0	-2,6	

Commentary

Between the first and the third complete diagrams of convergences, certain developments are worth pointing out.

The state manufacturers' convergence over objectives becomes noticeably stronger and appears twice as important as the state residents' convergence over objectives, which initially appeared comparable. The convergence over objectives between Paris Airport and the scheduled airlines and charter companies is confirmed as much stronger than the convergence of interests between the companies (scheduled and charter), and is probably a card to be played by Paris Airport.

THIRD COMPLETE DIAGRAM OF CONVERGENCES OVER OBJECTIVES

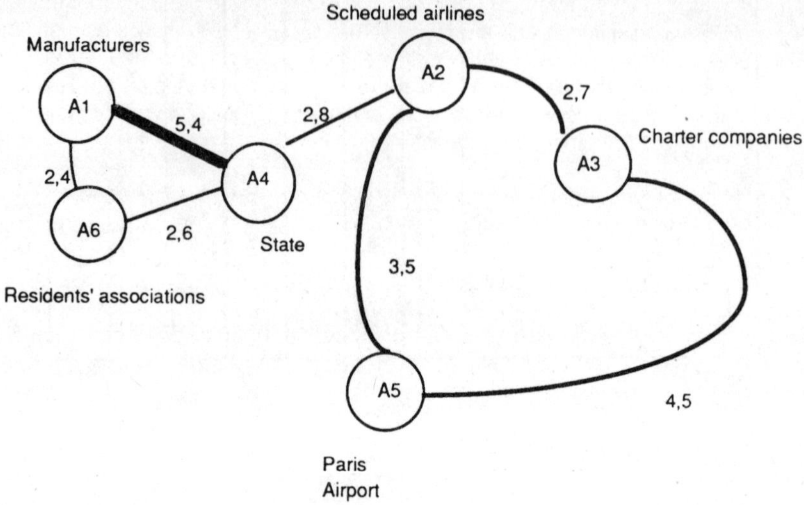

THIRD COMPLETE DIAGRAM OF DIVERGENCES OVER OBJECTIVES

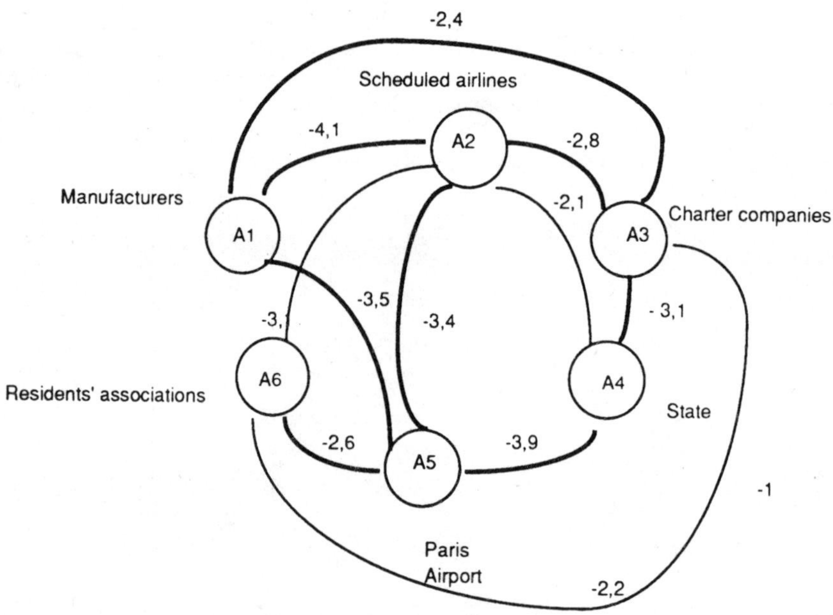

Comparison of the diagrams of divergences over objectives allows us to note certain remarkable changes in the actors' strategy when hierarchy of objectives and balance of power are taken into account. Thus, for example, the opposition of interests between the scheduled airlines and the manufacturers seems to be twice as significant as that between the charter companies and the manufacturers or scheduled airlines, which initially appeared comparable. In the same way, the conflicting objectives of the state and Paris Airport become much more critical than the conflict of objectives between the state and the airline companies.

From the above, it is not unreasonable to conclude that the state should support the manufacturers in their struggle for market share, and should strengthen regulations and standards which favour the development of new aircraft. Paris Airport, which is subject to the powerful protection of the state, must above all rely on the scheduled airlines to exert pressure on the state, for the charter companies are in a much less favourable position of power. In doing so, Paris Airport should logically tone down its support for development of charter flights, because the scheduled airlines are opposed to this.

In the example we have considered, taking into account hierarchies of objectives and relationships of power did not cause major upsets to the first analysis. Other scales of notation would probably provide a clearer contrast in results. Other indicators of power relations could also be tested, for example, by relying on the matrix of net balance of power between actors (derived from MAI matrix through the difference between aij and aji).

		A1	A2	A3	A4	A5	A6	
Manufacturers	A1		6	8	0	6	-2	+18
Scheduled airlines	A2	-6		6	-3	0	-5	-8
Charter companies	A3	-8	-6		-8	-6	-10	-38
State	A4	0	3	8		-3	8	+16
Paris Airport	A5	-6	0	6	3		-7	-4
Residents' associations	A6	2	5	10	-8	7		+16
		-18	+8	+38	-16	+4	-16	

Three actors (manufacturers, state and residents) are overall in a very favourable position of power in relation to the group comprising Paris Airport and the scheduled airlines, which are overall neutralized ; and the charter companies are completely dominated, ie, in an unfavourable position of power in relation to all the other actors. Paris Airport is better placed in relation to the state than one would think a priori. The potential threat comes primarily from the manufacturers and the residents.

We shall not pursue this simplified example any further. For the most complex cases -around 15 actors or 10 strategic issues and about 40 objectives - one certainly has to break down the problem by studying each battlefield separately. This modular utilization of the MACTOR method implies of course a never-ending task of developing a coherent overall picture with each further addition.

6. Key questions for the future

The evolution of relationships of power between the actors can be presented in the form of hypotheses which may or may not be realized within the time horizon under consideration. These hypotheses are concerned with trends, as much as with events or discontinuities.

The subsequent application of the scenarios method consists of using expert methods to reduce precisely this uncertainty over hypotheses concerning futures hypotheses deriving from the actor strategy analysis.

We believe that MACTOR will disseminate rapidly, as it is a simple and appropriate tool which will lead to a better understanding of the actors' games and power relationships. The air transport example developed here was rather illustrative. We assume that the use of MACTOR by Paris Airport Authority and by the French Electricity Authority to face the new European context proves that MACTOR certainly has a promising future.

CHAPTER VI

REDUCING UNCERTAINTY : EXPERT CONSENSUS METHODS

In the same way that the past can be summarized by a series of significant events, possible futures can be identified by a list of hypotheses which, for example, demonstrate the persistence of a trend, its disruption or the developmental genesis of a new trend.

In concrete terms, these hypotheses relate to the key-variables and the balance of power between the actors as analysed when the base was constructed. Scanning possible futures is done through morphological analysis. The implementation or otherwise of the hypotheses within a given time-frame is marked by a degree of uncertainty which can be reduced with the aid of subjective probabilities provided by experts.

In fact, when one looks to the future, personal judgement is often the only way to account for events which might occur (there are no statistics of the future). Expert methods prove useful for reducing uncertainty and also for comparing the views of one group with those of others (bell-weather function) and, at the same time, to become aware of the scope and span of opinions held.

The Delphi method, developed in the 1950's, is the best known expert method. It suffers from a number of weaknesses however, notably in its failure to account for interdependence of the questions asked. A new method then appeared at the end of the 1960's in the United States and at the beginning of the 1970's in Europe : cross-impact matrix. Following an inventory and historical review of these tools, we provide as an example a method which we developed in 1974 : the SMIC method.

1. Scanning possible futures: morphological analysis[1]

This is a sophisticated title for a very simple, yet often unappreciated (or forgotten) method which should be reinstated, for it can prove very useful for stimulating the imagination, helping to identify hitherto unknown products or processes, and scanning the field of possible future scenarios.

The originator of the method, F. Zwicky, envisaged that this method would "make invention routine", i.e., a common-place procedure. Zwicky, who was the first to imagine dwarf stars, developed the method in the 1940s while working for the American Army. According to legend it was through this method that Polaris missiles were first thought of.

[1] To learn about morphological analysis, cf. E. JANTSCH (1967), 'La prévision technologique', OECD and also R. SAINT-PAUL and P. F. TENIERE-BUCHOT (1974) 'Innovation et évaluation technologique', Entreprise Moderne d'Edition, 1974. Unfortunately these two excellent studies have been out of print for several years now... F. ZWICKY, Morphology and nomenclatura of jet engines, Aeronautical Engineering Review, June 1947.

1.1. The field of possible futures, a morphological space

The principle underlying the method is extremely straightforward. The system or function under study is broken down into sub-systems or component parts. These components must be as independent as possible and yet represent the totality of the system under study.

An aircraft is composed of wing structures, tail units, engines, etc... and each of these components could be assembled in different configurations, for example : one, two, three, or more, wings. A given aircraft will therefore be characterized by the chosen specific configuration of the components. There are therefore as many possible technical solutions as there are possible combinations of the configurations.

A system of 4 components, each having 4 configurations represents no fewer than 4 x 4 x 4 x 4 = 256 combinatory possibilities. This field of possible combinations is called the *'morphological space'*.

In the example proposed by E. JANTSCH[2], concerning propulsion units, there were more than 10 components, each with 2 to 4 possible configurations : thus the total number of imaginable solutions was 36,864. Fortunately, constraints exist (technical incompatibility, for example) which make several families of solutions unworkable and thus reduce the morphological space. It is also possible to give preference to those combinations of configurations which appear more propitious than others, in terms of such criteria as development costs, safety factors, feasibility, etc....

It is useful to compare the existing with the total morphological space : the harvest of new ideas will be all the richer in that the potential space is unknown (the ratio of the number of known solutions to the number of possible solutions is particularly interesting in this respect).

Areas of application are numerous and extend to many innovation and research procedures. R. SAINT-PAUL and P. F. TENIERE-BUCHOT remind us of the amusing example of the shaving function

[2] E. JANTSCH (1967) 'Technological forecasting', OECD.

Shaving

Energy sources	° Electrical	° Chemical	° Manual	° Mechanical	
Shaving agents	° Heat	° Electricity	° Blade	° Chemical	° Bacteria
Dynamics	° Circular	° Linear	° Static		

This morphological space contains 4 x 5 x 3 = 60 possibilities. We recognize the currently used methods in the above table : the linear dynamics manual blade and the circular blade electric shaver. The authors cite some solutions worth studying, such as *"selective burning of the beard hair, or bacterial ingestion of the beard by static application of a cream"*.

Curiously, morphological analysis has been used primarily in technological forecasting and far less in general futures studies. However, it lends itself well to the construction of scenarios. Let us consider a global system broken down into components : demographic, economic, social and organizational factors, with a certain number of possible states (hypotheses or configurations) for each of these components.

Configurations (hypotheses)

Components (dimensions)					
demographic factors	°	°	°	°	
economic factors	°	°	°	°	°
technological factors	°	°	°		
social factors	°	°	°	°	

In essence, a scenario is no more than a path combining a given configuration for each component. The morphological space defines the range of possible scenarios very precisely. It is probably the fear of drowning in the huge number of possible combinations that has curbed the utilization of morphological analysis for the construction of scenarios. We propose below a methodological approach which side-steps this obstacle and enables one to make the most of the analysis.

1.2. Problems and limitations

Specifically, the utilization of morphological analysis poses several problems relating to the question of comprehensiveness and to the limitations and illusions inherent in the number of combinations.

Firstly, the choice of components is particularly critical and requires considerable thought. By multiplying the number of components and configurations, the system expands very quickly, to such an extent that analysis rapidly becomes practically impossible ; on the other hand, with too few components the system is impoverished. Hence the requirement that there should be a compromise value. One must be careful to ensure that the components (dimensions) are independent and that they are not confused with the configurations (hypotheses).

Secondly, scanning all possible and imaginable solutions may give the illusion that all combinatory possibilities have been explored, whereas in reality the field has no definitive limitations but is simply evolving with time. Should one leave out some component or configuration which is essential for the future, one risks missing a whole facet of the field of possibilities (had such a study been applied to time-pieces at the start of the 1950s or 1960s, everything would have been imagined except the quartz watch).

Lastly, the user is very quickly submerged by the number of combinations and simply articulating the possible solutions becomes physically impossible once they exceed several hundred in number (we saw above that for a system with 4 components and 4 configurations each, there were already 256 possible combinations!). In such conditions, how can we identify the useful morphological sub-space ?

1.3. The useful morphological sub-space

Reducing the morphological space is necessary because it is impossible for the human mind to cover, step by step, the whole field of possible solutions generated by the combinations ; it is also desirable since there is no point in identifying solutions which in any case will be rejected once certain selection criteria (technical, economic...) are taken into consideration. Choices are therefore imperative to identify the key and secondary components which relate to these criteria. In a recent example, concerning a future, we suggested the following procedure :

- first identify the economic, technical and strategic selection criteria which can be used after the morphological analysis, to assess and select the best solutions among the total number of possible solutions (the morphological space) ;

- then identify those components which are deemed crucial according to the above criteria and classify these components in terms of criteria weighted differently according to the policy decisions adopted ;

- initially restrict exploration of the morphological space to the key components identified in this way ;

- finally introduce constraints of exclusion or preference (these combinations being excluded). In fact, many technical solutions are meaningless or irrelevant, either because of their intrinsic incompatibility (impossible combinatory associations) or once certain criteria (e.g., cost, competitivity) are taken into account.

This procedure enabled us to give priority to examining four main components out of nine under consideration. The initial morphological space, comprising 15,552 possibilities was thus reduced to a useful sub-space containing about 100 solutions (i.e., a reduction factor of 150). Taking the technical incompatibilities into account enabled us to eliminate more than half of these. The remaining half were subjected to individual assessment, each criterion being assigned a weighting value according to its importance in the policies under investigation. Thus, for each policy (set of criteria weightings) we were able to rank the 50 or so remaining solutions. A comparison of the various rankings then led to the identification of a hard core of twenty solutions, comprising : the best solutions in terms of all criteria and policies, as well as certain solutions which were outstanding in terms of certain specific criteria, and which for this reason were supported by a particular member of the working group.

The twenty solutions at the hard core of the useful morphological space were then grouped into families, i.e., in terms of their relative degree of kinship (identical solutions, give or take one or two configurations). Each of these twenty solutions was then subjected to detailed analysis and evaluation, specifying those configurations relating to the five secondary components.

From this experiment, we note two important lessons for the implementation of morphological analysis :

1) it forces us to think in a structured way about which components and configurations should be taken into consideration and enables a systematic scan through the range of possibilities ;

2) although the sum of possible combinations should not give the illusion of comprehensiveness, it should not be allowed to paralyse the thought process. It is fairly easy to reduce the analysis to a useful morphological sub-space (10, 100 or 1,000 times smaller). To do so, one only has to introduce selection criteria (with the help of Multipol, a multi-criteria method) and, for example, constraints of exclusion or preference.

The method developed above is now integrated into a micro-computer software package (MORPHOL). Morphological analysis can no longer stand accused of being difficult to implement. It is our feeling that this method will be the subject of renewed futures studies. Theory can only be credible when confronted with the test of a practical application.

2. An inventory of expert-consensus methods

Methods involving expert consultation can be ranged under three headings : "Delphi", the voting machines and "cross-impact".

2.1. The Delphi method

The Delphi method[3] involves "The systematic use of the intuitive evaluation of a group of experts" N. Dalkey and O. Helmer (1963). According to O. Helmer, one of the founders of the technique, "Delphi" was developed from the middle of the 1950's to meet the needs of the US army[4]. According to some authors, it has seen several thousand applications in the United States and several hundreds in Europe. These estimates should be viewed with some caution inasmuch as O. Helmer himself refuses to propose figures.

The Delphi method interrogates experts by means of successive questionnaires in order to bring out convergence of opinions and to identify clearly a possible consensus. The enquiry is carried out by mail and is anonymous in order to adjust for "leading opinions". The questions, by way of an example, deal with the probabilities of implementation of a certain hypothesis or event. The quality of the results is heavily dependent upon the care taken when drawing up the questionnaire and in the choice of the experts.

To be relevant, the method presupposes, on one hand, that genuine experts are consulted, i.e., people who are really able to answer the questions ; on the other hand, it is assumed that the view of a group of experts is superior to that of a single expert.

The Delphi method compounds a series of mailed questionnaires, their analysis and interpretation. As G. Ducos (1983) reminds us, each expert is offered "compensation and asked to answer only those questions for which he regards himself as most competent, or better still, to evalute his own level of competence with regard to each question".

The aim of successive questionnaires is, as R. Saint-Paul and P.F. Teniere Buchot (1974) note, "to reduce the interquartile space while specifying the mean value". To illustrate the method we will take an example which is very similar to that in their book.

This Delphi enquiry covered a whole range of economic questions. We will follow up one of them, viz, in what year will the gross individual income in France be double that for 1984.

[3] The word Delphi commemorates the town of Delphos, and its famous oracle.

[4] Interview given in September 1984 at Carmel (California) where Dr. Helmer is in retirement.

The first questionnaire aims at identifying the mean value and the interquartile space[5]. The distribution of the responses to the first questionnaire (see bar-chart) shows that mean is located in 2000 and the interquartile space (Q1,Q3) is between 1997 and 2005.

Response Former ⁀ new	Justification : when replying outside range (Q1, Q3)

The second questionnaire is aimed at reducing the interval (Q1,Q3) by asking for justifications of the extreme values. Each expert is informed of the first round results, is asked to supply a new response and to justify where it lies outside (Q1,Q3).

It is easier to conform, viz., to answer in the interval (Q1,Q3), than to maintain thereby an extreme point of view that has to be justified (if you think like everyone else, no-one asks you why). The simulated convergence gives a new reduced interval (Q1,Q3) 1998-2004 and a new mean value 1999.

The third questionnaire is designed to oppose the two extremes by bringing their arguments together. In addition, each expert is asked to criticize those who fall short of Q1 (1998) or beyond Q3 (2004).

On this occasion the convergence is forced, and even manipulated, since only the extremes are opposed, whereas taken together, they represent as many replies as are in the interval (Q1,Q3). Also, those at the extremes are not asked to criticise the views of those situated in the interquartile space.

Arguments 'short of Q1'	Arguments 'beyond Q3'	New response	Criticism and arguments

The fourth questionnaire gives the final response : 1999 for the mean value, 1998 for Q1 and 2003 for Q3.

The Delphi method, as described, to the extent that there seems to be a convergence of opinions around a central value, provides the right way to prepare a consensus for certain types of decision-making (technological investment with high economic and social risks). However, convergence does not imply coherence and consensus does not necessarily mean a correct forecast (everyone could be wrong at the same time). The history of forecasting errors teaches rather that we should distrust predominant ideas ; the correct viewpoint is often to be found in the minority.

[5] Here the mean value (second quartile) is the year that 50 % of the experts think that the doubling will occur 'before', and 50 % think it will take place 'after'. In taking the 25 % and 75 % thresholds, then 75 % and 25 % , we define respectively the first quartile (Q1) and the third quartile (Q3). The interquartile range is the interval (Q1, Q3).

In short, if the Delphi process appears to be well adapted to normative applications in its classical form, it could prove more misleading than useful for forecasting applications. There is naturally no reason why one should not alter the method and make Delphi a more useful forecasting tool by abstaining from reducing the extremes. There is less need to put out several rounds of questionnaires, which proves long, costly, painstaking and sometimes risky (since at each iteration a certain number of the experts evaporate).

Question : In what year will the gross individual income in France be double that for 1984 (in constant Francs) ?

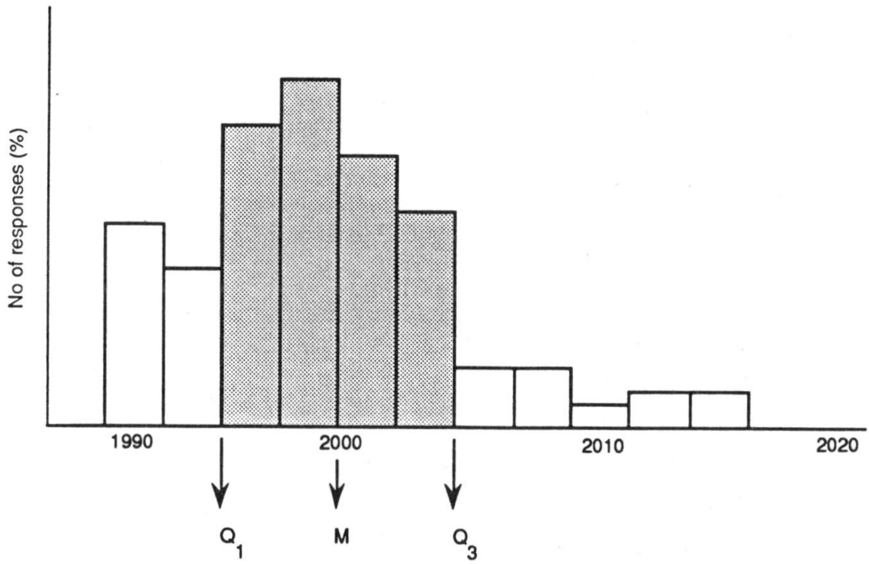

For forecasting applications the mini-Delphi technique -cf. G. Ducos (1983)- seems more appropriate. Using this technique first experimented in the early 1970's -cf. O. Helmer (1972)- the experts are in the same venue and discuss each question before responding individually. The Mini-Delphi process is likely to experience a vogue in various forms due to the new possibilities opened up by micro-computers in the use of voting machines. We must mention here two promising developments, one in France : Regnier's Abacus, and the other in the United States : Consensor.

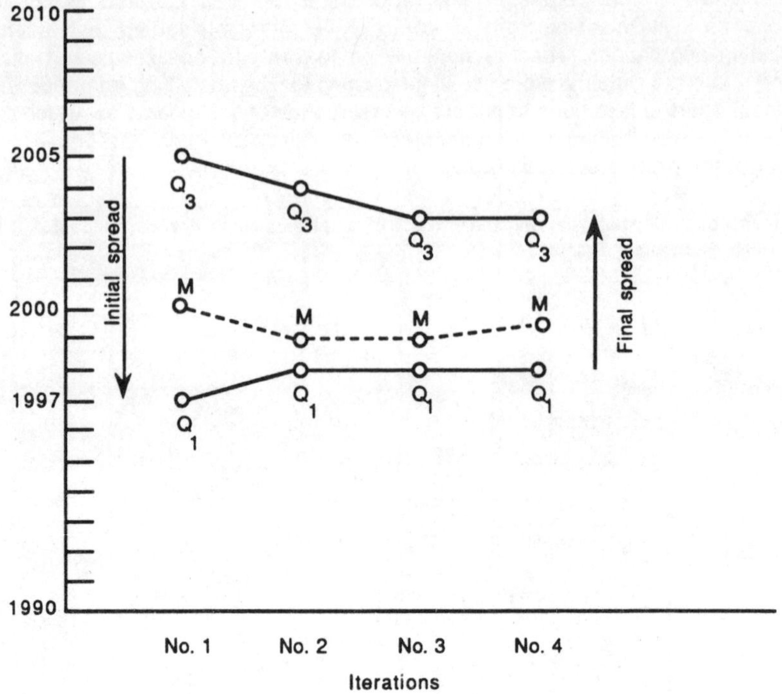

(A classical poll result) (Delphi result)

2.2. Voting machines : Regnier's Abacus and the Consensor

Regnier's Abacus (1983) is a novel method for expert consultation. Its originator, Dr Regnier, a consultant economist specializing in organization and communication methods believes that the method (successfully used in the pharmaceutical industry), could now be developed more systematically.

The main idea of the Abacus is to start with the three traffic light colours of green, amber and red, and then to add pale green and pink to allow more shades of opinion. White is a blank vote, black is an abstention. The colour-coded votes are then placed on a grid like a crossword puzzle. Each participant has a column and each element of the problem a row.

The mosaic image sketches out a map which guides verbal discussion. Nevertheless the procedure remains open and anyone can change their colour at any time. The Abacus is not a test but a tool which stimulates interaction among individuals. While we can only talk in turns, the Abacus image reveals everyone's opinions on the problem simultaneously. The Abacus is therefore an instrument tending to make communication efficient, for example, in a group where certain individuals are often stifled. What is more, the act of announcing a colour before the discussion expresses an individual's feelings and goes beyond mere rationalities.

Questions	Green	Light green	Orange	Pink	Red	White	Black
1							
2							
3							
4							
5							
6							
7							
8							
9							
10							
11							
12							
13							

How to make your choice using this grid.
The colours have the following meaning :
Green, like traffic light green, is a rather favourable response. *Red*, like traffic light red, is a somewhat unfavourable reply. *Orange*, like the traffic light amber, is the intermediate color between red and green. *Light green* is a shade more positive than orange, but less positive than green but not as unfavourable as red.
Thus we have a decision scale with five steps : five shades : *green, light green, orange, pink, red.* Moreover, a sixth colour *white* (= blank vote) implies you do not wish to decide on a colour. *Black* means you wish to abstain from voting.

Regnier's Abacus was published, with its associated pack, in 1975. It comprises four coloured cubes which slot into a honeycomb tray and has been used in various firms and institutions and in higher education (the National Polytechnic Institute of Lorraine, the Strasbourg Institute of Social Psychology, the Ecole Supérieure de Commerce de Paris etc.).

The automated Abacus, programmed by microcomputer is more recent. Image processing, for example, the permutation of the rows and columns for sorting, has become instantaneous. This manipulation of the coloured texture allows an easier reading of the pattern in the mosaic.

The tool also has the attributes of efficiency, time saving and simplicity. Learning time is very short and the meaning of the image is understood internationally. The Abacus reconciles the individual with the group through exchange and it introduces an approach which allows us better to exploit qualitative aspects with which our society is less familiar than quantitative analysis.

In its current form Regnier's Abacus makes clever use of familiar colours, to exploit collective opinion, yet it possesses certain characteristics specific to manual coding that limit its applicability.

Consensor, is an electronic voting machine developed in the USA by the firm *Applied Futures*[6], allows a synthesis that is :

- immediate - a histogram shows participants' reactions within a few seconds ;
- confidential - the anonymous votes of each individual can be transmitted ;
- scaled - the votes range from 0 to 10 ;
- weighted - the opinions of the participants are weighted according to their respective competence ;
- continuous - the expert can change his vote in the course of the discussion.

Consensor is portable and allows a group of up to 20 or so experts to express their opinions at a time. Given that tools such as Regnier's Abacus and Consensor are apparently simple to use and inexpensive, why have they not yet received the development they merit in Europe ? There are apparently numerous applications, both in prospective studies and in decision-support. Consensor would also appear to be useful for collecting information necessary for cross-impact analysis and for Regnier's Abacus.

2.3. Cross-impact methods

Although the Delphi method enables a fairly good synthesis of opinions to be obtained from which a convergent result can be determined, its shortcoming is that it does not allow for interaction between events. On the other hand, the cross-impact method (CIM)[7] has the advantage that it takes into account expressed opinion and simultaneous interdependence between questions providing an interpretation grid which proves coherent.

The cross-impact method is the generic name for a family of techniques which attempt to evaluate changes in the probability of occurrence of a given category of event, following a previous occurrence of such an event. The method starts with a list of events and their associated probabilities ; the basic hypothesis of the method is that the individual probabilities account for interactions, but only incompletely. Taking the interdependencies into account allows us to move from a system of unprocessed initial probabilities to a set of net probabilities, i.e. corrected probabilities.

The rest of the method consists, first, of analysing the sensitivity of the event analysis system, and, second, of building scenarios. The working out of the scenarios is implemented by highlighting the most probable final images.

In practice, if we have a system of N hypotheses ($h1$, $h2$ ... hn) there are 2^n

[6] Applied Futures, 22 Greenwich Plaza, Greenwich, Connecticut, 06830, USA.

[7] Some authors like G. Ducos (1980) speak of interaction analysis.

final images (interacting hypotheses), *viz* all the scenarios possible for the system. For example, let there, be $h1, h2, h4 \ldots hn$ but not $h3$: this is one of the 2^n. If we take into account the order in which the events occur, there are $N! \, 2^n$ development scenarios.

Several methods of cross-impact analysis have been put forward. To start with T. J. Gordon (1968), interactions are evaluated with impact coefficients ranging from + 10 to - 10, the transition between rough and final probabilities usually being achieved by fairly sophisticated techniques : the Monte Carlo iteration method. Later research, mainly that of J. Kane (1972), fell into the methodological framework set up by T.J. Gordon and continued to mix impact coefficients with rough probabilities in the formulae leading on to final probabilities. From this viewpoint, N. Dalkey (1972) was an exception : his model relied on a conditional probability matrix existing between every pair of events, to modify the original system of probabilities. This approach, which represented a definite improvement with respect to CIM as proposed by Gordon and developed by Dalkey, is not very credible.

In effect, the results obtained depend on the transition formula adopted for calculating the final probabilities. Several formulae have been proposed, often a judicious mixture of quadratics, mathematical expectations and coefficients with subjective weighting. In practice none is convincing and, as Florentin and Dognin demonstrate (1973), there can be as many results as formulae tested for a given single example.

Moreover, the method ought to be used to control the coherence of the estimates relative to the classical constraints on the probabilities. In practice, most methods, whatever their degree of complexity, result in clearly incoherent probability values, with, for example, results such as $P(i) < p(i/j).\ P(i/not\ j)$, which is not compatible with the relationship $P(i) = P(i/j)\ Pj + P(i/not\ j).P(not\ j)$ which must always be valid. Many writers confuse convergence with coherence : because results are coherent, that does not mean that the process is necessarily convergent.

Two methods, EXPLOR-SIM and SMIC[8], presented in 1974 represented a decisive step forward by insisting on working with homogenous data (probabilities only) to seek coherent results and work out scenarios. The first method was developed by researchers at the Battelle Institute, Geneva (C. Duval, E. Fontela and A. Gabus (1974) and the second by J.L. Duperrin and M. Godet (1974).

Other methods have been proposed since, and have been the subject of numerous presentations and polemic debates in *Futures* and *Technological Forecasting and Social Change*. Several French researchers have played an active role in this development, such as, for example ; J. Eymard (1975) with a Markovian model or G. Ducos (1980) with the MIP (1) and MIP (2) methods.

The debate mainly centres on one essential point, namely : "What questions may reasonably be put to an expert and how does one derive coherence from the answer?"

[8] The SMIC method (French acronym for Cross Impact Systems and Matrices) developed at the programmes department of the Atomic Energy Commission (C.E.A.) from 1972-3, and further developed at SEMA.

Under certain conditions, an expert can answer with simple conditional probabilities for several pairs of hypotheses *i* and *j*. Unfortunately it is practically impossible that his responses will validate the classic axioms governing probability : summing and product rules (constraints b and c)[9].

The search for coherence is all the more delicate in that it is legitimate to presuppose that some answers are more reliable than others (unevenly distributed incoherence). Each method provides a specific solution to the problem of coherence, but none is totally satisfactory. Thus, for example :

- EXPLOR-SIM only asks the experts for simple probabilities $P(i)$ and certain conditional probabilities $P(i/j)$ to calculate $P(i/not\ j)$ taking into account the summing rule. Although this practice has the advantage of constructing a matrix coherent with respect to constraints that are anyway insufficient, it nevertheless has the serious deficiency that it regards the estimate for $P(i/j)$ for example,as fully reliable .
- SMIC invites the experts to answer a grid of all questions $P(i) P(i/j)$, $P(i/\ not\ j)$ and seeks to develop information as coherent as possible to the initial set of data, by minimization of a bounded quadratic form. In so doing, however, data with different degrees of reliability are processed identically .

The debate is still open, though at a standstill, and the methodological progress of the past few years, with only a few exceptions[10], relates to minor refinements (cf. the excellent summary by O. Helmer (1981)).

Finally, on both sides of the Atlantic, certain methods, despite imperfections, have demonstrated their usefulness through a significant number of practical applications. Such is the case, at any rate, with the SMIC method which is described below.

3. The SMIC method

Among cross-impact methods, the SMIC method offers the advantage of very simple and inexpensive implementation (drawing up a questionnaire), provides rapid results and is generally easy to interpret.

The SMIC method consists of interviewing a panel in the most rational and objective way possible. A set of formal interviews could be conducted and an overall measure of agreement obtained, but unless a great deal of time was devoted to this, it would be difficult to see many more than 20 persons. With the method used here, two or three times that number can be questioned. Thus it is possible to exceed the threshold (around 30 people) beyond which past experience shows that the law of large numbers operates within a somewhat restricted overall professional environment. In other words, much the same results will be obtained, whether we ask

---

[9] (a) $0 \leq P() \leq 1$;

(b) $P(i.j) = P(i/j)\ P(j) = P(j/i)\ P(i)$;

(c) $P(i) = P(i/j)\ Pj + P(i/\ not\ j).P(not\ j)$

[10] Cf. Dr. Enzer's INTERAX Method (1980) at the Center for Futures Research of the University of Southern California.

100 or 150 people.

The method usually takes the form of a mailed enquiry, thus allowing the elimination of subjectiveness due to the researcher's presence, since, instead of a verbal opinion, evaluation will be based on replies couched in figures. The inaccuracy of expert answers is reduced : experts are asked to estimate the probability of a hypothesis occurring, on a scale from 1 (very low) to 5 (event highly probable). They are also asked to estimate in the form of conditional probabilities the likelihood of a hypothesis coming true as a function of the other hypotheses. The value 6 corresponds to the independence of a hypothesis. As a result of this, the expert has to revise his assessment several times and, to some extent, he must reveal the implicit coherence of his reasoning.

The reverse side of the coin is the difficulty of representing the future of a complex phenomenon by a limited number of hypotheses, which runs contrary to the approach in some opinion gathering methods. These, however, do not take account of the interdependence among the questions and quite often result in contradictory answers. That too can prove an advantage : the method requires the preparation of information and that the issues be considered carefully before selection of the key hypotheses. This underlines the importance of structural analysis and the need to understand actor's strategies in order to identify key variables and formulate strategic hypotheses.

The amount of information gathered in the course of a SMIC enquiry (60 to 80 questions usually answered by 40 to 60 experts), is of the same order as the amount furnished by a conventional survey asking a representative sample of 1000 people two or three questions. Thus, the choice lies between canvassing a wide spread of opinion for a small number of questions and an in-depth analysis of the " global vision" of a small number of experts.

3.1. The principle and the aim of SMIC

An event is a hypothesis coming true at a given time horizon and the set of hypotheses constitutes a reference frame within which there are as many possible states, i.e., final images, as there are combinations of outcomes of the hypotheses. The SMIC method, starting from information supplied by experts, allows a choice to be made from among the 2^n possible images to select those which merit a more detailed study, alllowing for their probability of occurrence.

The experts are asked (as a group of individuals) to tender information on :

- the list of *N* hypotheses considered fundamental to the objectives of the study : $H = (H1, H2, ...H_N)$;
- the probabilities of an implementation at a given time horizon : *P(i)* probability of hypothesis *Hi* ;
- the conditional probabilities of the hypotheses (paired) :
  P(i/j) probability of i if j occurs
  P(i/not j) probability of i if j does not occur.

In practice, the opinions supplied in response to some specific questions regarding non-independent hypotheses are not coherent with respect to the conventional constraints bounding probabilities.

These unprocessed opinions must be corrected in such a way that the final results validate the following conditions :

(a) $0 \leq P() \leq 1$
(b) $P(i/j).P(j) = P(i/j).P(i) = P(i.j)$;
(c) $P(i/j).\ P(j) + P(i/\ \text{not}\ j).P(\text{not}\ j) = P^{*}(i)$.

The principle of the SMIC method is to adjust the experts' unprocessed opinions in such a way as to obtain coherent final results (satisfying the normal constraints bounding probabilities) which remain as close as possible to the initial estimates.

We could envisage optimizing some function of the individual or conditional probabilities subject to the above constraints. However non-linearity of the constraints governing the isolated hypotheses imposes specific conditions on the optima ; this leads us to concentrate on the combinatory probabilities of hypotheses, i.e., situational scenarios.

The principle adopted attempts to obtain coherent final probabilities from the hypotheses[11] which result from the combined probabilities of the hypotheses, and which form global, unexpressed but implicit opinions relating to the scenarios.

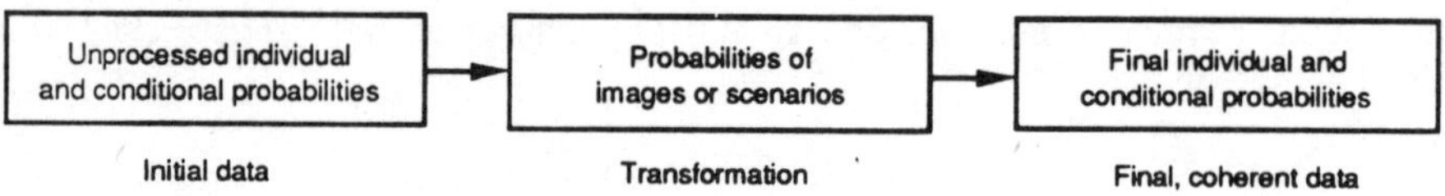

Obtaining coherent, final probabilities

3.2. Relationships between hypotheses and scenarios : the search for coherence

The $2^N = r$ possible situations of the system *Er* comprising *N* hypotheses, are :

E1 = (h1, h2, ... hi .... h_N)
E2 = (not h1, h2, ... hi .... h_N) (h1 not implemented)
....
Er = (not h1, not h2, ... not hi .... not h_N) (no hypothesis implemented)

[11] In some cases when it is preferable to speak of events rather than hypotheses, this number is restricted to five or six.

Each situation (or image) *Ek* has an unknown probability Π_k which we would like to identify.

Individual or conditional theoretical probabilities, expressed as a function of Π_k, can be associated with each isolated hypothesis *hi*.

(1) *Probability of* hi

$$P^* (i) = \Sigma_k \Theta_{ik} \Pi_k \qquad (1)$$

where $\theta\, ik = 0$ if *hi* does not occur in *Ek*
$\theta\, ik = 1$ if *hi* occurs in *Ek*

The relation (1) expresses the fact that the probability of hypothesis *i* is the sum of the probabilities of the situations where *hi* in fact occurs.

(2) *Probability of* hi *if* hj *is realized*

$$P^*(i/j) = \frac{\sum_{k=1}^{r} T(ijk)\, \Pi_k}{P^*(j)} \quad \forall(ij) \qquad (2)$$

where $T(ijk) = 1$ if *hi* and *hj* occur in *Ek*
$T(ijk) = 0$ if *hi* or *hj* do not occur in *Ek*

In fact we have $P^* (i.j) = P^* (i/j).P^*(j)$ and the probability that *hi* and *hj* occur simultaneously is equal to the sum of the probabilities of the situations where *i* or *j* both occur simultaneously .

(3) *Probabilities of* i *if not* j

$$P^*(i/\text{not } j) = \frac{\sum_{k=1}^{r} S(ijk)\, \Pi_k}{1 - P^*(j)} \quad \forall(ij) \qquad (3)$$

Where $S(ijk) = 1$ when hi and not hj are part of E_k
$S(ijk) = 0$ when hi and not hj are not part of E_k

The necessarily valid conditions are :

(a) $0 \leq P^*() \leq 1$;
(b) $P^*(i/j).P^*(j) = P^*(j/i).P^*(i) = P^*(i.j)$;
(c) $P^*(i/j).P^*(j) + P^*(i/\text{not } j).P^*(\text{not } j) = P^*(i)$.

Constraints (a), (b) and (c) are verified by the theoretical probabilities but not by the estimated probabilities : as a result the objective function that we propose to optimize consists of minimizing the difference between the products $P(i/j).P(j)$

which result from the estimates supplied by the experts and the theoretical products $P^*(i/j).P^*(j)$ which are expressed as a function of the Πk.

This is equivalent to seeking the probabilities ($\Pi 1$, $\Pi 2$, ... Π_k ... Π_r) of the r situations possible, which minimize for example :

$$\sum_{k=1}^{r} \left\{ \begin{array}{l} \left[\sum_{i} \left\{ P(i) - \sum_{k=1}^{r} \theta(ik).\Pi_k \right\}^2 \right. \\ \quad + \sum_{ij} \left\{ P(i/j).P(j) - \sum_{k=1}^{r} T(ijk).\Pi_k \right\}^2 \\ \quad \left. + \sum_{ij} \left\{ P(i/\text{not } j).P(\text{not } j) - \sum_{k=1}^{r} s(ijk).\Pi_k \right\}^2 \right] \\ \text{Subject the constraints} \qquad \sum_{k=1}^{k=1} \Pi k = 1 \\ \qquad\qquad\qquad\qquad\qquad\quad \Pi_k \geq 0, \forall k \end{array} \right.$$

This is a standard quadratic minimization programming problem under linear constraints.

At this stage it can be shown that there are multiple solutions for the Πk while the P^* remain singular. A choice criterion is introduced : the solution taken to be optimal is that which corresponds to the set of the Πk in such a way that the most likely scenario has the highest possible value, corresponding to "reality", most of the experts bearing in mind that when they responded to the SMIC questionnaire, this was a final image that they considered more likely than any other.

The solution corresponding to this criterion, *viz*, Max (Max Πk) is obtained easily using the simplex algorithm, since it is a linear function in Π, to be optimized under linear constraints.

3.3. Results : hierarchy of scenarios and sensitivity analysis

For each expert the SMIC programme gives the probability sequence ($\Pi 1$, $\Pi 2$, ... Πr) of the r scenarios which provide the highest value of the most probable scenario Max (Max Πk).

We thus obtain a *cardinal sequence of possible scenarios*, which enables us to define the *domain of the possible outcomes* retaining only those which have a non-zero probability.

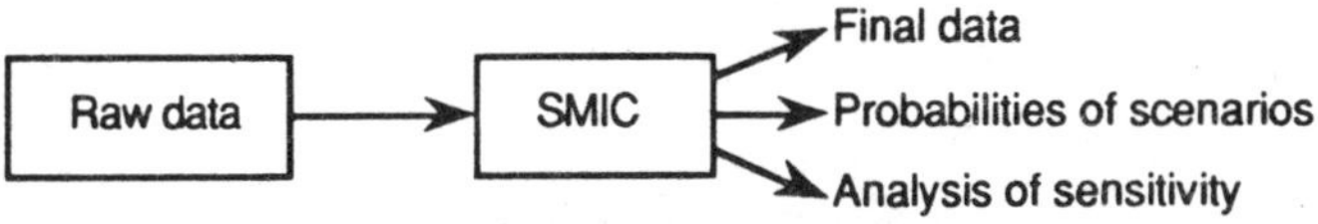

Within the domain of the possible outcomes we can distinguish those scenarios which are more probable than others, from which the reference situations and the contrasted situations can be chosen. From the probabilities of the scenarios we can deduce the coherent, simple and conditional, probabilities of the hypotheses, i.e., satisfying (a), (b) and (c). The rest of the method consists of sensitivity analysis to identify the driver or dominant variables and the dependent variables.

Sensitivity analysis. This is a matter of estimating the variation ΔPJ of the probability Pj of the event j following a variation ΔPi of the probability Pi of the event i. The results take the form of an elasticity matrix :

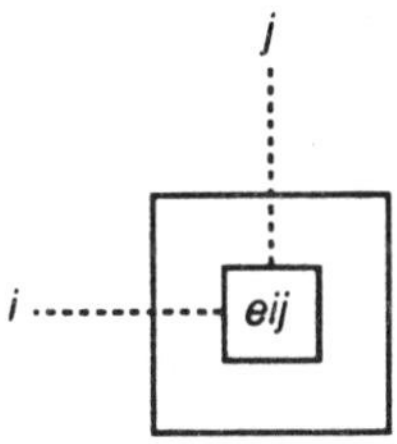

$$e(ij) = \frac{P(i).\Delta\ P(j)}{P(j).\Delta\ P(i)}$$

The effects of an action on each hypothesis are measured by the coefficients of elasticity eij. We construct an elasticity matrix whose row totals give the sums of the relative induced in the probabilities of the other hypotheses for a relative probability variation of i (10% for example). To some extent this sum translates the driving force of the hypothesis i on the others. Similarly the column totals allow an estimation of the degree of dependence of the hypotheses.

Sensitivity analysis informs us as to which hypotheses should be enhanced or inhibited, thus orienting the system in a desired direction. These elasticities can be calculated by simulation (cycling the model of the relationships several times through the probabilities). However, for technical and financial reasons, it is established practice to measure the impact of one event on another by shifting the bar-chart of the P(i), P(i/j) and P(i/not j).

Choice of the final images. For each expert consulted, we now have a list of the 2^N images, ranged in decreasing order of probability. A list of some of these images (ten or so) can then be drawn up such that :

- for each expert the sum of the probabilities of the images absent from the list is small ;
- for each image retained on the list, there is at least one expert who assigns a large probability to it ;
- we then calculate the mean of the assigned probabilities for each image,

obtaining a hierarchy of final images, and the corresponding scenarios.

The reference scenario (a scenario often quoted and with a high mean probability) and contrasted scenarios are then chosen from among the available scenarios.

The SMIC method can be summarized in essence as highlighting the most likely futures that will be dealt with by the scenario technique (Cf. figure above).

Once the final images have been worked out, the aim of the scenario method is to describe coherently the various pathways by which - starting from the present situation and including evolutionary mechanisms and the behaviour of the actors analysed in the base - the future can be predicted.

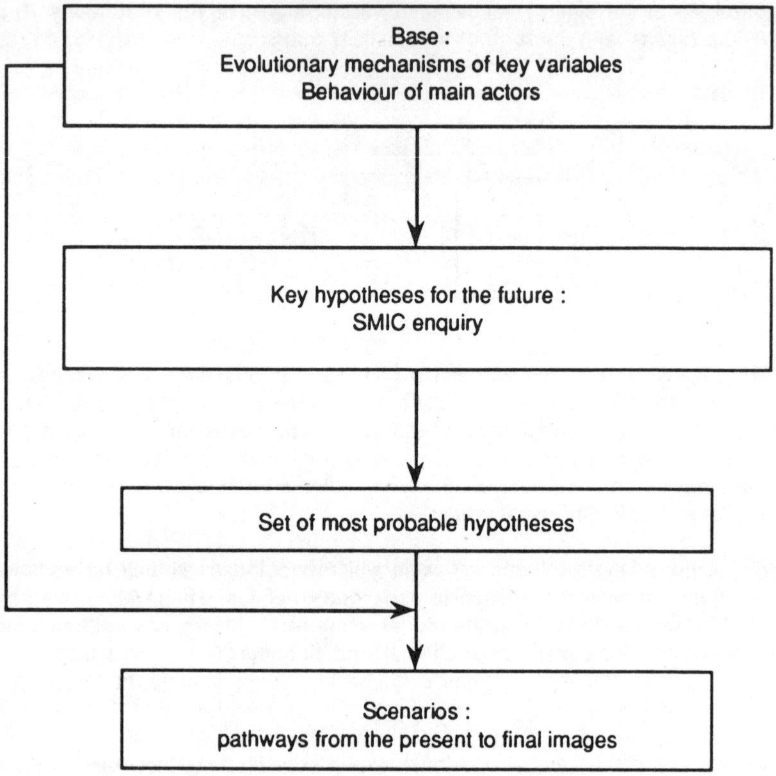

Domain of possible outcomes

3.4. Applicability and limitations

Several criticisms were levelled at the SMIC method, at least as regards its first applications. Notably :

- a too limited mechanical application ;
- the objective function and the multiplicity of solutions ;
- the amalgamating of the responses of several experts.

It is worth considering each of these points :

Limited and mechanical application. Every new instrument requires a learning period, during which time its use becomes an end in itself. Fortunately, for the SMIC method, this was a short period and today it is only with great circumspection that it can be used within the framework of the scenarios method. The number of hypotheses or events that can be handled by the SMIC method is generally limited to six, this figure being chosen less for mathematical reasons than to limit the maximum number of questions that can reasonably be put to the experts.

Objective function and the multiplicity of solutions. First, the objective function is in some ways arbitrary. Another function could be chosen. Nevertheless, the one we have used has the advantage of conforming to the 'philosophy' of least squares. In effect, as in linear regression, we have a host of points (the unprocessed answers) and we seek the "best fit" result that respects certain constraints (a straight line relation for the regression and the axioms of probability in our case). In any case, it is true that the optimum of the objective function is not unique and that there is an infinity of solutions for the probabilities of the k scenarios.

In 1976 we suggested introducing a choice criterion and retaining-as the optimal solution among the infinity of solutions-that which gave the highest value to the most likely scenario. The solution corresponding to this criterion, i.e., Max (Max Πk), can easily be obtained by using the simplex algorithm. This criterion has the advantage of partly removing the contradiction we have often noted among SMIC results, which tends to assign a relatively low probability to the most likely scenario as well as to the initial viewpoint held by the expert being questioned, according to whom one or two scenarios were clearly more likely than others.

Amalgamating responses. Given computing costs, it is not possible to run as many passes of the SMIC method as there are experts polled ; besides, there would be as many solutions as experts and arbitration problems would constantly arise. The solution we offer is to construct a typology of experts, as a function of the proximity of their responses and to retain only those scenarios which seemed most probable to the majority of experts, grouped by type ; i.e., as representatives of a category.

Given these limits, the usefulness of cross-impact methods such as SMIC remains considerable when it comes to choosing the most likely scenarios that are relevant, also to gain better understanding of the strategic behaviour of the actors driving the system by closely examining the image of the future that they generate. To better appreciate the technique's usefulness, we can now look at some examples.

4. Case studies

Around fifteen international surveys have been carried out using the SMIC method by mail and with very satisfactory response rates of the order of 25% to 30%. The results have always provided an invaluable source of information for the relevant prospective studies.

To illustrate the SMIC method, we refer to two early applications to show the extent to which they have stood the test of time (which seems to us the least that can be expected of a prospective study). The first example concerns the probable trends in air transport in the Paris region to the year 1990 as they were envisaged in 1974 when a SEMA study was carried out for the Paris Airport Authority.

SOME AREAS OF APPLICATION OF SMIC
OVER THE PAST DECADE

Long-haul passenger demand to 1990-2000
Aircraft construction
Air transport in the Paris region
The French post office in 1990
World geopolitical evolution
France and world developments
The consequences of a left wing victory in France in 1978
Firms in late 1978
The world petrochemical industry
Offshore industries
The European automobile industry
The cosmetics industry
Fairs and exhibitions in France
The Nuclear industry in the year 2000
Corporate activities and jobs to the year 2000

In this application, there was no enquiry involving outside experts, but a group opinion survey was undertaken by a working party which wished to test the coherence of their views as they resulted from the exercise together with certain assumptions about the "most likely" scenarios. The issues in this prospective study were not trivial, since the aim was to assess whether the traffic outlook for the year 1990 required the construction of a third airport in the Paris region in addition to Roissy. In the event of a positive response it would have been necessary as of 1974 to acquire the land for this future development.

Thinking back on events, it appears that the negative conclusion of the study was well founded. In any case the study clearly identified bottlenecks like passenger handling on the ground, average take-off delays, etc., the importance of which has since been confirmed. However, the conclusions which turned out to be relevant relied partly on hypotheses that were not borne out by facts : for example, the forecasts for economic growth were excessively optimistic (in 1974 the economic crisis was not generally considered likely to last).

The second application relates to the global needs and prospects for nuclear energy to the year 2000, incorporating some results of the international survey published in Economia in 1977 and which, despite the passage of time, remain accurate today.

By as early as 1977 it was clear that new forms of energy would not prove economic by the year 2000 compared with oil and nuclear power. It also seemed that the experts were divided about the development of nuclear power ; some, particularly those outside France, maintained that nuclear power was only an intermediate step of minor importance, as an abundance of oil was expected : oil would be more abundant because of high prices (we were then on the eve of the second oil crisis)[12].

Since then, history has shown that although the development of nuclear energy was necessary, it should have been carried out in a more flexible and less massive way because of the high degree of uncertainty about economic growth, the energy component of future growth, energy prices and conventional energy resources. In 1977, at any rate, very few experts believed in the development of breeder reactors. The decisions taken in 1984 with regard to Creys Malville confirm the soundness of this opinion.

4.1. Air transport scenarios[13]

We examined those events which could affect traffic at Paris airport for the period 1974-1990, an event being defined as the materialization of a trend to which a threshold is assigned even if this trend is at present only a potentiality. We identified six events which could be taken to characterize certain specific trends in air transport in the Paris region.

The question asked was : given that a system with six events can assume $2^6 = 64$ states at the given time horizon, what states (or scenarios) are most likely, or, the most unlikely ? The six events were :

(e1) *More than 50 million tourist class passengers.* This event characterizes an extrapolation of two trends : on the one hand, continued growth of passenger traffic, and on the other, a growing proportion of the tourist class in passenger traffic.

(e2) *An average of over 150 million passengers per aircraft movement.* This event implies a certain load factor and also assumes increased and widespread use of wide-body aircraft.

(e3) *An average take-off delay in excess of 20 minutes.* This event includes a number of phenomena such as, the saturation of airspace, which could be aggravated by the banning of night flights.

(e4) *Air ticket prices decreasing by more than 3% per annum, in constant terms.* This means for example that if the price of an air ticket in 1974 is 100 Francs, the same ticket would cost less than 63 Francs in 1990, in 1974 Francs. It could be said that if this particular event does not occur, air transport has little chance of becoming a mass transport option.

---

[12] These results are akin to those quoted previously.

[13] Study carried out by SEMA for the Paris Airport Authority, See M. Godet (1975).

(e5) *French gross national product growing in volume at more than 4% per annum.* This event is favourable to air transport, to the extent that economic growth creates some business class traffic and that a rise in real income increases the potential market for air traffic in general. In the long term this event seems to be a limiting factor for the development of air traffic in the Paris region. Growth in traffic is often accompanied by urban development, notably around airport zones. This in turn threatens to aggravate environmental problems.

(e6) *Regulatory constraints involving a 20% reduction in potential traffic movements.* This could lead to limits being imposed on the total number of movements or even a ban on night movements.

Unprocessed data. Events up to 1990 are characterized as shown below :

a) by the probability of occurrence of isolated events.

	P(ei)
e1 more than 50 million tourist class passengers in 1990	0.4
e2 an average of more than 150 passengers per flight	0.7
e3 an average take-off delay of more than 20 minutes (air-traffic control saturation)	0.6
e4 constant Franc ticket price falls by more than 3 % per annum	0.4
e5 French GNP grows by more than 4 % per annum	0.6
e6 regulatory constraints involve a reduction of 20 % in potential traffic movements	0.7

b) by the conditional probabilities of paired events :

	e_1	e_2	e_3	e_4	e_5	e_6	
e_1		0.5 / 0.3	0.7 / 0.4	0.8 / 0.1	0.6 / 0.1	0.4 / 0.5	e_1
e_2	0.8 / 0.3		0.5 / 0.7	0.9 / 0.6	0.7 / 0.7	0.9 / 0.6	e_2
e_3	0.7 / 0.6	0.4 / 0.7		0.7 / 0.6	0.7 / 0.6	0.8 / 0.4	e_3
e_4	0.8 / 0.1	0.6 / 0.3	0.4 / 0.4		0.4 / 0.1	0.1 / 0.7	e_4
e_5	0.7 / 0.6	0.6 / 0.6	0.6 / 0.6	0.8 / 0.6		0.6 / 0.6	e_5
e_6	0.5 / 0.8	0.8 / 0.5	0.5 / 0.7	0.7 / 0.7	0.9 / 0.7		e_6

P(i/j)
P(i/$\bar{j}$)

Matrix VI-1

This information is incoherent if one refers to the meaning described above. To obtain corrected results, we calculate the probabilities of the states, which at the same time indicate the most likely scenarios.

The final values. To facilitate the explanation, we shall first present and comment the corrected individual and conditional probabilities. We then discuss the probabilities of the states that enable us to modify the initial information.

P(i)		e_1	e_2	e_3	e_4	e_5	e_6
0.41	e_1		0.55 / 0.14	0.50 / 0.29	0.83 / 0.13	0.50 / 0.25	0.35 / 0.57
0.67	e_2	0.89 / 0.51		0.57 / 0.83	0.85 / 0.55	0.66 / 0.69	0.77 / 0.42
0.60	e_3	0.72 / 0.52	0.51 / 0.79		0.63 / 0.58	0.60 / 0.60	0.63 / 0.54
0.40	e_4	0.81 / 0.11	0.51 / 0.18	0.42 / 0.38		0.47 / 0.28	0.31 / 0.62
0.64	e_5	0.78 / 0.54	0.63 / 0.67	0.64 / 0.64	0.75 / 0.57		0.66 / 0.61
0.70	e_6	0.59 / 0.78	0.81 / 0.48	0.73 / 0.66	0.54 / 0.81	0.72 / 0.68	

Cell (row i, column j): $P(i/j)$ / $P(i/\bar{j})$

In the above example the initial individual probabilities are hardly modified : in general, without being fundamental, the changes are a little larger. On the other hand, some of the conditional probabilities have undergone non-negligible modifications and this can easily be explained : of course it is often easier to estimate a simple rather than a conditional probability.

Thus, large corrections have been made to :

- the probability of a tourist class traffic level of 50 million passengers in 1990, knowing that the average take-off delay will, by then, be over 20 minutes : P (e1/e3) moves from 0.7 down to 0.5 (this probability had clearly been overestimated by the group of experts).

- the probability of a decrease of over 3% per annum in ticket prices in constant terms, under the hypothesis that the French GNP growth rate would not exceed 4% per annum in volume : P(e4/e5) moves from 0.1 to 0.28

(this probability is much higher than that estimated by the experts).

The probabilities of the scenarios. For 6 events there are $2^6 = 64$ possible states.

	e_1	e_2	e_3	e_4	e_5	e_6
E_1	1	1	1	1	1	1
E_2	0	1	1	1	1	1
E_3	1	0	1	1	1	1
E_4	-	-	-	-	-	-
E_5	1	0	0	0	0	0
E_6	0	0	0	0	0	0

For each state E*k* there is an associated probability Π*k* with $\Sigma\Pi k = 1$ since it is certain that one of the states will occur.

The most likely scenarios, in decreasing order of probability are :

E_{12} (001011) Where $\Pi_{12} = 0.158$
E_{14} (010011) where $\Pi_{14} = 0.110$
E_{30} (010001) where $\Pi_{30} = 0.097$
E_1 (111111) where $\Pi_1 = 0.092$
E_{60} (001000) where $\Pi_{60} = 0.070$
E_{37} (110110) where $\Pi_{37} = 0.063$
E_{33} (111110) where $\Pi_{33} = 0.057$
E_{26} (011001) where $\Pi_{26} = 0.056$
E_{17} (111101) where $\Pi_{17} = 0.051$
E_9 (111011) where $\Pi_9 = 0.046$
E_5 (110111) where $\Pi_5 = 0.035$
E_{35} (101110) where $\Pi_{35} = 0.032$
E_{48} (000010) where $\Pi_{48} = 0.029$
E_{56} (000100) where $\Pi_{56} = 0.027$
E_{25} (111001) where $\Pi_{25} = 0.021$
E_6 (010111) where $\Pi_6 = 0.021$
E_{18} (011101) where $\Pi_{18} = 0.017$

E_{63} (100000) where $\Pi_{63} = 0.014$
E_{53} (110100) where $\Pi_{53} = 0.004$

Some 20 states in all have a non-zero probability ; they comprise the domain of possible scenarios. The other 44 states with a zero probability must be considered as not realistic ; however, this does not mean that it is not worth commenting on them : for example :

- E_{64} with $\Pi_{64} = 0$, the probability that none of the events take place is zero : this result shows that we have chosen sufficiently relevant events for at least one of them to occur during the period.
- E_{40} (000110) with $\Pi_{40} = 0$. If the price of a ticket, in constant terms, falls by more than 3% per annum and if, at the same time, French GNP grows at more than 4% per annum in volume, then one of the following four events must necessarily occur :
  e1 : more than 50 million tourist passengers by 1990 ;
  e2 : an average of more than 150 passengers per flight ;
  e3 : an average takeoff delay of more than 20 minutes ;
  e4 : regulatory constraints that reduce traffic by 20%.
- E_8 (000111) with $\Pi_8 = 0$. It is not possible that the last three events e4,e5,e6 occur, without at least one of the events e1,e2,e3, occurring too. If one considers that the last three events e4,e5,e6 are external variables and e1,e2,e3 internal variables of the Paris region air transport system, this shows that the system is necessarily sensitive to domestic developments.
- *the basic trend.* There is an 80% chance that the situation in 1990 will correspond to one of the first ten scenarios on the list given above. More precisely, E_{12}, E_{14}, E_{30}, E_1 constitute *the basic trend* : if E_{60} is added, there is a more than even chance that one of these scenarios will actually happen between now and 1990.
- E_{12} (001011) with $\Pi_{12} = 0.158$, *the saturation scenarios without strong traffic growth.* There are less than 50 million tourist passengers and less than 150 passengers per flight and the ticket price, in constant terms, is not reduced ; on the other hand, the average take-off delay is more than 20 minutes, French economic growth is strong and regulatory constraints involve a reduction of 20% in potential traffic movements.
- E_{14} (010011) with $\Pi_{14} = 0.110$. *Traffic growth is limited by the number of flights.* Only e2,e5,e6 occur. There is strong French economic growth (e5), urban development continues around the airports of the Paris region, environmental problems worsen and regulatory constraints(e6) are enforced, restricting traffic. In order to absorb the growth in traffic, without increasing movements, the airlines extend the use of wide-bodied aircraft and there are more than 150 passengers per flight (e2) etc.
- E_{30} (010001) with $\Pi_{30} = 0.097$. *Economic growth is weak and traffic growth is restricted by the number of flights.*
- E_1 (111111) with $\Pi_1 = 0.092$. This is *the conflict scenario*, in which everything happens. Problems do not inhibit the growth of the economy or air traffic, but this growth reinforces the difficulties, creating a tense situation.
- *The contrasting scenarios.* Other scenarios could be described as contrasted,

traffic, but this growth reinforces the difficulties, creating a tense situation.

- *The contrasting scenarios.* Other scenarios could be described as contrasted, and consist of less probable states. Examples would be :

  E_{33} (111110) with Π_{33} = 0.057.This is the scenario of *uncontrolled growth.* It is highly improbable that the first five events will occur, viz., that the growth of air traffic would be strong without regulatory constraints being enforced at some time or other.

  E_{48} (000010) with Π_{48} = 0.029. *This is the scenario for an air transport system independent of economic growth.* It is unlikely that sustained economic growth would have no consequences for air transport.

Strategic sensitivity analysis. It is necessary for policy makers to be aware of the possible states or scenarios for the evolution of the system under study in order to determine their strategy. In addition, the choice of actions available is conditioned by a previous examination of the direct and indirect effects that each decision could have upon the whole system. In particular, decisions with "boomerang" effects often tend to work against the person taking them and ought to be identified ; that is, actions whose primary effects are as desired, but whose secondary effects run counter to initial objectives.

On the other hand, it is often more efficient, for attaining a given objective to operate indirectly on the target variable, and the desired effect can thus be obtained in an indirect way : these are decisions with "ricochet" or "sling-shot" effects.

Sensitivity analysis consists of measuring the variation ΔPj of the probability Pj of the event j following a variation ΔPi of the probability Pi of the event i. Constructing an elasticity matrix allows the driver or dominant events and the dominated events to be deduced. Beginning with the final results, we then calculate the elasticity eij.

As a reminder, we recall the list of events :

- e1 More than 50 million tourist class passengers in 1990.
- e2 An average of more than 150 passengers per flight.
- e3 An average take-off delay of more than 20 minutes air-traffic control saturation.
- e4 Constant Franc ticket price falls by more than 3% per annum.
- e5 French GNP grows by more than 4% per annum.
- e6 Regulatory constraints involve a reduction of 20% in potential traffic movements.

The following table summarizes the results. The calculations have been performed with a step function ΔPi = 0.1 for all i.

	1	2	3	4	5	6	$\sum_j \lvert e_{ij} \rvert$
1		-0.12	-0.24	-0.47	-0.23	-0.54	1.60
2	0.40		-1.10	0.24	-0.71	-0.21	2.66
3	-0.28	-0.96		-0.64	-0.74	-0.64	3.26
4	0.37	-0.20	-0.39		-0.30	-0.61	1.87
5	-0.13	-0.71	-0.74	-0.26		-0.69	2.53
6	-1.32	-0.09	-0.73	-1.60	-0.76		4.50
$\sum_j \lvert e_{ij} \rvert$	2.50	2.08	3.20	3.21	2.74	2.69	

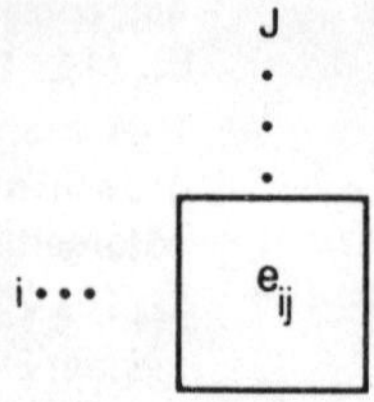

Reading the marginal row totals we can observe that the impact of some events is greater than others ; e.g., e6 and e3 with :

$$\sum_j \lvert e_{6j} \rvert = 4.50 \text{ and } \sum_j \lvert e_{3j} \rvert = 3.26$$

Regulation and take-off delays are *determinant events* for the development of air transport in the Paris region.

We can likewise note that :

$$\sum_j \lvert e_{4j} \rvert = 1.87 \text{ and } \sum_j \lvert e_{1j} \rvert = 1.60$$

Ticket prices, in constant terms, and the number of tourist class passengers have no great impact on the system of events.

Reading the column totals, we see that certain *events* are more *dominated* than others. Noteworthy, in this respect, are e3 and e4 with :

$$\sum_j \lvert e_{i3} \rvert = 3.20 \text{ and } \sum_j \lvert e_{i4} \rvert = 3.21$$

As far as e3 is concerned, this result is mainly explained by e23 = -1.10, which means that if the probability of e2 increases by 10%, then that of e3 reduces by 11%. *Utilization of wide-bodied aircraft considerably reduces the risk of saturation of controlled airspace in the Paris region.*

Regarding e4, the result is likewise explained by e64=1.60 which means that if the probability of e6 rises by 10%, that of e4 falls by 16%. *Airlines will have to offset the ticket price with the extra cost due to regulatory constraints.*

Event e3 is both a determinant and an influential variable. The saturation of controlled airspace is therefore the most sensitive event from the point of view of the development of the air transport.

As a special case of elasticity, we may note the value e61 = -1.32. The enforcing of regulatory constraints is thus a very unfavourable event for the development of tourist class traffic via chartered flights.

On the other hand for e51 = -0.13, air traffic generated by a demand for tourism is not very senstive to economic growth. We may note in any case that e24 = + 0.24. The general use of wide-bodied aircraft does not result in any measurable reduction of tariffs.

4.2. Nuclear energy scenarios to the year 2000

In this example we rely on the results of an investigation into global nuclear energy to the year 2000, carried out by SEMA and Economia in 1977 - cf. M. Godet and A. Maalouf (1977). The experts from 30 countries from whom some 90 replies were received, were asked to determine the probability of occurrence of around thirty hypotheses relating to the economic growth rates, the availability of oil, the competitiveness of nuclear power, the proliferation of nuclear weapons, the price of oil, the risk of accidental nuclear catastrophes, etc[14].

The main conclusions

- The experts considered that nuclear power would be the main source of energy in the year 2000 but they also considered that it was not yet a clear-cut success.
- If nuclear energy became predominant, opposition to nuclear power would be quelled : but if, for any reason, opposition remained significant, that would jeopardize the future of the nuclear industry. At the end of the century there would be a final struggle between opponents and proponents.
- If a serious accident were to occur, this battle would turn in favour of the opposition. It would be impossible to dispel opposition and the chances of pursuing the development of nuclear power would be considerably diminished as a result. Such an accident, however, was seen as unlikely, but a significant number of experts did not exclude the possibility.
- The proliferation of nuclear weapons, on the other hand, would only have a limited influence on the opposition and would not affect the future of the nuclear industry.
- Nuclear energy would undoubtedly be the most economic source of energy in the year 2000 but oil - much more so than new forms of energy - would remain a serious competitor.
- The price of oil would double between now and 1985 reaching $25 a barrel in constant prices.
- The development of nuclear power will be aided by sustained economic growth ; reciprocally it is necessary to guarantee growth.
- Measures for energy conservation will not be effective unless the economic crisis prevails.
- Western Europe will be among the leaders in the nuclear world by the year 2000, both technologically and commercially. Elsewhere, the nuclear industry will be at a stand-still especially in the Third World.

[14] See Appendix 1, 'Excerpts from the SMIC questionnaire'.

The unprocessed results of the study are given in the bar-charts in figure VI-5. The significiance of such bar-charts lies not only in clearly identifying consensus or several differing schools of thought, but also who said what.

At the end of the day, it matters little which responses are reliable and which give an accurate forecast : from the prospective point of view what counts is identifying rightly (or wrongly) *what image each expert questioned has of the future* (in principle representing a group of actors at least to some extent), *since it is in relation to this image of the future that each actor makes up his mind in the present.* In short, *prospective* investigation throws a powerful light on the actors' strategies, this analysis being essential for constructing scenarios. Let us not forget that the SMIC method will transform the unprocessed results in order to discern the most likely and the least likely scenarios.

What is the probability that by the year 2000, nuclear energy will be more economical than any other energy source ?

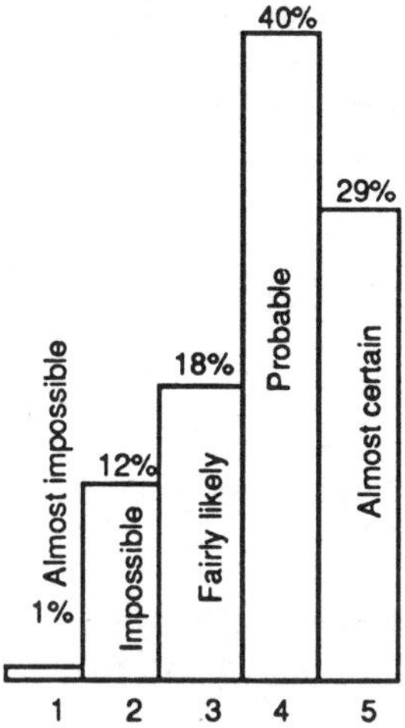

Nuclear energy should be more economical than new energy sources.

What is the probability that the price of oil will reach $25 per barrel in 1985 (in 1977 $) that is, twice the present price ?

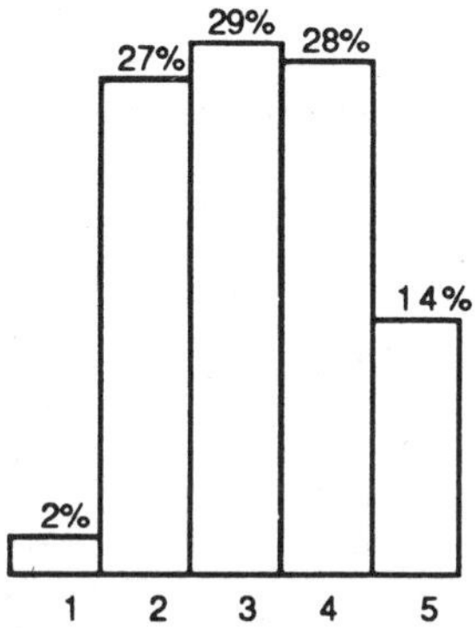

In 1977 the experts were divided on the question.

What is the probability that oil and other fossil fuels will remain widely available by the year 2000 ?

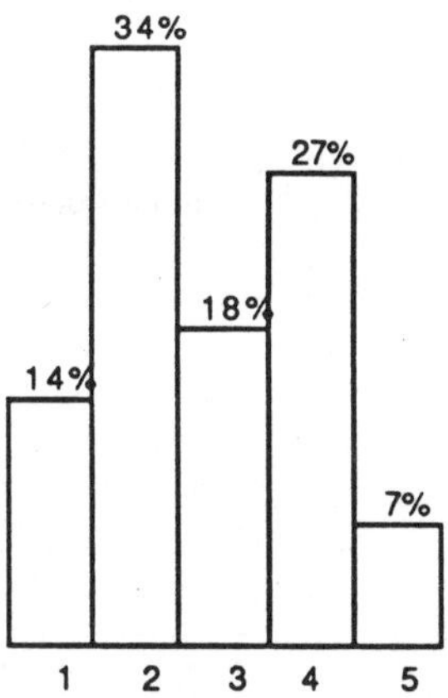

The experts are divided on the question of resources : some think that there will be a glut, others that supplies will run short.

What is the probability that 13 countries will possess nuclear weapons by the year 2000 (compared with six today) ?

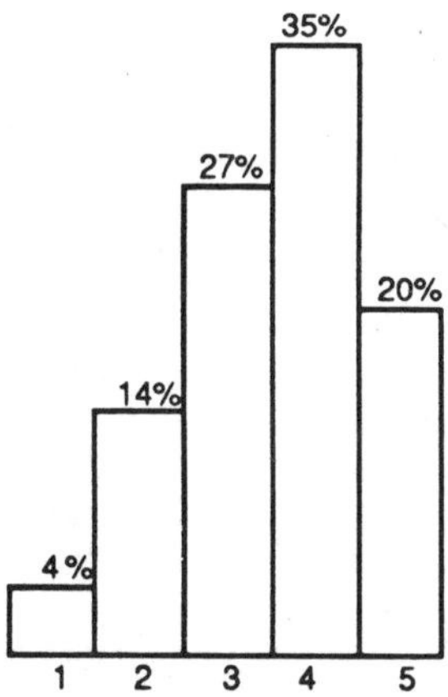

Accelerated proliferation of nuclear devices appears very likely.

Figure VI-5

The experts' answers to our questions about the nuclear industry, opposition to it, new forms of energy, oil, and growth have been reduced to only two responses : "yes" or "no" for each item. Therefore, 32 scenario outcomes were possible. The method has assigned a probability to each scenario, according to the experts' estimations. In Table VI-2 we summarized the 15 most likely scenarios, numbered in order of probability and representing nearly 80% of the total probabilities. The scenarios were ranged into four groups according to the relationship indicated between nuclear energy and growth.

The nuclear industry and economic growth : the possible scenarios and...

	Nuclear energy	*Opposition*	*New energy*	*Oil*	*Growth*	
1	Yes	No	Yes	No	Yes	The nuclear world :
2	Yes	No	No	Yes	Yes	unchallenged power with strong
3	Yes	No	No	No	Yes	economic growth
4	Yes	No	No	No	No	Nuclear energy at any cost :
7	Yes	Yes	No	No	No	well-developed nuclear, weak economic
9	Yes	Yes	No	Yes	No	growth
11	Yes	No	No	Yes	No	
13	Yes	No	Yes	Yes	No	
6	No	No	No	Yes	No	The ecological world :
8	No	No	Yes	Yes	No	weak nuclear energy, weak economic
10	No	Yes	No	No	No	growth
12	No	No	Yes	No	No	
14	No	Yes	Yes	No	No	
15	No	Yes	No	Yes	No	
5	No	Yes	Yes	Yes	Yes	Sober growth : economic growth without nuclear energy

... the impossible outcomes

I1	No	Yes	No	No	Yes
I2	Yes	Yes	Yes	Yes	No
I3	No	Yes	Yes	No	Yes
I4	Yes	Yes	Yes	Yes	Yes
I5	No	No	Yes	No	Yes

Table VI-2

The five scenarios which exhibited a zero or very small probability were every bit as revealing as the 15 most likely ones. They reveal both what the experts rejected as impossible and illuminate their opposites i.e., an image of the possible. Let us begin with the least likely :

- In scenario I1 without nuclear energy, oil or new forms of energy, economic growth would be sustained. In fact, it is difficult to see how the world economy could enter an expansionary phase without a source of energy ;

- Scenarios I2 and I4 are similar with one exception : growth is slow in one and rapid in the other. The meaning is clear : if there were oil, new energy sources and strong opposition to nuclear energy, it is impossible to see how nuclear energy would develop, whether growth were strong or not.
- Scenarios I3 and I5 are also similar with only one negligible difference : opposition. If the experts rejected them it was because they computed that if economic growth were to be rapid and there was a shortfall of oil,new energy sources would not be sufficient to supply the world economy and it would be inconceivable that nuclear energy would not develop, whatever the opposition.

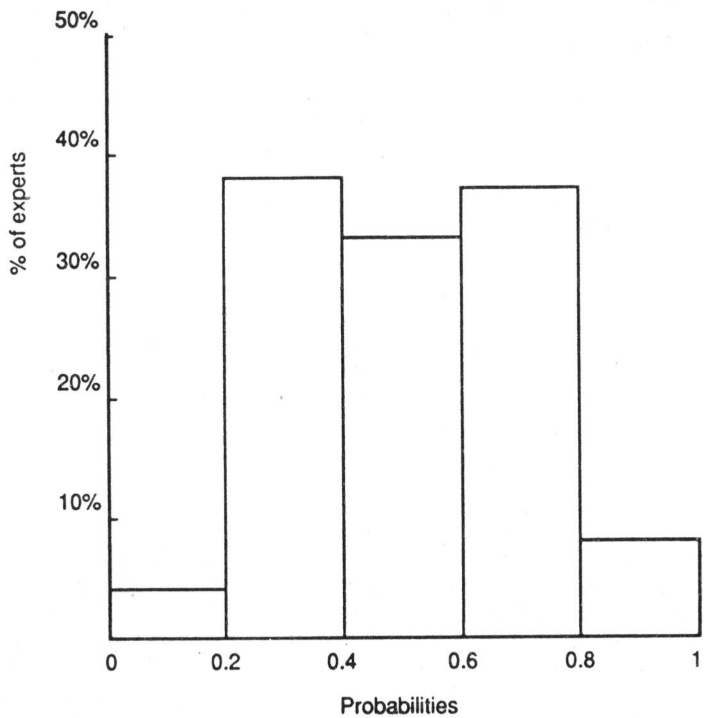

Figure VI-6
Solidarity of the oil-exporting countries

On the whole, it can be seen that the experts have a stereotyped view of the energy problem : if the world economies are expanding, oil and nuclear energy will be necessary. If the crisis is prolonged, one of the two will be sufficient and it is not impossible that it would be oil.

As another example, when we asked in 1975 "*Whether or not the solidarity of the OPEC countries would be intact in 1990*" the experts appeared divided on the question, which, naturally, implied two scenarios : on the one hand, maintenance of the solidarity of the OPEC countries and on the other the breaking-up of the cartel (see Figure VI-6).

In addition it was interesting that, on the whole, the experts close to the American administration and the oil companies thought that the break-up of OPEC was unlikely, while this idea was often considered likely by energy experts of OPEC member countries. This has obvious strategic implications. *It is important for an actor (in this case OPEC) to be aware that even if he feels he is weak or vulnerable, others may think him strong.*

There are numerous examples that spring to mind. It is not our intention to present them all here, but rather to reiterate that it is always prudent and stimulating for a future studies group within a firm, a government department or a research centre to juxtapose its own ideas about the future with those of other experts outside the group. The practice of conducting an external enquiry is an excellent intellectual safeguard and often serves to test critically the certainties and received ideas in which any group is likely to become enmeshed.

We now end this survey of prospective methods which allow the degree of uncertainty about the future environment of the enterprise to be reduced. Illuminating strategic action by the light of future studies is the route which leads from prospective to strategic management.

4.3. Excerpts from the SMIC questionnaire[15]

SEMA-Prospective and the international economic and political monthly journal ECONOMIA are organizing an enquiry among 300 international experts on the theme, 'An evaluation of future nuclear energy worldwide to the year 2000'. We would be grateful for your participation in this novel type of enquiry by replying to the attached questionnaire before 15 August.

The method used[16] has already been established in the political field and in the area of energy prospects, where the unforeseeable nature of certain developments during this decade have shown the need for new methods of prospective study. By taking twenty minutes or so to reply, you will allow us to evaluate the significance of the interaction between different aspects of the nuclear question.

The detailed results of the survey will be sent to participants. The main conclusions will be published in ECONOMIA, as well as a list of the persons questioned. In the event that you prefer that your name does not appear, please let us know.

Thanking you in advance for your contribution, we are, yours sincerely,

[15] Enquiry carried out in 1977.

[16] The SMIC method.

Michel Godet
SEMA-Prospective

Amin Maalouf
Economia

Name of participant ....
Adress ....
Street ....
Town ....
Country ....
Telephone ....

The detailed results of the survey will be sent to you at this address. The main conclusions will be published in ECONOMIA and you will be sent them on publication. If you prefer your name not to appear on the list of people who participated in the enquiry, please say on this page.

Please return before 15 August to : 'ECONOMIA', NUCLEAR ENQUIRY, 51 Avenue des Ternes, 75017 PARIS - France.

Evaluation of the future of nuclear energy worldwide up to the year 2000

This particular study was fairly unusual. While taking only a little time for the selected respondents, it enabled a wide range of the facets of the question to be examined in detail. In most surveys on major international problems, the questions asked are treated separately, ceteris paribus, and the subtleties of opinion are distorted in the general conclusions.

We consider it is important not only to evaluate the probability of this or that hypothesis, but also to work out the conditional probability resulting from the interaction between various hypotheses, since these are rarely independent. The survey is enhanced by a series of supplementary questions which allow the overall value of the opinions expressed to be assessed.

The latter are proffered by persons who know more and have greater influence on the course of events in their field, allowing new knowledge relating to the problem to emerge. To this extent, the results of the enquiry themselves are to be viewed as an event.

Main hypotheses

The five hypotheses for the development of the future of nuclear energy worldwide up to the year 2000 are a follows :

H1 - Predominance of nuclear energy (nuclear-generated energy will represent more than 20% of total energy production in the world by the year 2000 : the present figure is 2%).

H2 - Popular opposition reduced (the various forms of opposition to nuclear energy will reduce rapidly by the year 2000).

H3 - New, economic forms of energy (new forms of energy, mainly solar energy, will be competitive in the year 2000).

H4 - Oil available (reserves of oil and other fossil fuels will continue to satisfy world demand in the year 2000).

H5 - Sustained economic growth (the average annual growth rate of GNP for the developed countries will be higher than 4% during the period 1978-2000).

The enquiry method

The five main hypotheses above are presented for assessment, in three phases :

(1) First, a simple probability : all other things being equal, what probability would you assign to the accuracy hypothesis ;

(2) Second, the conditional probability : we correct the simple probability by considering in turn that each hypothesis is -then is not- accurate, and then by evaluating the impact of this event on the four other hypotheses ;

(3) Finally, we evaluate the probability of ten subsidiary questions which will serve to clarify certain important aspects : simple probability first, followed by conditional probability as related to one or other of the main hypotheses[17].

Meaning of the probability scale

(1) Event nigh-impossible
(2) Event improbable
(3) Event of average probability
(4) Event likely
(5) Event quasi-certain
(6) The two events under consideration are independent.

Examples of answers

- Simple probabilities

1	2	3	4	5
			X	

- Nuclear predominance

Meaning : all other things being equal, I estimate that it is likely that energy of nuclear origin will be predominant, worldwide, in the year 2000.

- Conditional probabilities (and associated subsidiary questions).
- What is the probability in your opinion that each of the following four hypotheses will be implemented, given that hypothesis H2 (reduced popular opposition) *is not verified.*

[17] If the number of hypotheses *(h)* is large, the number of scenarios *(2(h))* would make the reading of trends difficult. By reducing the number of main hypotheses to 5 we obtain 2 (5) = 32 scenarios and the subsidiary questions serve to refine the results by introducing further nuances.

	Improbable ← 1	2	3	4	5 → Probable	6
H1 - Nuclear predominance	X					
H3 - New economic forms of energy					X	
H4 - Oil available					X	
H5 - Sustained economic growth						X

Meaning : if popular opposition does not weaken, it is almost impossible that nuclear energy will be dominant in the year 2000 ; it is almost certain that the development of new energy techniques will be more rapid and that new oil reserves will be discovered. There is no connection between opposition and economic growth.

Simple probabilities

	Improbable ← 1	2	3	4	5 → Probable	6
H1- Predominance of nuclear energy						

	Improbable ← 1	2	3	4	5 → Probable	6
H2 - Reduced popular opposition						

	Improbable ← 1	2	3	4	5 → Probable	6
H3 - New economic energy forms						

Improbable ←					*Probable* →
1	2	3	4	5	6

H4 - Oil available

Improbable ←					*Probable* →
1	2	3	4	5	6

H5 - Sustained economic growth

Conditional probabilities as a function of H1

What is the probability in your view, that each of the following hypotheses will turn out to be true, assuming that H1 (predominance of nuclear power) *is true ?*

	Improbable ← 1	2	3	4	5	*Probable* → 6
H2 - Reduced popular opposition						
H3 - New economic energy forms						
H4 - Oil available						
H5 - Sustained economic growth						

What is the probability, in your view, that each of the follwing hypotheses will turn out to be true, assuming that H1 (predominance of nuclear power) *is not true ?*

Improbable ← → *Probable*

	1	2	3	4	5	6
H2 - Reduced popular opposition						
H3 - New economic energy forms						
H4 - Oil available						
H5 - Sustained economic growth						

and so on for 2, H3, H4 and H5.

Subsidiary questions (examples)

What is the probability that event Q1 will occur : 'A non-similar nuclear catastrophe causing more than 100 deaths between now and the year 2000' ?

← *Improbable* 1	2	3	4	5 *Probable* →

What is the probability that event Q1 will occur, assuming that hypothesis H1 (predominance of nuclear power) *is true ?*

← *Improbable* 1	2	3	4	5 *Probable* →

What is the probability that hypothesis H2 (reduced popular opposition) will be true, assuming that event Q1 occurs ?

Improbable 1	2	3	4	5 *Probable*

What is the probability that event Q6 will occur : 'The price of oil will exceed $25 per barrel (double the present price) by 1985, in constant 1977 dollars' ?

Improbable 1	2	3	4	5 *Probable*

What is the probability that event Q7 will occur : 'Nuclear energy will be the most economic form of energy in the year 2000' ?

Improbable	1	2	3	4	5	*Probable*
	☐	☐	☐	☐	☐	

What is the probability that event Q7 will occur, assuming that hypothesis H4 (oil available) *is true ?*

Improbable	1	2	3	4	5	*Probable*	6
	☐	☐	☐	☐	☐		☐

What is the probability that event Q8 will occur : 'Accelerated nuclear proliferation : more than 12 countries will possess nuclear arms by the year 2000 as compared with present' ?

Improbable	1	2	3	4	5	*Probable*
	☐	☐	☐	☐	☐	

What is the probability that event Q10 will occur : 'Fast breeder reactors will represent more than half of all nuclear power stations built between now and the year 2000' ?

Improbable	1	2	3	4	5	*Probable*
	☐	☐	☐	☐	☐	

CHAPTER VII

IDENTIFYING AND EVALUATING STRATEGIC OPTIONS

1. Decision process : identify, evaluate, choose and implement

Decision-making is a classical question of strategy, over which many writers have laboured. I. Ansoff (1965) distinguished three types of decisions (see table VII-1) :

- *Strategic decisions*, concerning the external affairs of the company ;
- *Administrative decisions*, relating to manpower management, to the organization of labour, circulation of information and to organizational structures etc ;
- *Operational decisions*, which aim to improve the efficiency of transformation of internal resources into added value (production programmes, rationalization programmes, price policy, sales promotion etc).

Although interesting, this typology is now somewhat out of date as the setting-up and possible success of the strategy have become increasingly dependent on decisions of an administrative or operational nature. Four stages are ordinarily distinguished in the decision process :

- Perception of the necessity of making choices ;
- Formulation of possible decisions ;
- Evaluation of options ;
- Decision and implementation.

The necessity for choice is not always perceived : how many companies unreasonably retain at least some declining activities with a glorious past whose losses they consider only temporary ? How many firms launch out in a particular direction without serious consideration of all the diversification possibilities that are available ?

Table VII-1
Principal decision categories

	Strategic	*Administrative*	*Operational*
Problem	Choice of the range of products and markets which have the chance of giving the company an optimum return on investments	Structure of corporate resources to achieve optimal success	Trading in conditions of optimum return on capital
Nature of problem	Judicious distribution of resources between products and markets	Organization, acquisition and development of resources	Budget allocations to departments Planning the application and conversion of resources Management and control of operations
Key decisions	Definition of strategic objectives Measures of diversification Measures of expansion Administrative stra-tegy Financial strategy Choice of growth media and their distribution through time	Organization : structure of authority, respon-sibilities and communications Structure for the conversion of resources : distribution of work and assignments Acquisition and development of resources : financial equipment, personnel, raw materials	Operational objectives Fixing prices and production levels Production planning and stock management Marketing policy R & D policy Controls
Nature of decisions	Centralized Made in part ignorance Non-repetitive Non-regenerative	Conflict between strategy and commercial activity Conflict between individual and collective goals Close link between economic variables and social factors Decisions required by strategic issues and/or operational problems	Decentralized Carrying risk and uncertainty Repetitive Very numerous Limited ability to optimize due to complexity of issues Regenerative

Source : I. ANSOFF (1965)

Areas	Possible actions
1. Products	**Change the product range :** • discontinue unprofitable lines - add-on item(s) to the range offered • replace some outdated products • change the quality of certain products (improve or reduce the quality) • change the packaging of some products • change existing product prices (higher or lower)
2. Markets	**Remain in the same market :** • seek a greater market share, either by selling more to existing customers or looking for new customers • select existing customers, seeking to eliminate the least profitable • diversify customers for greater sales' security • extend the market (other areas in the home market, exports, possible new users in existing geographical areas etc)
3. After sales service	**Improve the service offered, or reduce its cost, or make it more selective (types of customers etc)**
4. Distribution channels	**Improve the utilization of existing channels :** • to make them more effective (more customers affected) • to reduce the cost • look for new channels
5. Sites	**Look for better sites :** • for manufacturing (present or extensions) • for warehousing
6. Production costs	**Search for new production methods :** • by internal research • by sub-contracting • seek supply economies • stock levels • purchases
7. Organization	**Seek a more dynamic organiztion :** • for the whole of production and sales for product lines • slim down functional or support departments • sub-contract some activities
8. Personnel	**Change the profile and the recruiting methods for any new managers needed** • improve training • improve career policy (assignments, promotion etc)
9. Finance	**Expand financing capability :** • through leasing • reduction of assets (buildings, stocks etc) • look for less expensive sources of finance • improve the ratios : $\frac{\text{shareholders' funds}}{\text{permanent capital}}$ $\frac{\text{fixed assets}}{\text{permanent capital}}$
10. Management	**Introduce a management information system (budget forecasting)** **Make existing controls more effective**

Becoming aware of a *strategic gap* between corporate objectives and its growth trend should lead a company to explore first of all the expansionary possibilities identified by the product-market matrix - improvement of market shares in traditional markets, sales of new products in old markets, and old products in new markets. It is only when expansion is not sufficient to fill the strategic gap that one has to resort to total diversification (new markets for new products), since, as Ansoff emphasizes, this is always riskier.

In certain cases one also has to revise growth objectives, and take financial and human characteristics into account, aligning them with corporate culture and the existence of possible synergies. Finally, growth is not an end in itself, and must first of all be effective. For many companies, a return to profitability is achieved via intelligent surgery of its activities and, as a result, a reduction in turnover, while not forgetting to look for improved internal efficiency for a given level of production.

Some authors such as de J. de Guerny and J. C. Guirriec (1979) have developed useful checklists for strategic idea-seeking (TableVII-3).

Once the possible decisions have been formulated, they have to be evaluated. This phase is often side-stepped because of a desire to get on with the job. It is a rough evaluation of possible actions according to certain criteria which have been weighted in some way. We have already made reference to the fact that it is better to use multicriteria choice methods for an uncertain future, such as Electre, for such an evaluation and selection. These methods allow us to consider the most likely scenarios for the strategic environment and the enterprise diagnosis, in order to identify which actions should be undertaken, which rejected, and which are in some way risky.

2. Relevance trees : from objectives to action

This method, originally used mainly in the technological and military fields, aims to rationalize the selection of elementary actions or operations (the trunk of the tree) with a view to achieving overall objectives (the top of the tree).

2.1. The qualitative hierarchy : aims, objectives, means and action

Although the process is similar to a flow-chart, we shall use the term "relevance tree". The aim of the method is to relate the different hierarchy levels of a problem, moving from the general level (the top) down to the more detailed levels (the lower levels). This process, characteristic of trees, excludes reaction from lower to higher levels.

A distinction is made between the general aims (higher levels, including policy decisions, missions and objectives) and the means (lower levels, including resources, sub-systems and sub-sets of actions and elementary actions). The various levels therefore correspond either to the increasingly detailed objectives of the decision system or to the means implemented (the tree is usually organized into 5 to 7 levels).

RELEVANCE TREE

GENERAL OBJECTIVE

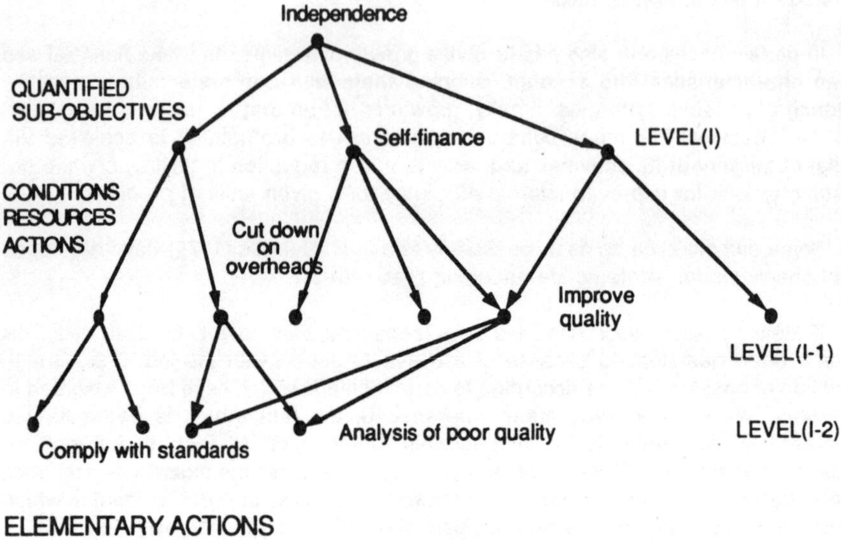

When, for instance, the overall corporate aim is to strengthen the company's independence, level (I) will contain "increase self-finance" as a sub-objective. To achieve this sub-objective, a certain number of conditions (I-1) will be needed, among them lowering overheads, or improving quality. To satisfy the latter condition, one would need to comply with standards or carry out an analysis of decline in quality, among other things.

The apparently simple process of constructing the tree must comply with the following conditions :

- there are no links between nodes at any given level, i.e. elements at the same level are independent ;
- there is no direct link between nodes on non-adjacent levels ;
- when filling in the contents of the levels at the top, one must balance them out at the base in order to stabilize the construction : what one loses in terms of generality one gains in variety (and vice versa).

The definitive choice of objectives and actions can only be made after prior analysis of the system under consideration, using two complementary approaches :

- *the ascendant approach* starts with the actions considered relevant and then studies the objectives to which these actions lead ;

- *the descendent approach* starts with the list of final explicit objectives and seeks out and analyses the appropriate resources needed to attain such objectives, and variables liable to modify them.

Each item (action or objective) must be clearly specified so as to maintain a precise and detailed sense of meaning (so that we know at all times what we are talking about).

In practice : the use of a writing board and self-adhesive notelets will enable a dynamic and evolving construction of the relevance tree.

2.2. Flow chart notation and action evaluation

The objective of this phase is to measure the contribution of each action to the objectives of the system ; in order to do so, a relevance grade is assigned to each line of the chart. The grade assigned to an action at level (l-1) specifies its contribution to the achievement of actions at the level immediately above (l).

At this stage of the study, different methodologies (Pattern, CPE (1)) can be used to rank the decision paths according to the significance of their contribution to the achievement of the initial objective (l-1), viz. the aggregation stage. What we propose here is a simple methodology whereby the action at level (l) constitutes an evaluation criterion for actions at level (l-1).

Matrices (multi-criteria grids) are set up for each level. The rows contain the m items (actions) at level (l-2) and the columns the n criteria at level (l-1) ; for each criterion we evaluate the contribution of each action towards satisfying that criterion.

Level l-1 Level l-2	Criterion 1	Criterion 2	Criterion n
Action 1			
Action 2			
Action m			

A grid matrix can be established for each pair of levels: the actions at level (l-2) can be graded in terms of the actions (criteria) at level (l-1). Actions at level (l-1) are considered as the criteria for those at level (l-2) and they in turn are considered as the actions for criteria at level (l).

The matrix calculation explained in the box overleaf enables us to ascertain the quantitative contribution to realization of the initial objectives of the actions at the lowest level : it is also possible to identify the most relevant paths which allow optimum attainment of the objectives.

PATTERN : a grading and aggregation method

Each level of the tree is characterized by a certain number of specific criteria which constitute performance measurements for actions at the lower levels. In this method, the nodes of the system at level (l) (actions) and the criteria used to assess level (l-1) are not equivalent.

The grades are assigned on a spectrum (from 0 to 1) ; the assessment of each criterion and the weightings are standardized. The relevance of each node also lies between 0 and 1, with the total relevance factors equal to 1, for a given level.

The fact that the different levels are graded independently enables us to identify the most relevant paths which will ensure attainment of the general objective under optimal conditions. The relevance of a path, which follows the links to the tree, is equal to the product of the relevance values of the nodes passed on the way.

EVALUATION OF OVERALL RELEVANCE OF THE LOWER LEVELS IN RELATION TO THE GENERAL GOAL

Level (l)	☞	p sub-objectives
Level (l-1)	☞	n means
Level (l-2)	☞	m elementary actions

p Evaluation of the m elementary actions at level (l-2) in terms of the n criteria (means) at level (l-1) : matrix A (m ; n).

p Evaluation of the n means at level (l-1) in terms of the p criteria (sub-objectives) at level (l) : matrix B (n ; p).

p Evaluation of the p sub-objectives of level (l) in terms of their contribution to the general objective of level (l+1) : vector column C (p ; 1)

Evaluation of the overall relevance of the elementary actions at level (l-2) in terms of the general objective of level (l+1) is obtained by multiplying the matrices :

$$\underset{(m,\ n)}{A} \times \underset{(n,\ p)}{B} \times \underset{(p,\ 1)}{C} = \underset{(m,\ 1)}{P}$$

Within each Evaluation t matrix (A, B, C) the items in rows are graded in terms of the n items in columns (criteria). In order to facilitate the calculations, the criteria are weighted on standardized scale (total weighting points amounting to 1).

2.3. Usefulness and limitations

A partial qualitative utilization, i. e., restricted to construction of the tree, is relatively easy and can prove very useful and productive at certain stages of the prospective thinking process or of drawing up action strategies by a group of actors.

This method is an excellent thinking aid and allows one to avoid redundancy (there must be no imbalance in the tree) ; to discover new ideas by throwing light on obscure areas : objectives which have no connection with resources and vice versa ; to clarify choices made ; to improve coherence ; and finally to structure objectives and the resources to achieve them.

The relevance tree method when applied fully (grading of the flow-chart and aggregation) can prove difficult and awkward to implement : representation of the tree form is somewhat inflexible, there being little room for taking uncertainty into account...

It is worth considering this method in many cases, because of the rigour it imposes, and because of the simple and appropriable nature of its qualitative element.

Before stating how multicriteria choice of strategic action can be made, it is appropriate to review other possible methods which could be called on, notably those commonly used for investment options in an uncertain future (J. C. Holl, J. P. Plas and P. Riou, 1973).

3. Classical methods for options evaluating

There is a broad gamut of classical methods. We discuss below the weighting method and methods arising out of the theory of investment choice based on the analysis of forecast discounted cashflow : the method of average cashflow, and 'minimax' methods.

Weighting

Suppose there are five new products, judged on five criteria (launch cost, supply risk, correspondence with image, sales, profits etc) in order to decide which products are to be launched as a priority.

The weighting method gives the following classification :

6, 5, 4, 1, 2, 3 : therefore 6 and 5 will be launched.

There are drawbacks to relying on a classification, if, for any reason, there is a supply interruption (criterion 2) halting production. Products 5 and 6 are badly placed with regard to this criterion, while for product 1 there is no risk of supply interruption. A policy seeking to spread risk factors (absolutely essential in a period of uncertainty) ought to lead to the launching of products 1 and 6.

Weighted sums	Points of view / Products	3	2	3	1	1
		1	2	3	4	5
111	1	10	20	5	10	16
51	2	0	5	5	16	10
43	3	0	10	0	16	7
120	4	20	5	10	10	10
148	5	20	10	15	10	13
166	6	20	10	20	13	13

Methods of investment choice for an uncertain future

To simplify the presentation we make the assumption that the future is totally uncertain : the company is not in a position to assign probabilities to the different possible outcomes. We draw widely on the example given by J. C. Holl, J. P. Plas and P. Riou (1973) - a company is seeking to determine the best policy to apply to ensure the success of its development strategy in an overseas country where the course of events is uncertain. We assume that three policies, denoted *P1* to *P3*, are open :

- *P1* : to export finished products and conclude an agreement with a local distribution chain ;
- *P2* : to export finished goods and create the company's own distribution chain ;
- *P3* : to export parts, build factories for local assembly and set up a distribution chain.

The discounted cashflows which each strategy would generate will depend on the policy pursued by the host country with regard to domestic investment. We assume that the company considers the future policy to be followed by the country being studied as completely unknown, but that five attitudes, denoted *E1* to *E5*, are possible :

- *E1 :* low customs duty and total freedom of foreign investment ;
- *E2 :* low duties on parts but high duties on assembled products, together with freedom for foreign investment ;
- *E3 :* very high duties on all imports, but freedom of investment ;
- *E4 :* nationalization of foreign investments, but freedom for imports ;
- *E5 :* nationalization of foreign investments and limitations on imports for every policy option.

Presented with each outcome the firm estimates the forecast discounted cashflow below :

outcomes

Policies	E_2	E_2	E_3	E_4	E_5	C
P_1	+10	+ 3	+ 3	+ 3	+ 2	4.2
P_2	+15	+ 6	+ 6	-10	-12	1.0
P_3	+13	+13	+ 5	-12	-13	1.2

A first idea, which requires some thought before adopting a policy in the light of the five outcomes, is to compare the average discounted cashflow corresponding (C) to each policy. This criterion leads us to choose policy P1.

If we knew the probabilities of the scenarios' outcomes we would only need to calculate an average, weighted by the subjective probability of each outcome, to determine the optimal policy from the point of view of weighted average discounted cashflow.

A second idea would be to play safe and choose a policy which would maximize the normal foreseeable gain - hence the term 'minimax' given to this criterion. From this point of view, *P1* is again the best policy. However, this decision rests on a fragile base. If, for example, the policy *P2,* faced with the outcome *E1,* corresponded to a cashflow of 15000 instead of 15, then the minimax criterion which leads to adopting policy *P1* would be very questionable, since the maximum loss from policy *P2* (-12) is a drop in the ocean compared with the gain forecast, if outcome *E1* occurs. One can entertain the idea of risking a little to gain a lot.

A third, more subtle, idea consists of considering the misgivings the company would experience as a result of not having taken the right decision. 'Let us suppose, for example, that the company adopts policy P1. If the attitude of the country concerned turns out to be *E1,* the best policy would have been policy *P2,* since this would have produced the largest discounted cashflow. In relation to this policy, policy *P1* leads to a loss of 5 in terms of extra gain. The "misgivings" corresponding to policy *P1* and attitude E1 are valued at 5. We can construct a table of misgivings for each policy and each stance of the foreign country' :

	E_1	E_2	E_3	E_4	E_5
P_1	5	10	3	0	0
P_2	0	7	0	13	14
P_3	2	0	1	15	15

Making a choice is tantamount to giving up other options : once the decision is made, one must accept the consequences of the chosen course, thus 'regretting' not taking the others. From this point of view, it is reasonable to fix, as a criterion for the choice of policies, the minimum value for the maximum misgivings (the Savage criterion). This criterion also leads to policy choice *P1*.

If all the decision criteria lead to the choice of a given policy, that in itself is an additional argument in favour of that policy. However this case is rare ; in most cases one must decide by necessarily favouring certain criteria.

At the end of the day, the 'minimax' criterion is also subject to criticism. The writers envisage a fourth policy for the firm (P4), characterized by the following distribution of discounted cashflows :

	E_1	E_2	E_3	E_4	E_5
P_1	+ 4	+ 20	+ 10	- 10	- 12

The introduction of this new policy significantly modifies the 'misgivings' table :

	E_1	E_2	E_3	E_4	E_5
P_1	5	17	7	0	0
P_2	0	14	4	13	14
P_3	2	7	5	15	15
P_4	11	0	0	13	14

The minimax misgivings criterion leads the policies to be preferred in the order *P4*, *P2*, *P3*, *P1*: 'otherwise expressed, the order of classification of policies *P1*, *P2*, *P3* according to the Savage criterion depends on whether policy *P4* is taken into account or not. This conclusion is obviously embarrassing'.

Here we run up against the external problem of the sensitivity of the results to a change in the initial data. Testing the initial data, which are usually both unreliable and not comprehensive in coverage, leads to the rejection of the results derived from the use of a single method. An appeal to pluralism and employment of a complementarity of approaches before deciding on a particular strategic direction is recommended. Faced with future uncertainty, multicriteria methods of choice appear the most appropriate since they lend themselves to such sensitivity analyses because of the way that they are constructed.

4. Multicriteria methods

Decision support provides 'models' comprising a set of variables and relationships, and of a unit which is a function of its values, called the economic function, or the criterion. The latter represents the preferences of the decision-maker. In these models, a so-called optimal solution is sought, ie a solution that gives the highest possible value to the function.

For some problems these methods are still perfectly satisfactory. However, for many other problems they do not appear adequate. They neglect the non-quantitative aspects : require the evaluation of all quantitative aspects in a common unit of measurement : put emphasis more on seeking a theoretical optimum than on correctly modelling preferences. They then take on an artificial appearance with false accuracy.

Devising a single criterion raises serious problems in most cases. Indeed, every decision-maker must take into account the multiple consequences of the decisions he is thinking of making. And these cannot necessarily be analysed in a natural and obvious way in terms of a common unit : a civil engineering project for a motorway for example, will have consequences for finance, the environment, urbanization, traffic, etc.

In this way, the problem of press support for an advertising campaign amply illustrates the risks of using only a single criterion. We have worked over a long period in this area, using only numerical data which we tried to optimize. The unit decided upon was the cost per thousand effective readers. In terms of budget, one first took out maximum coverage in the periodical with the lowest cost per thousand readers, then the second, then the third and so on until the budget was exhausted.

Many other aspects have to be taken into account, eg the affinity of the periodical for the message : the impact of an advertisement for perfume in a do-it-yourself magazine, even one for women, would be poor since the reader is not sensitive to this type of advertisement ; the gap between his or her current interest and the message of the advertisement is too wide. Technical aspects are involved, e.g. colour, coupon offers, cutting out ads (it is known that the readers of some magazines do not like to cut them up). Reader loyalty can be seen as an essential criterion for an advertisement that is designed for a series.

Analysis of the results of the decision must therefore be carried in a way which seeks to avoid translating everything into a single formula, or considering only what can be reduced to figures.

4.1. Aid to decision-making

A decision can generally be framed in one of the three following problem areas :

- in favour of a single action ;
- in favour of all 'good' actions, rejecting all 'bad' actions (a bank which authorizes overdrafts to firms can duly authorize them to all customers who have a

clean bill of health) ;

• decide on a list of priorities that are sufficiently satisfactory (for a programme of long and costly research on operations).

Whatever the problem area in which the decision lies, multicriteria analysis will be of assistance to the decision maker :

• in taking different points of view into account (or criteria) ;

• in defining the trade-offs between these criteria explicitly in terms of the objectives ;

• in formalizing this global view into a model, without a sophisticated mathematical process which would risk producing an illusory optimum founded on schemas which do not correspond adequately to reality. In this way we can come up with practical advice which relates to the responsibilities of the person or the company whose preferences we wish to reveal.

The analysis of 'situations' calling for choices (decisions) leads us to define the characteristics of the consequences of these choices. Thus the time element in the problem of routing motorways will be taken into account when comparing the different possibilities through the users' time-saving dimension as they transit from town A to town B. Time-saving must be specified : is it at peak times or off-peak times ? The time-saving dimension will be introduced by means of an indicator which could be the time saved in going between town A and town B.

In the same way the element of 'noise' generated by the motorway could be brought in by means of an indicator, 'number of people suffering from a certain level of noise' (sleeping difficulty, difficulty in hearing television, in conversation etc).

The analysis continues by identifying the significant indicators : from this emerges a certain number of criteria through which various aspects are taken into account, sometimes simply ranked and not measured.

For an anti-pollution campaign project, for example, costs are considered, using money indicators, ie the cost to the local authorities and to the users.

We likewise introduce savings in human lives as a result of the expected reduction in severe illnesses. Again, the sulphur dioxide content of the atmosphere can be used as an indicator to take into account less serious illnesses. Finally we look at acceptance by public opinion (excellent, moderate, no view, hostile). The analysis being complete, one must then evaluate each project along each dimension.

Multicriteria procedures allow for a comparative assessment on different courses of action, and the result lies in identifying the best action or set of actions, or a ranking depending on the nature of the problem studied.

It thus appears both desirable and possible to improve the quality of major decisions which are taken every day : defining regional development policy making a rapid transport connection or siting a new factory, launching a new product, selecting an advertising campaign, adopting a research project, choosing a personnel policy etc. All such decisions can be prepared by using multicriteria methods, implementation of which must be incorporated in a fairly systematic set of procedures.

Experience in the accepted methodology and practice of decision support allows us to point to a set of solutions in five major phases which stem from implementation of such procedures, viz :

- phase 1 : taking stock of all possible actions ;
- phase 2 : analysing the consequences of actions undertaken ;
- phase 3 : specifying the criteria and assessment, according to criteria ;
- phase 4 : definition of policies ;
- phase 5 : ranking the actions and sensitivity analysis.

4.2. Listing possible actions

Every decision process necessarily begins with a survey and definition of the opportunities or the actions open to the decision maker. There is more than one way of going about implementing procedures that will provide an inventory of the possible actions.

Intervening in the selection of research projects is a typical method. The consultant (in liaison with the Director of Research) draws up a questionnaire, i.e. a presentation of ideas for research, and then organizes meetings in research centres to explain the objectives of the Research Division and circulate the questionnaires. Afterwards, the ideas or plans for research accumulated are structured to constitute the set of all possible projects.

This example shows that the collection process must necessarily be organized around the systematic search for ideas, and that actions must, where possible, be collected by questionnaires as well as by personal interaction (brainstorming sessions).

4.3. Analysis of the consequences of actions

The results of various actions usually appear unclear, intermingled and badly differentiated. If we exclude difficulties associated with factors of multiplicity, the analysis will encounter further obstacles, for four main reasons :

- the consequences to be understood sometimes require long and costly investigation ;
- the consequences are often marked by uncertainties that can, to some extent, be probabilized ;
- the consequences are closely related to the actions of other partners ;
- the consequences are not directly measurable and require qualitative estimates.

The way in which the consequences of various actions are to be understood depends on the nature and size of these difficulties.

Thus, in the choice of a motorway route, SEMA carried out a series of open, undirected conversations within a broad brief, in which the interviewees were invited to imagine the changes that would come about - mainly as regards traffic patterns and the environment - and the repercussions on their way of life. The interviewees then enumerated various aspects of the consequences which should be taken into account to make comparisons between the various motorway routes - investment costs, time savings, compulsory purchases, noise, aesthetic considerations etc.

4.4. Defining criteria and evaluating actions in terms of these criteria

The originality of multicriteria methods lies above all in the fact that, to build a criterion, we convert every statistical indicator or qualitative magnitude into a simple system of notation, consisting of a scale with a limited number of levels. The number of levels varies according to the importance or the uncertainty appertaining to the results. However, it is most important to ensure that the assignment of values should not be open to discussion : it is unnecessary to use too fine a scale of values, but it is important to attain a precise definition of the method of assessment.

To define a commercial strategy, the criterion 'advertising expenditure' will be expressed, for example, on a scale with four levels. At the same time, when it comes to assessing each product, in terms of its quality as perceived by the consumer, the associated criteria are expressed only in terms of qualitative measures of evaluation. These should, however, be defined accurately : the product is identified not only by the norms of competitive standards but also with respect to the customers' reactions to differences in quality.

Once the criteria have been defined, each action is evaluated as a function of each criterion. This phase of the procedure can sometimes involve returning to the definition and notional limits of the criteria.

Assessment of actions is attained either by addressing a questionnaire to qualified individuals - researchers, users, etc - and collecting the responses, or by organizing meetings of experts, during which actions and criteria are compared and the actions evaluated, the rule being to obtain a consensus.

4.5. Definition of policies and ranking actions

In order to advise on a given action or set of actions, one must necessarily define explicitly the main objectives of the decision-maker ; in other words, he must specify the weight that he assigns to the different criteria.

In choosing the technical activities for the promotion of certain computer hardware, the decision-maker involved hesitated between a policy of immediate market development or a policy of a more long-term development : the first led to emphasis on the weights for criteria, favouring the short-term items such as rapidity of implementation, commercial costs, response time in the market place, and assigning little, if any, weight to the criterion 'long-term profitability', while the second approach led to an entirely different set of weights.

As soon as the evaluations of each action by the various criteria are available (be they quantitative or qualitative) and once the different criteria have been weighted, the problem then becomes one of comparing the different actions, using appropriate methods, that reflect the preference of the decision-makers.

Three methods (the method of comparative reverse ranking, the Electre II and Multipol method) which allow the ranking of comparisons are described below.

It is then necessary to verify the stability of the rankings, by checking whether slight changes in evaluation of actions or the weighting of criteria basically affect the result : this is known as sensitivity analysis.

4.6. Multicriteria decision in strategic management

A strategy is built up from a set of actions such that :

- their consequences in the short, medium and long term do not run counter to the objectives, but, on the contrary, lead towards their attainment ;
- they are internally consistent ;
- at all times the set of actions to be undertaken or continued with is relevant to developments in the environment.

This latter point is fundamental. Although it is relatively simple to define a strategy which seems well adapted to the present situation, one should be prepared to bend it to take account of internal and external changes in its context. It could turn out that these changes are slight and that the change of direction can be achieved by sail-trimming (contingency actions). However, it could also be that these changes force us to question decisions already taken and to make a fresh start with a new set of actions (structural actions) in order to adapt effectively. These actions could be directed towards :

- working, if possible, to implement those scenarios most favourable to corporate objectives ;
- limiting the damaging consequences of developments as envisaged in the pessimistic scenario ;
- facilitating the company's future involvement in an environment undergoing constant change.

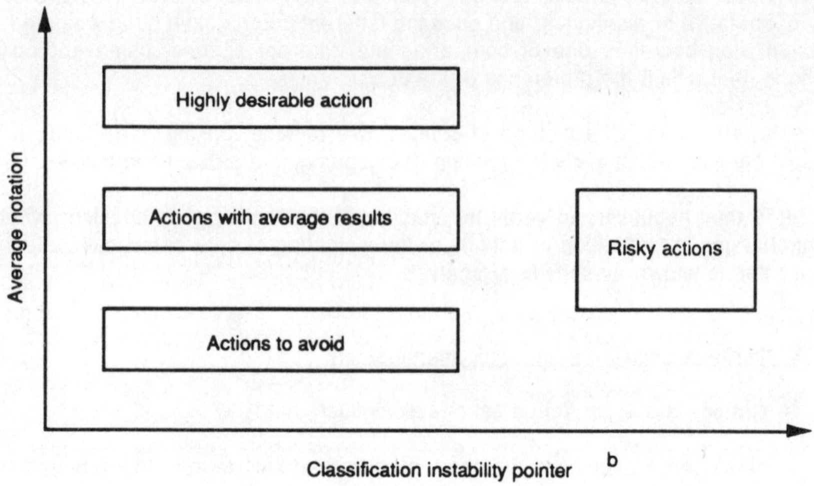

Figure VII-1

Evaluation of risks of actions
(a) The average classification pointer for an action can, for example, be the average of the classifications of actions under the various hypothetical scenarios, weighted by the scenario probabilities.
(b) For example : standard deviation - min - max deviation.

The multiplicity of possible actions raises the problem of choosing the most judicious among them, taking into account the objectives being sought by the company and the constraints that are present. Methods of choice (in the face of an uncertain future under multiple criteria, e.g. Electre II) allow :

- an evaluation of the consequences of each possible action, in the different contexts described by the scenarios ;
- a judgement of each action according to the criteria the company must take into consideration (financial, technical, strategic and commercial etc) ;
- highlighting the set of priority actions to be undertaken, allowing for the likelihood of the different scenarios coming about.

Certain actions are correct under all scenario hypotheses, while others are only right under specific hypotheses and therefore carry a risk which needs to be assessed, and which can be represented as in Figure VII-1. Hence the risk being taken in the choice of strategy is specifically accounted for by multicriteria methods.

4.7. Sophisticated tools, limited applications

The originality of multicriteria methods lies in their ability to exploit the information made up of actions and criteria, and the evaluation of actions according to criteria. If one action is better than a second according to certain criteria, less good according to others, and equivalent according to a third group of criteria, the decision-maker cannot actually state a priori that one of these two actions is preferable to the other. He needs a tool which will enable him to make an objective decision.

All that has been said above regarding the interest of multicriteria methods is true. However, these methods have not really been taken up widely. There has even been a tailing off in their application and diffusion. At the same time, these methods have become the subject of academic research and of adulteration.

In other words, by becoming more complex, the methods have become inappropriable and have been implicitly rejected by potential users, who have contented themselves with rudimentary evaluation based on two or three criteria, all generally calculated manually on a corner of the table. It is to avoid a return to the Stone Age that we dreamt of the development of a simple and appropriable tool : this was how Multipol was born, which we shall present after two other methods : comparative reverse ranking and Electre II.

By considering these two methods, we can identify the problem which determines whether one method rather than the other should be employed first.

The method of comparative reverse ranking

(1) Actions are first ranked in equivalent classes. The classes are then placed in a hierarchy such that within the same class all actions are considered to be equal.
(2) The list of actions is not closed : at any time, new actions can be considered. This method is, therefore, particularly appropriate to new products coming out of research laboratories over a period of time : the new product, once evaluated according to the criteria, is immediately assessed as 'good' or 'bad'.
(3) The number of criteria is limited (less than ten or so in practice).
(4) The method is simple to implement.

The Electre II method

(1) It provides a ranking of actions.
(2) The list of actions is closed : introducing a new action means that the method must be reprocessed from the start.
(3) There is no limit to the number of actions or criteria.
(4) The method is computer-based (The Electre II programme).

5. The method of comparative reverse ranking

The method of comparative reverse ranking consists of drawing up a number of rules relating to the problem and the objectives of the decision-maker, which allow a summing matrix to be constructed. A scale (quantitative or qualitative) with several levels is associated with every criterion. The summing table allows an action to be assessed directly, taking into account the levels it reaches for each criterion.

The reverse ranking rules

The reverse ranking rules translate the policy or the objectives by showing how, all other things being equal, the movement of an action from one level to a lower one against a criterion reclassifies it, ie moves it from one class to another. Thus, in the selection of certain research projects, after assessing the different projects qualitatively according to all the criteria, it was first necessary to assign numbers to the various levels of one scale such that the numbers defined the scale levels and were representative of the reclassifications. Three criteria were used : the volume of sales expected, the cost of development and the technical chances of success, which for each of them gave the following levels :

C1 Sales	excellent	good	moderate	poor
	1	2	4	7
C2 Cost of development	low	average	high	
	1	3	5	
C3 Chances of success	excellent	good	poor	
	1	2	4	

There is thus a reclassification of one class if sales are good instead of excellent (1 to 2) ; of two classes if they are moderate instead of good (2 to 4) ; and of three classes if they are poor instead of moderate (4 to 7). The policy expressed by the decision-maker is thus interpreted by the way in which the levels vary within the various scales.

The criterion 'sales', therefore, has a relatively higher weight than the 'chances of success' criterion, since the maximum amplitude of a reclassification is twice as large for the first as for the second.

The ranking of actions

The evaluations for each project, according to the criteria, are aggregated by a summing matrix which allows a class number to be given each combination of possible estimates according to each of the criteria.

In the above example the criteria were aggregated by treating all other things as being equal ; the interaction of the criterion 'chances of success' with 'cost of development' gives the following matrix :

Chances / Cost	E	G	P
L	1	2	4
A	3	4	6
H	5	6	8

The second column of the grid is deduced directly from the first ; in effect, 'all other things being equal' the chances are good instead of excellent, and that leads to a reclassification of '1' (cf the rules defined above). As a result, the second column is equal to the first incremented by '1'.

The third column is deduced from the second in the same way that the second is from the first.

One needs however, to take account of sales (the third criterion) which could be excellent, good, moderate or poor. The principle is exactly the same as that above : reclassifications corresponding to this criterion are inserted and we finally obtain the *summing matrix* given on the following page.

The first column of this matrix corresponds to projects for which the chances are excellent *(E)* and the costs low *(L)*, medium *(M)* or high *(H)*. The chances being *E*, the projects considered are in class 1, as long as costs are low. If costs, instead of being low are medium, a reclassification of '2' takes place and the project in question moves to class 3 etc.

The consolidation grid, enables a comparison of projects with different modes of assessment ranked in ordered classes. Thus, for example, all projects with the following assessments will be ranked in class 6 :

- sales *E*, chances A, costs *L* ;
- or sales *E*, chances *G* costs *L* ;
- or sales *G* chances *E*, *costs H* ;
- or sales *A*, chances *E*, costs ***M***.

At the end of the aggregation procedure used in the reverse ranking method, the whole set of actions is ranked in a certain number of classes numbered 1, 2, 3... in decreasing order of priority. In this way the number of classes is reduced with respect to the number that could have been created if a class had been set aside strictly for actions with the same evaluation mode according to each criterion, since the degree of uncertainty which clouds the results of any action does not warrant using too precise a classification.

Thus, in the above example all the projects end up ranked within a previously established classification ; the choice is generally made by setting up three groups of research projects :

- a group of projects with a high enough ranking and whose total cost does not exceed the resources available as incorporated in the research programme ;
- an intermediate group of projects retained either as information or in expectation of further or more resources ;
- finally, a group of projects with too low a ranking and which, at least provisionally, are put to one side.

Although the purpose of the method is to decide in favour of several actions, it is sometimes necessary to consider them as no longer independent.

When considering these interconnections. it is enough to accept actions sequentially, class by class so as to be able to transform the various estimates attached to an action which has links with other actions once they have been accepted.

Summing Matrix

Sales excellent

Cost \ Chances	E	G	P
L	1	2	4
A	3	4	6
H	5	6	8

Sales good

Cost \ Chances	E	G	P
L	2	3	5
A	4	5	7
H	6	7	9

Sales moderate

Cost \ Chances	E	G	P
L	4	5	7
A	6	7	9
H	8	9	11

Sales poor

Cost \ Chances	E	G	P
L	7	8	10
A	9	10	12
H	11	12	14

Reclassification of 1 ... of 2 ... ... of 3

Different reclassification rules can be adopted to account for non-independent viewpoints where 'nothing is equal to anything else'. In this example, the more costs rise, the more the 'chance' viewpoint predominates and vice versa.

Cost \ Chances	E	G	A
L	1	2	4
M	3	4	8
H	5	7	12

6. The Electre II method

The Electre II method is based on the idea that, from developing a comparison of actions in a hierarchy one can thus determine their priorities. The ranking takes into account the evaluation of every action in terms of every criterion and weightings representing the objectives of the decision-maker. Ranking is obtained from the definition of 'super-ranking' between the products.

'Super-ranking' relationships

If one action is at least as good as another in terms of each criterion, we can deduce, without too great a risk of error, that that action is better.

In general, one action will be better than another on some criteria but worse on others and equivalent with respect to some third group of criteria. In this case we have to define the conditions under which we can say that that action is better overall. This concept of 'globally better' is formalized by the so-called 'super-ranking' relationship : *a* is globally better than *b* (or *a* outclasses *b*), if two conditions are simultaneously fulfilled :

- *Condition I :* the sum of the weights of the criteria according to which a is assessed is at least as good as b, is sufficiently high (concordance) ;
- *Condition II :* for every criterion on which *a* is worse than *b*, the difference in value is not too large (non-discordance condition).

Example : Ranking regional development projects within the framework of a development assistance study. The projects to be ranked could be in education, research, sanitation, technical training, etc. There are seven projects: *A, B, C, D, E, F, G.* Each is evaluated according to ten criteria, among which are :

- the impact on mortality, estimated by experts ;

- sanitary and socio-economic priorities ;
- regional requirements ;
- technical feasibility.

The experts who met to estimate the relative importance of each criterion were divided into two groups. We wanted to obtain the rankings that corresponded to these two hypotheses. The numerical data were as follows :

Criteria \ Projects	A	B	C	D	E	F	G
1	20	10	5	5	15	10	0
2	9	6	3	6	12	0	3
3	6	9	3	12	6	3	0
4	8	4	2	4	6	0	2
5	4	8	2	4	6	2	0
6	8	6	0	4	4	2	2
7	2	4	4	6	8	2	0
8	6	4	2	8	4	0	2
9	6	6	2	9	4	2	0
10	2	4	1	3	3	0	1

Here criterion 1 is scored from 0 to 20, criteria 2 and 3 from 0 to 12, criteria 4, 5, 6, 7, 8, and 9 from 0 to 8, and finally criterion 10 from 0 to 4.

Combination of weights :

	(1)	(2)	(3)	(4)	(5)	(6)	(7)	(8)	(9)	(10)
Hypothesis 1	5	3	3	2	2	2	2	2	2	1
Hypothesis 2	4	3	3	3	2	2	2	2	2	1

If we designate by :

- P_+ (a, b) the weight of all the criteria for which a is better than b ;
- P_- (a, b) the weight of all the criteria for which a is worse than b ;
- $P_=$ (a, b) the weight of all the criteria for which a is equal to b ;
- C the threshold of concordance ;
- d_i the discordance for the criterion i ;
- $\gamma_i(a)$ the evaluation of the action a on the criterion i ;

a outclasses *b* if the following three conditions are true :

$$\frac{P+(a, b)}{P-(a, b)} \geq 1 \qquad (1)$$

$$\frac{P+(a, b) + P=(a, b)}{P+(a, b) + P=(a, b) + P-(a, b)} \geq C \qquad (2)$$

$\gamma i(b) - \gamma i(a) < di$ for every criterion i for which a is worse than b. (3)

The Electre II programme offers standard concordance thresholds and discordance values. There exist in fact two series of standard concordance thresholds and discordance values which enable definition of a 'super-ranking' relationship that is strong (maximum severity) and a relationship that is weak (minimum severity).

The procedure allowing actions to be compared, taken two by two, is easier to understand if we assume the various criteria are like the members of a jury having a number of votes which correspond to the weight of the criteria. The jury never advocates one action rather than another unless there is an adequate majority for it and unless the minority is insufficiently strong to oppose the views of the majority.

The ranking of actions.

From the set of outranking relationships of all the actions taken two by two, the Electre II programme generates a graph, the nodes of which are the actions and the arcs between them the 'super-ranking' relationships: a *strongly* outclassing *b* given by :

and a outclassing *b weakly is* given by :

If the seven actions *a, b, c, d, e, f, g* are to be ranked, a graph of the following type is obtained for the evaluations and weightings :

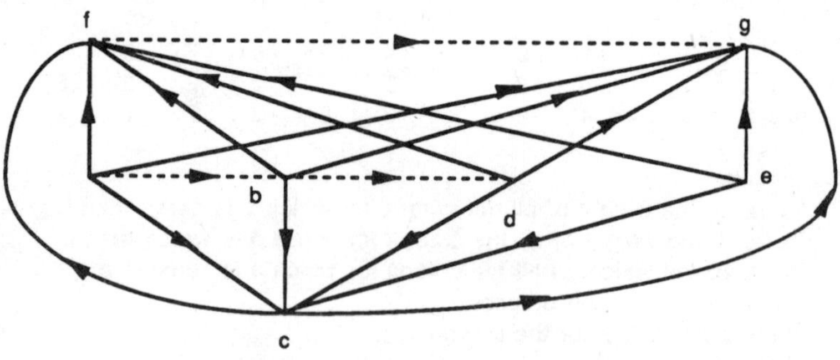

From a graph like this the Electre II programme supplies three rankings : direct, inverse and mean. These rankings are established from the *strong* 'super-ranking' relationships, the *weak* 'super-ranking' relationships serving to separate those that were originally considered equal.

The direct ranking

Direct ranking is obtained by considering the length of the routes *terminating* at each node, the length being measured by the number of nodes passed en route. A node that is not strongly outclassed by another will be ranked first, the node at the end of the longest path will be ranked last.

The direct ranking taking into account the strong outranking relalionships looks as follows :

- class 1 : *a, b, d,* c
- class 2 : *e*
- class 3 : *f, g*

If we consider the weak relations it becomes :

- class 1 : *a, e*
- class 2 : *b*
- class 3 : *d*
- class 4 : c
- class 5 : f
- class 6 : g

The inverse ranking

In this ranking, a node will be ranked all the higher, the longer the routes *away from* the node are ; the node at the origin of the longest route will be ranked first and the node that strongly outclasses no other will be placed last.

The inverse rankings are as follows :

- class 1 : *a*
- class 2 : *b*
- class 3 : *d, e*
- class 4 : *c*
- class 5 : *f*
- class 6 : *g*

The mean ranking

The mean ranking which will be retained as the final ranking is the average of the direct and the inverse rankings.

In the example given, the mean ranking is as follows :

- class 1 : a
- class 2 : *b, e*
- class 3 : *d*
- class 4 : *c*
- class 5 : *f*
- class 6 : *g*

We obtain as many rankings of actions as there are combinations of criteria weightings which correspond to the ultimate objectives of the decision-maker. We can then verify whether a later modification of the weighting of the criteria will change the basic results or not, and determine the set of actions that the decision-maker must decide upon and those he would be well advised to implement.

Conclusion

Multicriteria methods attempt come to grips with the reality of problems, by taking into account not only the quantitative, but also the *qualitative aspects*[1] *of* the consequences of various actions among which a choice has to be made. The methods developed by the SEMA group and the whole analysis system required, result in practical advice which involves the participation of the managers involved in decision-making or advising. The methods provide *a tool for dialogue* between the people involved, as it occurs through questionnaires, during meetings or brainstorming sessions which allow deeper levels of thought, by highlighting throughout the main factors which make up the environment of the decision. Considered opinions are then validated by a rational support method that allows the decision-maker to take *a global, structured view of problems.*

7. The Multipol method

7.1. A simple operational tool

The need to take account of the presence of multiple criteria in decision-making problems has motivated the development of multicriteria methods as decision-making aids and led to a very extensive range of concepts and procedures (fuzzy logic sets, the utility function, ...). The Multipol method (combining the terms multicriteria and policies) is certainly the simplest, but by no means the least useful. It is based on the evaluation of actions by means of a weighted average method, just as pupils in a class are assessed by credit weighted units.

As stated by B. Roy, any decision about a set of actions to be undertaken can be identified as belonging to one of the following problem classifications :

[1] We must emphasize again that the basic strength of this type of method lies in the fact that it suffices to be able to evaluate the different actions with respect to each criterion qualitatively. Therefore one does not necessarily have to commit oneself to costly investigations to obtain numerical information the accuracy of which is often quite misleading.

- selecting the best actions (choice) ;
- classifying the actions into sub-groups (sorting) ;
- ranking the actions.

The Multipol procedure responds to these three problematiques in that it enables a comparative evaluation to be made about the actions, whilst taking account of the different contexts of the study : envisaged policies and expected scenarios.

In Multipol we find the various classical phases of a multicriteria approach : listing of possible actions, analysis of consequences and elaboration of criteria, evaluation of actions, definition of policies and classification of actions. The originality of the Multipol method lies in its simplicity and flexibility of utilization. Each action is evaluated in respect of each criterion, using a simple grading scale (0-5) or (0-10). This evaluation is obtained through questionnaires or expert meetings in which a search for consensus is a necessary factor.

The assessment of actions is not undertaken in a uniform manner : one must take into account the different contexts linked to the objectives of the study. One policy is a weighting scheme applied to the criteria which interprets one of these contexts. Such weighted criteria could also correspond to the various value systems of the actors involved in the decision, to undecided strategic options, or to multiple scenarios and to evaluations which incorporate a time factor. In practice, the experts apportion a given total weight to the set of criteria, for each policy.

Finally, for each policy, the Multipol procedure assigns a mean score to the actions. In this way a table of comparative classification profiles of actions is drawn up according to the policies under consideration.

Accounting for the risk element related to the uncertainty factor or to conflictual hypotheses is done by means of a stability classification scheme for actions, according to policies. In this way one can test the robustness of the results.

7.2. Case study : launching a new product

Suppose we have five new products to be evaluated according to five criteria (launch cost, risk of supply break-down, image suitability, turnover profits...) in order to decide which two products should be launched as a priority.

The evaluation of actions according to criteria (here on a scale from 0 to 20) closely resembles the grading system used in French classrooms, with pupils obtaining one mark for each subject taught (criterion).

Table 1
Evaluation of actions according to criteria

	Launch Price	Supply Breakdown	Image Suitability	Turnover	Profit
PRODUCT1	10	20	5	10	16
PRODUCT2	0	5	5	16	10
PRODUCT3	0	10	0	16	7
PRODUCT4	20	5	10	10	10
PRODUCT5	20	10	15	10	13
PRODUCT6	20	10	20	13	13

We know that the general ranking of the pupils in a class depends not only on the marks obtained in each subject but also on the coefficients assigned to each course. If you change the weights, you are in essence adopting another selection policy.

Let us suppose that for the new products to be launched we define an initial policy P_1, the so-called short-term mixed policy, which puts prime value on low cost (weight 3 for criterion 1) and high profile image (weight 3 for criterion 3) and which distributes the other weighting values as follows : 2 for criterion 2 and 1 for criteria 5 and 6.

Sum well-balanced	Policy P1	3	2	3	1	1
	Products	1	2	3	4	5
111	1	10	20	5	10	16
51	2	0	5	5	16	10
43	3	0	10	0	16	7
120	4	20	5	10	10	10
148	5	20	10	15	10	13
166	6	20	10	20	13	13

According to policy P1, simple calculation of the weighted averages leads to the following ranking : 6, 5, 4, 1, 2, 3 ; we would therefore choose to launch products 6 and 5.

Relying on this ranking could present difficulties if for any reason there were a breakdown in supply (criterion 2), causing production to come to a standstill. Products 5 and 6 are badly placed in respect to the risk criterion, whereas for product 1 there is no risk of supply breakdown. A policy designed to spread the risk -vital in a period of uncertainty- would lead one to launch products 6 and 1.

In a multi-criteria choice, it is essential to ask oneself the following question : how stable is the ranking ? In other words, is the ranking obtained according to one given policy (set of criteria weightings) the same as for other policies that one might envisage ?

In general, rankings will vary from one policy to another and it is advisable to evaluate their sensitivity so that in making a decision one has a better awareness of the possible risks one is taking.

A. Product ranking in terms of policies

In practice, this entails defining a set of possible policies. In the example here, six policies are envisaged and translated into different sets of criteria weightings.

P_1 **Short-term mixed policy** emphasizes low launch cost and high profile product image ;

P_2 **Profitability policy** emphazises low cost, profits and turnover ;

P_3 **Medium/long-term mixed policy** which also seeks profitability (profit and low cost) but without risk in terms of security of supplies ;

P_4 **Image-Prestige policy**. In this policy economic constraints are secondary to concern for a strong image, even if limited in scope,where a flag-flier product is launched ;

P_5 **Market presence**. The policy here is to be aggressively present on the market-place, taking a high-profile stance. From this viewpoint turnover and image are important criteria ;

P_6 **Safe supply policy** with the single constraint of profitability.

We could also have considered a seventh undifferentiated policy according equal weight to all criteria. This policy was rejected as showing a singular lack of intentionality or sense of strategic priorities by the decision-makers. The table below shows the sets of criterion weightings. To facilitate calculations, the sum of weightings to be distributed is fixed at 10.

Set of Weights

Policies	Launch cost	Supply breakdown	Image suitability	Turnover	Profit	Total
ST mixed	3.00	2.00	3.00	1.00	1.00	10
Profitability	3.00	1.00	1.00	2.00	3.00	10
MT/LTmixed	2.00	3.00	1.00	1.00	3.00	10
Image-prestige	1.00	3.00	4.00	1.00	1.00	10

Market presence	1.00	1.00	3.00	4.00	1.00	10
Safe supply	1.00	5.00	1.00	1.00	2.00	10

Using this data, the Multipol programme immediately provides two tables of results and two sets of graphics synthesizing them.

For each action (product to be launched) the first table gives a score for each policy (on a weighted scale from 0 to 20). The ranking value is in parentheses. The general average (score average) and the mean deviation of the weighted scores appear in the last two columns.

Product ranking as a function of policies (scores and general averages)

Policies	PRODUCT N°1	PRODUCT N°2	PRODUCT N°3	PRODUCT N°4	PRODUCT N°5	PRODUCT N°6
ST mixed	11.10(4)	5.10(5)	4.30(6)	12.00(3)	14.80(2)	16.60(1)
Profitability	12.30(4)	7.20(5)	6.30(6)	12.50(3)	14.80(2)	15.50(1)
MT/LT mixed	14.30(1)	6.60(6)	6.70(5)	10.50(4)	13.40(3)	14.20(2)
Image/prestige	11.60(3)	6.10(5)	5.30(6)	9.50(4)	13.30(2)	15.60(1)
Market presence	10.10(4)	9.40(5)	8.10(6)	10.50(3)	12.80(2)	15.50(1)
Safe supplies	15.70(1)	6.60(6)	8.00(5)	8.50(4)	12.10(3)	12.90(2)
General average	12.52(3)	6.83(5)	6.45(6)	10.58(4)	13.47(2)	15.05(1)
Standard deviation	1.92	1.31	1.36	1.37	0.91	1.19

This table reads as follows : product N°1 scores 11.10 for policy P_1 and 12.3 for policy P_2 etc. Its general average for the policies overall is 12.52 with a standard deviation of 1.92. In policies P_1 and P_2, product N°1 is in fourth place and in third place overall.

SCORES and RANKS (same results ranked from best to worst)

Policies	PRODUCT N°6	PRODUCT N°5	PRODUCT N°1	PRODUCT N°4	PRODUCT N°2	PRODUCT N°3
ST mixed	16.60(1)	14.80(2)	11.10(4)	12.00(3)	5.10(5)	4.30(6)
Profitability	15.50(1)	14.40(2)	12.30(4)	12.50(3)	7.20(5)	6.30(6)
MT/LT mixed	14.20(2)	13.40(3)	14.30(1)	10.50(4)	6.60(6)	6.70(5)
Image/prestige	15.60(1)	13.30(2)	11.60(3)	9.50(4)	6.10(5)	5.30(6)
Market presence	15.50(1)	12.80(2)	10.10(4)	10.50(3)	9.40(5)	8.10(6)
Safe supplies	12.90(2)	12.10(3)	15.70(1)	8.50(4)	6.60(6)	8.00(5)
General average	15.05(1)	13.47(2)	12.52(3)	10.58(4)	6.83(5)	6.45(6)
Mean deviation	1.19	0.91	1.92	1.37	1.31	1.36

The second table provides the same information as the first one, except that the actions (products to be launched) are placed in order of rank obtained by the average policy values.

We note that the calculation of the general averages above is the result of a simple average of scores according to policies. Multipol software also allows policies to be weighted in terms of possible rankings.

The tables of results are visualized by two graphic representations (2). The first shows each product's ranking profile according to the different policies. The software enables one to select those sub-sets of actions whose profiles one wishes to display (a diagram of all the profiles would be unreadable). The ranking profile is independent of the possible weighting of policy.

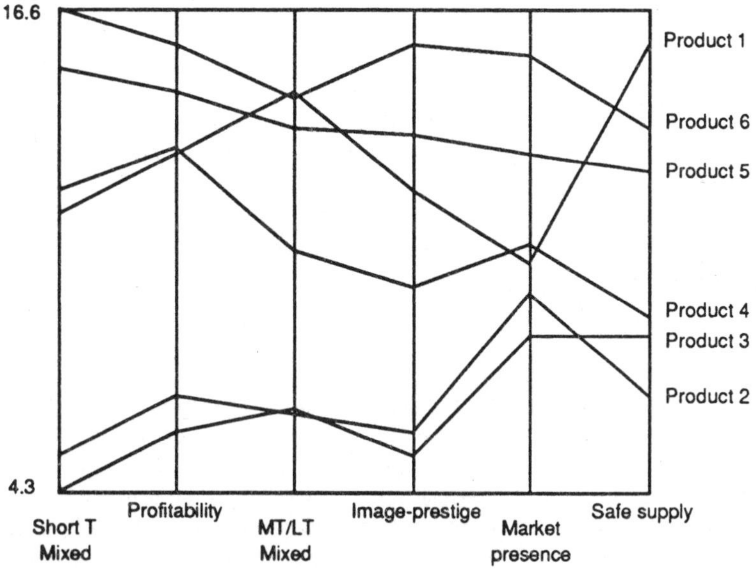

Diagram of profiles
Profile of product ranking graph according to policies

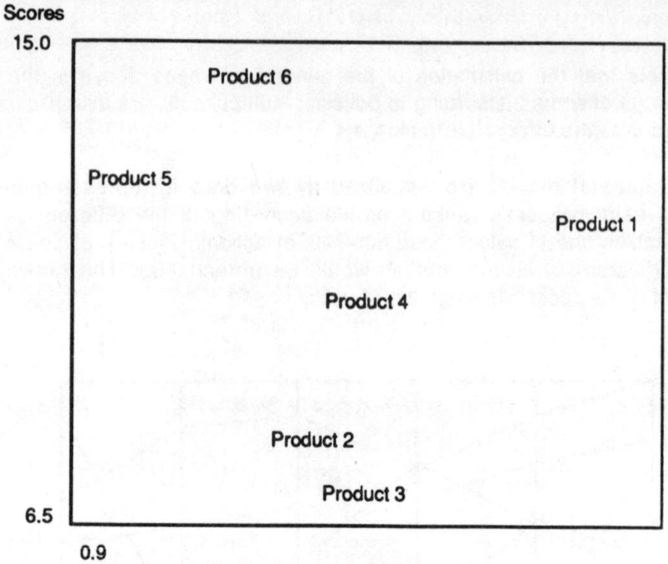

Mean deviation
Stability graph for product ranking according to policies

Notes :

The diagram of profiles allows us immediately to see the validity of the initial remark : products 5 and 6 have the same profile and have top ranking in respect to most policies, except for P_1 (the safe supply policy) where product 1 clearly outclasses them. However, this product ranks very low in terms of other policies. In other words, product 1 has a relatively high average score but with a high standard deviation (a strong variation in average score from one policy to another). If we have to launch two new products, it would probably be preferable to opt for products N°6 and N°1 rather than N°6 and N°5.

B. Ranking of policies according to scenarios

The decision regarding which products to launch depends on the policies envisaged. And these policies are more or less adapted to the most probable scenarios of the future environment. Hence the obvious idea of using Multipol once more to rank the policies according to the scenarios.

In the second Multipol run, it is as if the policies were "actions" to be ranked according to the "policies" (which are in fact scenarios). To facilitate our account, we shall assume that only three scenarios could occur.

- **Scenario A, the reference scenario**, characterized by slow but balanced growth, has a high probability of occurrence : 0.7 ;

- **Scenario B, financial shortfall**, has a probability of 0.2 ;
- **Scenario C, international political crisis**, has a probability of 0.1.

Ranking of policies with respect to scenarios

Data 1 input

Number of "objects"	:	*6 policies to be ranked according to scenarios*
Number of "criteria"	:	*5 the same criteria as before*
Number of "policies"	:	*3 the three scenarios*

Probabilities/weightings "of the policies"

Scenario	A 0.70	
Scenario	B 0.20	*the scenarios probabilities will*
Scenario	C 0.10	*be used to weight the "policies"*

Marking table

	Launch cost	Supply breakdown	Image suitability	Turnover	Profit
ST mixed	3	2	3	1	1
Profitability	3	1	1	2	3
MT/LT mixed	2	3	1	1	3
Image/prestige	1	3	4	1	1
Market presence	1	1	3	4	1
Safe supply	1	5	1	1	2

This table is simply the set of weightings for the five criteria according to the six policies studied in the first Multipol run ; only this time they are considered in a dual fashion : as an evaluation of the importance (relevance) of the criteria for each policy.

Sets of weights

	Launch cost	Supply breakdown	Image suitability	Turnover	Profits	Total
Scenario A	2.00	1.00	2.00	2.50	2.50	10
Scenario B	3.00	3.00	0.00	1.00	3.00	10
Scenario C	2.00	4.00	1.00	1.00	2.00	10

Scenarios A, B, C -the new 'policies'- also reflect different weightings. As before, we obtained results in table form and graphic representations (rank profiles and stability diagrams). Only the latter are shown here. Reading them suggests the following points : the safe supply policy is best for scenarios B and C but the least favourable for scenario A (slow growth). In this reference scenario, policies P_2 (profitability) and P_5 (market presence) are by far the most preferable.

What risk is one taking by favouring one policy rather than another ? To answer this question, we must take account of the scenario probabilities, since the profiles alone are not enough and we must examine the stability graph for policy ranking (which incorporates this dimension in the form of weighted scores).

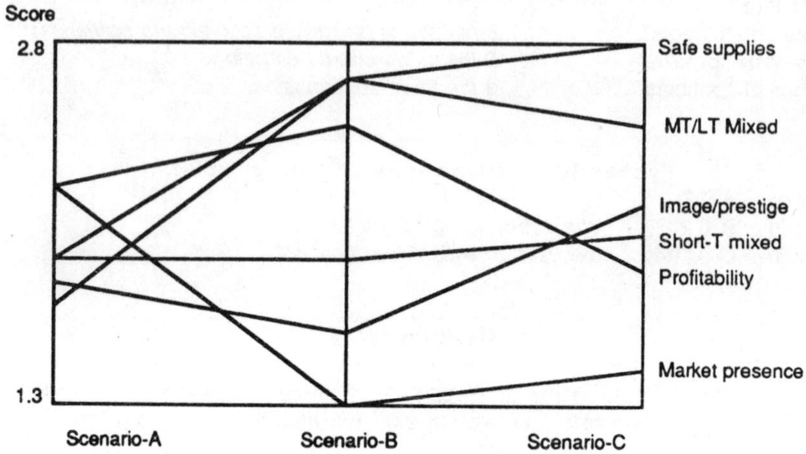

Profile of policy ranking graph according to scenarios

In this example, the scores are evaluated on a scale from 0 to 4, and as previously, the profile graph is independent of the weightings (probabilities) of the scenarios.

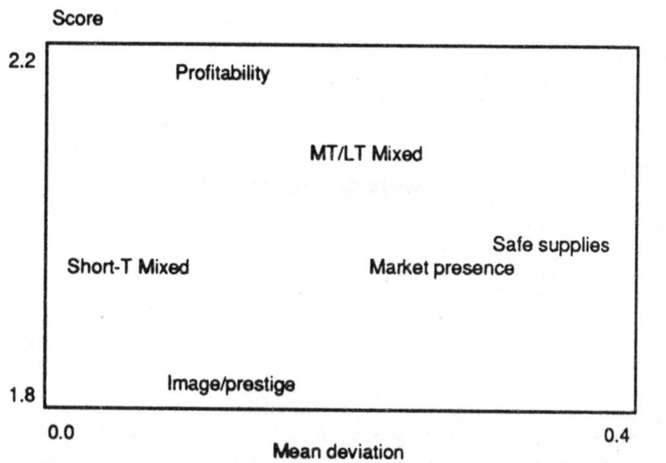

Stability graph for policy ranking according to scenarios

It emerges clearly that the profitability policy (P_1) outclasses all the others, while the medium-term mixed policy (P_3) is in second overall position. The safety policy (P_6) is much further down, in third position, and displays a high standard deviation in its scores : optimal for scenarios B and C but tail-end for scenario A (which is also the most likely). Finally, taking into account the probable scenarios, we would therefore recommend policies P_2 and P_3, according to which launching product 6 should be given priority and a choice made between products 5 and 1.

CHAPTER VIII

INTEGRATING SCENARIOS AND STRATEGY

1. Back to square one in strategic management

1.1. Two age-old concepts
1.2. Two exemplary models : the Church and the armed forces
1.3. Two pioneers : Henri Fayol and Frédéric Winslow Taylor
1.4. A prophet in the desert of management : Mary Parker Follet

2. The emergence and development of strategic management, from 1920 to the present

3. The inevitable encounter

3.1. Rise of prospective thinking
3.2. Questioning Planning

4. An integrated approach : strategic prospective

The prospectivist and the strategist are faced with the same challenge : to anticipate action ; yet their frames of reference and their forms of practice are very different. In 1985, in *'Scenarios and Strategic Management'* we identified a high level of synergy between these two complementary approaches, although without attaining total synthesis. This degree of integration is now possible, as is compensation of the weaknesses of one through the strengths of the other.

We can now envision a marriage between prospective vigilance and strategic determination. However, to be fruitful, this marriage must incorporate daily realities and lead on to a real mobilization of collective intelligence. This *'appropriation-incarnation'* is necessary for reflection and anticipation to crystallize and translate into efficient strategic action. These three golden rules (anticipation, appropriation, action) are the apexes of the Greek triangle.

The encounter between prospective and strategy is not the result of chance, but stems from need and the determination of several persons since the early 1980s.

Although integration of prospective and strategic management was inevitable, it has not brought an end to confusion between genres and concepts. If we liken strategy to flexibility and planning to rigidity, we are in danger of forgetting that reactivity is meaningless without the proactivity (the future project, the objective) which is characteristic of planning.

It is not so much planning itself which is in question, as the way in which it has been implemented. The grafting on of strategic planning can only be successful if it integrates the culture and identity of the organizations concerned. The levers of development are not only rational but also emotional and behavioural.

Are we concerned here with strategic management in the sense used by Igor Ansoff ? Not solely, since management is normally placed at the service of a strategy - it does not constitute a strategy in itself. Strategy shapes management but also presupposes the existence of objectives and associated tactics. It is therefore high time that all these concepts were clarified. The best way to do this is deliberately to return to original sources and use them. Most modern concepts in strategy and management have a long history.

1. Back to square one in strategic management

1.1. Two age-old concepts

In prehistoric times men came together in groups to hunt large animals. Tribes were formed and rules were established. The objective and the tactics were clear : to isolate a few animals, frighten them and make them rush headlong into some ravine or gully where the hunters were lying in wait. Is this not already an example of strategy and management ?

General André Beaufre (1963) defined strategy simply as : 'the art of uniting force in order to achieve political goals'. Strategy should not be confused with tactics : 'the art of employing arms to obtain the best possible outcome' ; nor with logistics : 'the science of movements and supplies'. So, there cannot be strategy without tactics (satisfactory and contingent decisions to reach the set objectives) ; in addition a minimum of logistics (resources) is needed in order to attain the goals. By integrating tactics into strategy we can concur with General Beaufre that 'The aim of strategy is to attain the objectives set by policy, by making the best use of the means at one's disposal'.

It is useful to remind corporate economists and strategists of these clear definitions, as it is often forgotten in such circles that a set of tactics has never been sufficient to make up a strategy. Reactivity is not an end in itself ; flexibility alone leads nowhere ; we need to know where we want to go in order to choose the 'best' tactic.

The concept of management is also often used but rarely defined. We shall take the simple definition proposed by Luc Boyer and Noel Equilbey (1990) : 'Management is the art of placing the organization at the service of strategy'. Note in passing that 'strategic management' is a pleonasm, since management is, by definition, at the service of strategy.

On the basis of these definitions we can see that the history of management and strategy goes back several millennia. People must have organized themselves in order to build the Pyramids, or to embark on conquests.

1.2. Two exemplary models : the Church and the armed forces

The continuance of certain models of organization -both military (the Roman army) or religious (the Catholic Church)- is evidence of their pertinence. As Luc Boyer and Noel Equilbey (1990) remark, 'The superiority of the Romans was based on discipline and organization ; this was how they were able to triumph over more numerous or more intrepid enemies'.There are several explanations for the longevity of the Catholic Church : individual commitment to a collective project, membership of a very structured community which works on the principle of subsidiarity and has a limited number of hierarchical levels (the priest, the bishop, the Pope) for such a varied mass organization.

Already we are talking of strategic centralization and operational decentralization. The Pope is the guardian of the doctrine, and the hierarchy affords a high degree of local autonomy to the priests, on the condition that they respect certain dogmas (obedience, the infallibility of the Pope...). A long and sound theological training gives priests what Henry Mintzberg (1982) would call a 'standardization of qualifications', and guarantees a degree of identitical behaviour.

Alongside the secular organizations in the Catholic Church we find monastic orders functioning according to different rules, outside the traditional hierarchy, fairly independent of the Pope, and revolving around a contemplative or productive set of aims. Is this not what Igor Ansoff, much later, would term 'dual project-oriented structures' ? Generally organizations disappear precisely because of their previous success : they gradually come to seem rigidly set, incapable of adapting to new contexts and changing strategy (the question of the celibacy of Roman Catholic priests is just one example of such rigidities which are suicidal for an organization).

The army is another organizational example which is too rarely called upon when looking at corporations, except when warlike language is being used. So it is of interest to quote Sun Tzu, a contemporary of Confucius (about 500 BC). In his book, *L'Art de la Guerre* ("The Art of War"), he insists on the importance of team spirit in the troops and of reciprocal confidence between the general and his army : he stresses the necessity of knowing the battleground and the environment, and the usefulness of taking into account the enemy's psychology. Some of his remarks remain surprisingly relevant today. In particular, he devoted a great deal of thought to the role of leaders, and saw 'too many rewards or penalities as the sign of a general's lack of authority to command' ; according to Sun Tzu, 'if punishments are to be effective and legitimate they should be perceived as such by the soldiers'.

Without going back so far, we could also draw some topical lessons from Machiavelli or Clausewitz. Clausewitz was a Prussian general, a theoretician during the Napoleonic Wars. He also noted the importance of troop adhesion and team spirit for the success of an army. He was one of the first to draw a comparison between economic and military organization. He insisted in particular on diagnosing one's own strengths and weaknesses and those of the opponent, and on taking the initiative in action (choice of battleground, timing and resources).

More recently, Claude Sicard (1987) points out clearly the similarities between the military world and the business world, and the elements of comparison : the leader, the enemies, victory, the army, the motive are all the same, it is only the fields of application which differ. For Sicard, Charles de Gaulle's book, *L'armée de métier* ("The Professional Army"), lists the modern components of any strategic effort : the project, opening up to the environment, anticipation, sense of structural reactivity, sense of behavioural reactivity.

Claude Sicard also remarks : 'The military does not teach strategy to the young sub-lieutenants, but only to officers who have acquired a degree of maturity and who already have significant experience of being in command'. So much for the (useless) teaching of strategy in our business schools !

For a more complete account of the lessons in economic strategy that can be learnt from military strategy, we would have to quote at greater length from General Beaufre. Here we shall restrict ourselves to a final remark from him : 'To be a good strategist, you need a great deal of resolution, a cool head so that your decisions are calculated, and a fierce desire to maintain your efforts towards attaining the set goal. These qualities are rarely found together, hence the scarcity of real men of war, for they have to be both thinkers and men of action'.

In 1934 Charles de Gaulle, in his book 'L'Armée de métier' (The professional Army), indicated five essential components which he believed were at the basis of any strategic effort :

- a project (in this case the defence of France)
- an opening onto the environment
  - international political environment
  - technological development (key role, for example, of the internal combustion engine)
- anticipation through prospective analysis
  - on one hand, Hitler's policies (attacks on weak countries)
  - on the other hand, future arrangements (armoured divisions, infantry, aircraft)
- a sense of strucutral reactivity
  - in the overall conception of the army
  - in the tactical use of this army
  - in the utilization of new communications systems (radio transmission)
- a sense, finally, of behavioural reactivity : thus, General de Gaulle requested at this time :
  - 100,000 trained professional soldiers
  - a new kind of officer, capable of taking initiative on the battleground
  - political will and determination on the part of the government (which, as we know, was ultimately lacking).

We should also mention Bernard Nadoulek's (1989) stimulating research on 'strategic intelligence', and his typology of conflicts : 'direct, indirect, anticipation'. His work forms part of the history of strategy management accumulated over the centuries, which we have only been able to outline here.

This brief history of strategy and management at least has the merit of relativizing the scope of contemporary 'discoveries' in strategy as applied in the field of economics. Every year the language is enriched with new words, but the underlying concepts have long been known. These lessons in the history of organizations were clearly set out as early as the beginning of the 20th century by the precursors of modern strategy and management : Henri Fayol, Frederick Wislow Taylor and Mary Parker Follet[1]. We shall now discuss the classics of modern management.

[1] In 1960 the American Management Association published a very interesting 'bible' of core writings, edited by H. F. Merril. It was translated into French and published in 1970, with the title 'Les classiques du management' (The management classics).

1.3. Two pioneers : Henri Fayol and Frédéric Winslow Taylor

The first attempts at corporate planning date from the end of the 19th century with the work of the French pioneer, Henri Fayol (perhaps better known in the USA than in France). His *General Principles of Administration* has withstood the test of time remarkably well. These principles form part of a publication entitled *General Industrial Administration*, which first appeared in France in 1916 (Fayol, 1979)[2].

Fayol spent his entire career in a French mining and industrial company, retiring as chief executive officer after achieving remarkable success in reorganizing and expanding the business. In his book, which was the result of several decades of experience, Fayol drew attention to the existence of an 'administrative [function, responsible for] drawing up a general policy programme of action for the company, constituting the corporate structures, coordinating efforts and harmonizing activities'.

'Administration', Fayol stated, *'is forecasting, organizing, directing, coordinating and controlling'* :

- *Forecasting* is examining the future and setting up an action programme.
- *Organization* provides the company with everything required to enable it to function -skills, tools, funds and manpower.
- *Directing* is ensuring that the staff carry out their functions.
- *Coordination* is to bind together, unify and harmonize all activities and efforts.
- *Control* ensures that activities comply with the orders given.

Although Fayol offers a list of 14 general principles of administration, he specifies that this list is not restrictive, and that the word 'principle' must be understood in a broad sense, which excludes any idea of rigidity, 'for there is nothing rigid or absolute about administration ; everything should be kept in perspective'. Fayol's 14 principles are :

1. division of labour ;
2. unique authority ;
3. discipline ;
4. single chain of command ;
5. single hierarchy ;
6. the subordination of private interests to the general interest ;
7. remuneration ;
8. centralization ;
9. hierarchy ;
10. order ;
11. fairness ;
12. stability of the workforce ;
13. initiative ;
14. unity among the workforce.

[2] It will be regretted that in the 1979 edition the word 'prevoyance' (foresight) disappeared from the subtitle of the 1947 edition.

Some of these principles, like 'single command', and 'single hierarchy' are well known. Others, like 'initiative' and 'unity among the workforce', or 'centralization' and 'decentralization' have been forgotten and then rediscovered under another name. In order to return directly to source, the reader may like to peruse an excerpt of the 14 principles of administration (see Exhibit VIII-I).

At the turn of the century, the development of rational organization and the division of labour under the influence of F. W. Taylor also saw the creation of large industrial conglomerates. Mass consumption implied mass production. Growth and diversification of activities raised organizational problems of a new order that are still relevant today.

For example, there is the problem of deciding between centralization and the organization of groups by main functions on the one hand, and decentralization of responsibility into sectors of activity on the other, in order better to identify those which are profitable and those which are not, but where a certain amount of coordination at the centre must be presupposed. This question had already been taken up by Fayol. Further, we see below that Taylorism is but a poor reflection of Taylor's own thinking.

He would perhaps been the first to bring Taylorism to trial. In fact, the fundamental goal he pursued was, in his own words, to 'achieve high salaries with a low cost in manpower'. To achieve this aim, it was of course necessary to install a 'precise time and motion study', but in his eyes this was only one of the many instruments of the 'scientific management' whose arrival he was ardently hoping for as early as 1912, and which would bring about a real 'mental revolution' in the company (see box on Scientific Corporate Management according to F. W. Taylor). These ideas, half a century old, found renewed youth with Hervé Serieyx's 'enterprise of the third kind'.

1.4. A prophet in the desert of management[3] : Mary Parker Follett[4]

Was it possible for a woman at the turn of the century to write about management ? Moreover, could she be understood if her innovative ideas were several decades ahead of conventional thinking ? Mary Parker Follett answers these questions.

[3] This description is cited by Dimitri Weiss (1988), and has been attributed to S. C. George a management historian.

[4] Mary Parker Follett (1868-1932) was an American who studied in the UK and France. In 1918 she published a book entitled "The New State".

Initiative. To conceive a plan, and successfully implement it, provides one of the deepest satisfactions that an intelligent man can experience : it is also one of the most powerful stimulants to human activity. This ability to conceive and execute (a plan) is called initiative. Freedom to make proposals and freedom to carry them out are different aspects of initiative.

Unity among the workforce. Every chief executive should reflect on the fact that corporate harmony and a united workforce are great assets, or, as the proverb has it : 'Power stems from unity'. One must respect the principle of the single chain of command and avoid two dangers :

- *Dividing the workforce* - dividing the enemy's forces in order to weaken them is a clever strategy ; but dividing one's own troops is a grave error committed against the enterprise. No special skill is needed to create discord and strife ; it is within easy reach of any imbecile among subordinates. On the other hand, real talent is required to coordinate effort, to stimulate zeal, to use each individual's capabilities and reward them, without arousing jealousy and without disturbing harmonious relations.
- *Overusing written communication* - it is generally simpler and quicker to communicate verbally than in writing. Fayol also shows that memos are 'sources of complications, conflicts and delays, damaging to the enterprise'.

Division of labour aims at producing more, better, and with the same amount of effort.

Authority and responsibility. Authority is the power to issue orders and the right to be obeyed.

Official authority in a manager (which is a right of office) is distinct from personal authority derived from intelligence, knowledge, experience and moral strength... To make a good manager, personal authority is the indispensable complement of official authority.

There can be no authority without responsibility, that is without some sanction -be it reward or punishment- accompanying the exercise of power. Responsibility is the corollary of authority.

Discipline. Discipline is compliance with the conventions agreed between the company and its employees. The state of discipline in a social entity depends essentially on the quality of its leaders. I have always found French workers obedient, even devoted, when well managed. It is important that the conventions be clear and, as far as possible, give satisfaction to both parties. Discipline is as relevant to the highest executives as to the humblest employees.

Single chain of command. For any action, an employee must receive his orders from a single superior ; people cannot stand having a dual authority above them, which is a source of conflict and inefficiency.

Single authority. This principle may be expressed as having one boss and one programme for one set of operations with the same goal. A single chain of command cannot exist without single authority, but does not follow on automatically from it.

Centralization. Centralization is not, of itself, a good or bad system of administration and can be adopted or abandoned at will by the directors according to circumstances ; it always exists to some degree, and centralization (or decentralization) is purely a matter of balance. The problem is one of finding the limit which is best for the firm. The goal to aim for is the best conjugate use of resources and the workforce as a whole.

Inasmuch as the absolute and relative weights of the executive and the employees are continuously changing, it is understandable that the degree of centralization (or decentralization) itself can vary constantly.

'Scientific management is not a recipe for efficiency... it is not a time and motion study nor the printing, filling in and circulation of a ton of forms to a team, saying "Here's your system, sort yourselves out and use it". It is not a system of divided or functional management... Scientific management implies a general mental revolution by both workers and managers...

The major revolution which will occur in mental attitudes by the two parties when scientific management is initiated, is that both will cease to consider the sharing of added value as the most important point and that they will turn their joint attention to the growth of the added value.

The two parties will understand that in replacing antagonism and conflict by amicable co-operation and mutual assistance, they can jointly carry this added value to such a degree... that there is a possibility of a steep rise in the wages and an equally high rise in the profits...

But this increase is only the smallest item of the project. The harmony which scientific management will introduce between the employer and the employee is the best mutual outcome that could happen'.

Her ideas are disturbing because they are unclassifiable ; for a long time they were considered no more than a psychological approach bordering on manipulation. However, the school of Behaviourism invented nothing - it is to Mary Parker Follett that we owe the formulation of the principle of integration in order to make group interests coincide with those of the individual. In this her views were in opposition with those of Henri Fayol, for whom individual interest should be subordinated to the general interest. She believed in individual self-control and in the power of bonds between individuals within a group as a factor of integration (this is close to self-organization).

As Dimitri Weiss (1988) emphasized : 'She remains to this day one of the most neglected major early authors on management. She will remain unclassifiable due to the variety and richness of her interests, from industrial relations to international relations'. Some modern writers, such as William Ouchi (1981) have become famous for concepts such as Theory Z, whose discovery should without doubt be credited to Parker Follett. In her writings we find most of the modern ideas which can be grouped together under participative management : decentralized decision-making, the integrating rôle of groups, the authority of competence, hierarchical control replaced by trust and communication, 'the logic of responsibility rather than the logic of obedience'.

Mary Parker Follett still seems to be ahead of the times when she lists the essential qualities of a leader : 'The rôle of the man at the top is not to take decisions for his subordinates but to teach them how to resolve their problems themselves. The best manager does not persuade people to follow his wishes, he shows them what they must do in order to carry out their explicitly defined responsibilities. Such a manager does not wish to think for others ; on the contrary, he trains them to think for themselves.

'In fact, the best managers try to train their disciples to become managers themselves. A second-rate executive will try to suppress the initiative of his subordinates for fear of rivalry'.

The message here is that the real power of a leader cannot be measured by the domination which he exerts over others, but by his capacity to develop autonomy and responsibility among his subordinates.

Z theory and its precursors

'It was William Ouchi who coined this term in his book of that title, published in the USA in 1981. It is a deliberate reference to the distinction established previously by Douglas Mc Gregor, (1906-1964) in his book on '*La dimension humaine de l'entreprise*' ("The human dimension of the company") (1957), between what he called theory X and theory Y'.

According to theory X, people are passive, have an aversion to work, and try to avoid it. They must be constrained, controlled, managed, and threatened with disciplinary sanctions, in order to elicit from them any effort in line with the pursuit and accomplishment of the organization's objectives. A person is driven to work by acting on the negative aspects of his character and on what, according to Maslow's needs hierarchy, are his inferior needs - such as his physiological needs.

Theory Y assumes a person capable of acting in a responsible, participative and cooperative way - and able to set himself as objectives what are, according to Maslow's needs hierarchy, superior levels of motivation, such as the need for esteem, recognition and status... In theory Y it is necessary to ensure that particular interests are subordinated to the general interest.

The Z company is seen as a community of equals who cooperate to achieve common objectives. The company manages the behaviour of this community by relying on commitment, loyalty and trust, instead of counting only on hierarchy and supervision... The values of the clan give rise to a team spirit, working groups in which members feel solidarity towards each other, and workers who are well integrated into their company.

Probably, without knowing it, many successful writers on management have produced hits by (re)discovering some of the ideas of Parker Follett. K. Blanchard and S. Johnson's (1984) 'minute manager' - so-called because he or she requires so little time to lead staff to produce impressive results- obviously resembles Parker Follett's 'first class director', although less complete.

2. The emergence and development of strategic management, from 1920 to the present

In the USA, the inter-war years saw the birth, notably at Dupont and General Motors, of the first experiments in dissociating strategic (objective-setting) from tactical (ways of reaching objectives) responsibilities. Over the same period, statistical and financial control techniques to monitor plans and programmes multiplied, without, however, becoming integrated into any real corporate plan *per se*.

After World War II, large firms committed themselves much more systematically to forward planning and organizing for growth and diversification in their activities, beginning with short term analysis of products and markets under the familiar heading of *marketing*. It would not be a distortion to consider the development of corporate planning and marketing as two interrelated phenomena.

It was not until the 1960s that planning really became a fundamental activity within companies. In France, such companies were stimulated to plan by the existence of the national plans which provided economic projections that were sufficiently well defined and credible as to provide a frame of reference for companies. In the USA this kind of planning became known as long-range planning, to emphasize the fact that companies were moving beyond the horizon of the annual budget and wondering what was to happen to them, to their investments and to their physical organization over a span of several years.

It rapidly became clear that long-term planning efforts had to be directed to *planning and organizing the growth and diversification of the activities of the enterprise* in its entirety - hence the expression 'corporate planning'.

Over the same period long-range planning -now corporate planning- had become the object of theoretical inquiry. Chandler (1962) emphasized harmonization between a company's external strategy and the internal company structures ; I. Ansoff (1965) examined the evolutionary trends of planning and decision systems. Ansoff (1978), amply demonstrates the historical link, between the opportunities presented by the environment and the development of the hierarchy of production functions, and the development of intra-company structures - staff, line management, international project orientations, and so on.

During the 1960s, many factors contributed to the development of corporate planning and long-term strategic thinking. In particular, we can single out :

- The acceleration of technical and economic change, ie the change occurring in the competitive environment of the company.
- The development of factors that create inertia within the company with regard to ever-larger investments, the length of R & D time cycles and the dual structure of the workforce, this last factor being both quantitative (one could no longer hire and fire according to variations in demand), and qualitative (time was needed to train staff for the new skills required).
- This rising level of education among staff and lower ratios of managers to workers made it no longer possible to run the company efficiently without internal concertation. Preparing the plan offered exactly the right opportunity for dialogue within the firm.

Following the events of 1973, corporate planning has not escaped the wave of criticism and scepticism that all attempts at anticipation and forecasting encountered. In a rapidly changing climate, with shifting, fickle winds, and unreliable forecasts, it is often deluding (and even dangerous) to try to maintain a given direction. It quickly became evident, however, that *environmental uncertainty reinforced the need for corporate planning*, then aptly renamed 'strategic management'. Companies, then, must adapt their strategies and demonstrate *flexibility*. Increased efforts in *prospective* and anticipation of events are necessary, if one wishes action to be directed in ways likely to safeguard maximum flexibility.

In an increasingly turbulent world, the very concept of planning as an *a priori* objective becomes irrelevant, since it is not objectives which count most - even if they are indispensable. What really counts is the capacity to react and adapt to changes in the environment : G. Archier and H. Serieyx (1984) speak of *reactivity* ; I. Ansoff (1978) states that we have shifted from planning to strategic management.

Two apparently distinct research paths, in reality complementary, were initiated during the 1970s. The first approach, called strategic portfolio analysis was conceived at the end of the 1960s and made famous by the Boston Consulting Group (BCG), was enormously successful in popularizing some valuable tools of rational analysis for a public of business leaders, who really needed them (product life-cycles, experience effects, etc). Encompassing the competitive, technological and financial dimensions, the proponents of this rational approach were seeking universally applicable rules for strategic analysis (PIMS formulae, for example), the application of which would ensure economic success for the company.

The second path, which we can call heuristic, adopting Marie-José Avenier's (1985) term, singles out a corporate dimension which had been neglected by strategic analysis - the human factor. The key to a dynamic enterprise, in this approach, is to be sought in organizational structures and behaviour rather than in ready-made recipes of technological, economic and financial rationality. That is the main message repeated on nearly every page of a major work by T. Peters and R. Waterman (1982), which made a tremendous impact in the USA and Europe (if only in terms of sales), and was entitled, *In Search of Excellence*.

During a period of crisis and heightened economic competition, success depends on mobilizing total corporate intelligence (H. Serieyx, 1982) to attain objectives and counter constraints, and this will succeed all the better if these have been debated with concerted effort. Dialogue within the company has become a necessity (generals don't fight their own troops). Preparing the plan provides a special opportunity for introducing and implementing concerted agreement, which is indispensable for internal cohesion.

History does not repeat itself. This adage is undoubtedly true, except with regard to ideas. Numerous principles of strategic organization are curiously close to principles elaborated by the French pioneer, Fayol, and a little later by Taylor. Taylor's fame derives mainly from his division-of-labour axiom, although this was only a secondary element compared to Taylor's call for a total mental revolution on the part of both workers and management. In addition, we should of course mention Mary Parker Follett's prophetic views, described earlier.

After nearly a century of debate on organizational strategy and managment, can we distinguish a unifying message ? We shall retain one only, which is paradoxical, since it concerns the principle of contingency, which is presented in Chapter IX. Finally, we shall venture to make a forecast : there will be a return to the concept of the plan and the project.

Strategic planning has been laid to rest by strategic management ; does this not point to an unconscious camouflaging of the lack of objectives and the loss of direction which characterize modern societies ? Not knowing where we want to go and why, we take pleasure in commentary - ie, in analysis of tactical ways and means to adapt in the face of change. The ship no longer has a prow, but the captain knows all the secrets of the tiller and the ship's instruments ; preactivity and proactivity are alien to him, he knows only the reactivity of strategic management.

Being reactive should not be confused with being flexible. The first is improvised as an organization's appropriate response to external hazards. The second is kept up as an intrinsic capacity of the organization to react and adapt to the environment without losing its direction. In other words, internal flexibility is the condition for external reactivity. The first derives from physical condition, the second from reflexes.

Jean Cocteau put it so well : 'Fashion is what goes out of fashion'. Soon reactivity will have had its day and we shall rediscover, perhaps with new words, the virtues of strategic planning - a skillful mix of voluntarism and flexibility. For this comeback to happen the concept of the plan will first have to be definitively liberated from the bureaucratic corsets into which it has wrongly been laced.

3. The inevitable encounter

3.1. Rise of prospective thinking

In *Scenarios and Strategic Management* we put forward the strong potential synergy between these two complementary approaches. We did not, however, manage to realize the desired synergy. Since then, prospective has continued along its own path, and has spread into companies and public administrations. But it is primarily the prospective state of mind - global, systemic and long-term - which has been taken up. This attitude can be summed up by some simple formulae : 'Global vision for local action' ; 'Clarify present action in the light of the possible future' ; 'Mistrust the effect of fashion and conventional wisdom'.

At the same time, specific prospective methods, such as structural analysis, cross-impact studies, Delphi and scenarios, have not advanced significantly, but have been diffused. Theoretical research and sophisticated tools have been neglected in favour of multiple applications. Operational imperfection is worth more than inoperational perfection. In order to approach a complex world, we need simple and appropriate tools (appropriate because they are adaptable).

In fact, prospective increasingly often takes the form of collective thought - a mobilization of minds in the face of changes in the strategic environment. Such mobilization is indispensable in preparing for and successfully implementing action.

This trend towards wider diffusion and appropriation of prospective - formerly the preserve of experts - is to be applauded. But the methodological weaknesses - which are persisting and even becoming accentuated - are regrettable.

The plea for research in prospective is all the more justified as some people confuse simple tools with simplistic tools. We should recall that the scenario method, as conceived almost 20 years ago, remains as useful as ever, and has, above all, the great merit of demanding intellectual rigour : qualitative and quantitative analysis of marked trends, retrospective study of actors' moves, pinpointing seeds of change, tensions and conflicts, constructing coherent and complete scenarios (paths of progress and future images).

The word 'scenario' is increasingly misused and abused - it is used to refer to any use of a hypothesis at all, without checking the relevance and coherence of the hypotheses or considering their likelihood (probability). Another common confusion is to take one's wishes (objectives) for realities, to mix the exploratory and the normative. All possible scenarios are not equally probable or desirable, and a distinction must be made between environmental scenarios and actors' strategies.

Some specific tools of prospective, such as structural analysis and the MICMAC method, are today so successful as to be almost a cause for concern to the people who worked on their development. Structural analysis is too often applied in a mechanical fashion, without purpose and to the detriment of real thought. The lesson from this is that it takes time to diffuse a tool (over 15 years) and even more time for it to be used well. When we present a method in a manual, we should also tell the reader what to do if he or she wishes to avoid using it badly.

Rapid diffusion of such methods is now partly due to computer support software, which makes these tools highly accessible at low cost. We have put together a *Tool-box of prospective methods*, each identified in terms of the type of problem area one is working in (asking the right questions, understanding the past and actors' strategies, scanning the field of all possible futures and reducing uncertainties, identifying and assessing the strategic options).

The *tool-box* has recently been completed by adding the new tools, MACTOR, Morphol and Multipol, which join MICMAC and SMIC. The software is available on diskette for PC's and compatibles and MacIntosh. We believe that these tools in turn will become widespread. We should, however, remember their uses and limitations - they should be used to stimulate the imagination and reduce incoherence, but not as a substitute for thought or to restrict freedom of choice. Before going on to see how *prospective* can be integrated into a strategic approach, let us recapitulate on how the latter has developed over the past 15 years.

3.2. Questioning Planning

In the 1970s, there was an interesting correlation between the decline of national planning and the rise of corporate planning. Since the early 1980s, corporate planning too has apparently been falling into disrepute, or at least losing prestige. The French national plan that President de Gaulle considered to be a *'binding obligation'* may be seen as a useless form of agitation for the *analytical ivory towers* denounced by T. Peters and R. Waterman (1982).

Why should one set strategic objectives and invest the means necessary if, given the turbulent market-places and changing environment, these very objectives must themselves constantly be modified ? The technical use of 'sliding scales' of objectives does not satisfactorily solve this sort of dilemma.

Double crisis of strategic planning

First, there is the crisis of planning, which has been thrown into question by the turbulent environment and the rise of liberalism. The *laisser-faire* attitude towards market forces is considered the best remedy when faced with imbalances, for which governmental and regulatory intervention are held responsible - hence the deregulation movement originating in the USA, where planning has always been considered almost evil (eg, as in Gosplan).

In Europe, planning has above all been the victim of its own success. Adaptation in the face of uncertainty cannot accommodate sacrosanct and therefore rigid goals (whereby a project is rejected because it was not foreseen in the plan) ; nor can it accommodate procedures which have become oppressively bureaucratic and paper-generating (at a time when the paperless office is in vogue). At the same time, however, we have too often thrown out the baby with the bathwater, forgetting that the planning report is less important than the process of consultation which led to it (consultation without a final report is better than the opposite). Today, we could make the same observation about company projects ; it is better to undertake a company project without saying than to talk about it without doing anything.

Second : there is the crisis of strategic analysis - product-market segmentation and portfolio analysis, successfully popularized by Anglo-Saxon consultants (eg BCG, MacKinsey, ADL) were severely criticized because of their mechanical, reductionist approach. These methods have practically fallen into disuse by those who invented them, yet they are taught more then ever in management and business schools. It would be wrong to smile too readily at this irony, for obsolete though it may be, portfolio analysis remains a good tool for familiarizing oneself with the concepts of strategic analysis (segmentation, life cycle, the effect of experimentation/experience).

However portfolio analysis is improved, one of the main weaknesses of this method remains - it produces an image of the present (actually of the recent past, due to the delay in obtaining figures) from which it is often very dangerous to extrapolate - the future balance of a portfolio of activities can vary according to which environment scenarios are envisaged.

This crisis in strategic planning is also a crisis in the rationalist school of thought, which favours 'cold' values (reason, analysis, calculation, forecasting) and relies on economic and strategic tools of analysis, and operational research ; such methods have gone into decline, particularly in the USA, because of their success, misuse, and the effects of fashion. This has followed the classic pendulum phenomenon, with oversophisticated methods making way for common sense, and then for the simplistic ideas of the heuristic school of thought, whereby pragmatism became a religion recognizing only the 'warm' values of enthusiasm, charisma and will. This is how there was a gradual shift from research into excellence, to a passion for excellence, leading finally to 'chaos management'. We have already discussed what we think of this new fashion. Opposition between reason and passion is as useless and sterile as that between right and left brain. The human mind constitutes an indivisible whole : without reason, passion is blind, and without passion to activate desire and projects, reason leads nowhere.

The rationalist trend has not had its last say, however. Pioneers like H. Igor Ansoff have always preferred strategic pilotage to pilotage with vision, even though they have sacrificed the concept of planning to promote that of strategic management : their approach in terms of internal organizational strengths and weaknesses, and threats and opportunities presented by the environment, remains as valid as ever.

During the 1980s the rationalist school of thought experienced a revival through the works of Michael Porter (1980 and 1985). This Harvard professor demonstrated the importance of analysing the competitive forces in a given environment (eg, rivalry of competitors in the same sector, power of suppliers and customers, threats of potential new entrants and substitute products). He also identified two generic strategies (domination by costs and diversification) and finally he reestablished analysis in terms of value chains. The overall result is an improved analysis of the key factors of success in different corporate strategic domains of activity (SDA).

This revival is, however, inadequate : in particular it conceals the financial, human and organizational aspects of a company, and neglects the irrational framework, ie the identity and the values of the organization, which are indispensable for defining a full and coherent strategic project. In order to answer the question 'where do we want to go and where can we go' we need to know where we are and where we have come from.

The most radical advance with respect to classical rationalist approaches was made by Marc Giget (1989). He was able to deal with the deep-seated reality of the company : taking into account historical, economic, technological, human and financial aspects and calling on the prospective dimension as required.

There remains, however, one delicate question : although strategic analysis and the preparation of a developmental plan constitute exceptional opportunities to enhance communication and stimulate internal mobilization around common objectives, nevertheless the genres often have to be separated. If planning is really strategic, it must remain confidential or at least subject to restricted circulation. Diagnosis of internal strengths and weaknesses and threats and opportunities for a development provides strategic information which should only be circulated widely if it seems tactically opportune to do so. Unfortunately, as Thomas Durand (1982) stresses : 'this desire for secrecy contradicts the need to mobilize people around this common project : the company plan'.

Faced with this dilemma, companies have various responses, which go from one extreme to the other. At Thomson CSF, in Rhone Poulenc, France, for example, 15 copies of the plan are circulated. At Elf, several hundred copies of a single version of the plan are circulated to company executives. At the other extreme we have the RATP (Paris Public Transport System), which circulates several thousand copies of the company plan. Obviously what is possible for a public company with a monopoly is not possible for a company operating in a more competitive system.

4. An integrated approach : strategic prospective

For Marc Giget, the director of Euroconsult, a company must be seen as a tree of competence, and cannot be reduced to its products and markets. In a tree (Figure 1), the roots (technical skills and know-how) and the trunk (capacity for industrial implementation) are as important as the branches (product-market lines).

The image of the tree has its advantages. First, it appears that, to quote Giget 'the company must not die with its product'. Just because a branch is ill, one should not saw through the trunk. In this case it is better to redirect the sap (ie, the skills) towards new branches of activity which correspond to its genetic code. There are the French examples of Bollore-Technologies (from cigarette papers to specialized packages), Graphoplex (from slide rules to precision thermoplastics) or la Règle à Calcul, the well-known Boulevard Saint-Germain slide-rule distributor which became a distributor of calculators and electronic products.

The image of the tree also has its limitations. The dynamic of the tree is not unidirectional, from roots to branches - it functions in two directions - the branches in turn nourish the roots through photosynthesis and the humus produced from fallen leaves.

The image of the tree of competence was born out of a strategic analysis of large Japanese companies. It appeared that, implicitly or explicitly, most organizational structures in Japan are represented in the form of a tree ; thus, for example, three concentric circles to symbolize research, then production and finally commercialization, also represent a tree projected into a plan. Marc Giget's approach has attracted attention, and has been taken up, by major companies throughout the world.

Naturally, the strategic approach, defined through trees of competence, felt the need for prospective study of the competitive environment. It is therefore understandable that the marriage between prospective and strategy came about through a rapprochement between scenario methods and trees of competence. The marriage will be all the more fruitful in that there is total compatibility of blood groups between these two approaches ; both imply simple tools, capable of being appropriated by those who must use them, by and for themselves, within the company.

Before presenting in Figure 2 the integrated diagram, constructed with Marc Giget, we should recall the three stages of the scenario method :

(1) Identify the key variables. This is actually the aim of structural analysis.
(2) Understand the past and analyse actors' games in order to ask key questions about the future.
(3) Reduce uncertainty on the key questions and pick out the most probable

environmental scenarios with the help of expert methods.

These stages are represented in the left half of Figure 2.

The first stage is not limited to a structural analysis of the company in its environment, but also comprises a thorough X-Ray of the company, from know-how to product lines, achieved by use of the tree of competence.

Stage 2 concerns the retrospective dynamic of the company in its environment - its past development, its strengths and weaknesses in relation to the main actors in its strategic challenges - which allows us to locate the key questions for the future.

Stage 3 involves reducing uncertainty over key questions for the future. Eventually expert survey methods are used to show up marked trends, risks of rupture and finally to outline the most probable environmental scenarios.

Stage 4 aims to identify a coherent project, ie the strategic options which are compatible both with the company identity and with the most probable scenarios for its environment.

Stage 5 is devoted to the evaluation of strategic options. A rational approach would encourage reliance on a multicriteria selection method, but this rarely happens. This stage ends the preliminary phase of reflection before decision-making and action.

Stage 6, from project to strategic choices, is crucial, as it involves the transition from reflection to decision-making. Making strategic choices and prioritizing goals are tasks for the board of directors or its equivalent.

Stage 7 is concerned wholly with implementing the plan of action. It involves the negotiation or setting up of goal-oriented contracts, establishing a system of coordination and follow-up, and the development of (external) strategic vigilance.

This integrated approach does not proceed in a totally linear way. It includes a possible feedback loop from stage 7 to stage 2 : implementation of the plan of action and the results of strategic vigilance may lead, in some cases, to a reconsideration of the dynamic of the company in its environment.

Finally, the transition from prospective reflection to strategic action assumes that the actors concerned enter into the process. This means that the whole staff, and not just the managers, must be involved as far as possible in these different stages, without changing the necessarily confidential nature of certain strategic choices. For a successful transition from thought to action there must be appropriation - which brings us back to the three elements of the Greek Triangle.

Of course, this integrated diagram of prospective and strategy is aimed primarily at companies which can be represented in form of a tree of competences. There remain many other questions concerning global or sectoral (demographic, energy, industrial) prospective for which the classical scenario method is indispensable.

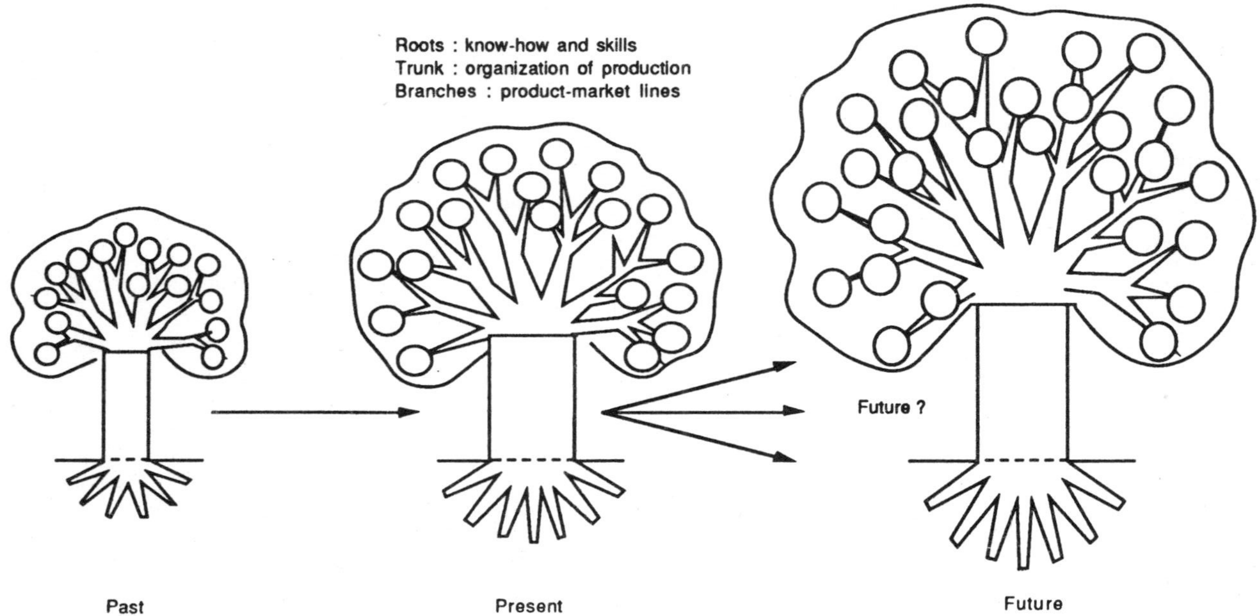

The past is unique ; analysing it allows us to understand the constants and continuity of the company's business, to improve our knowledge of the company project in its historical reality.

The future is uncertain ; its analysis allows us to identify the threats and opportunities presented to the company, and to define the issues and challenges it faces, in order to determine its desired future and to incorporate this into the company project.

Figure VIII-1
The tree of competence and its dynamic
Source : Marc Giget, *La conduite de la réflexion et de l'action stratégique dans l'entreprise* (Euroconsult, 1988).

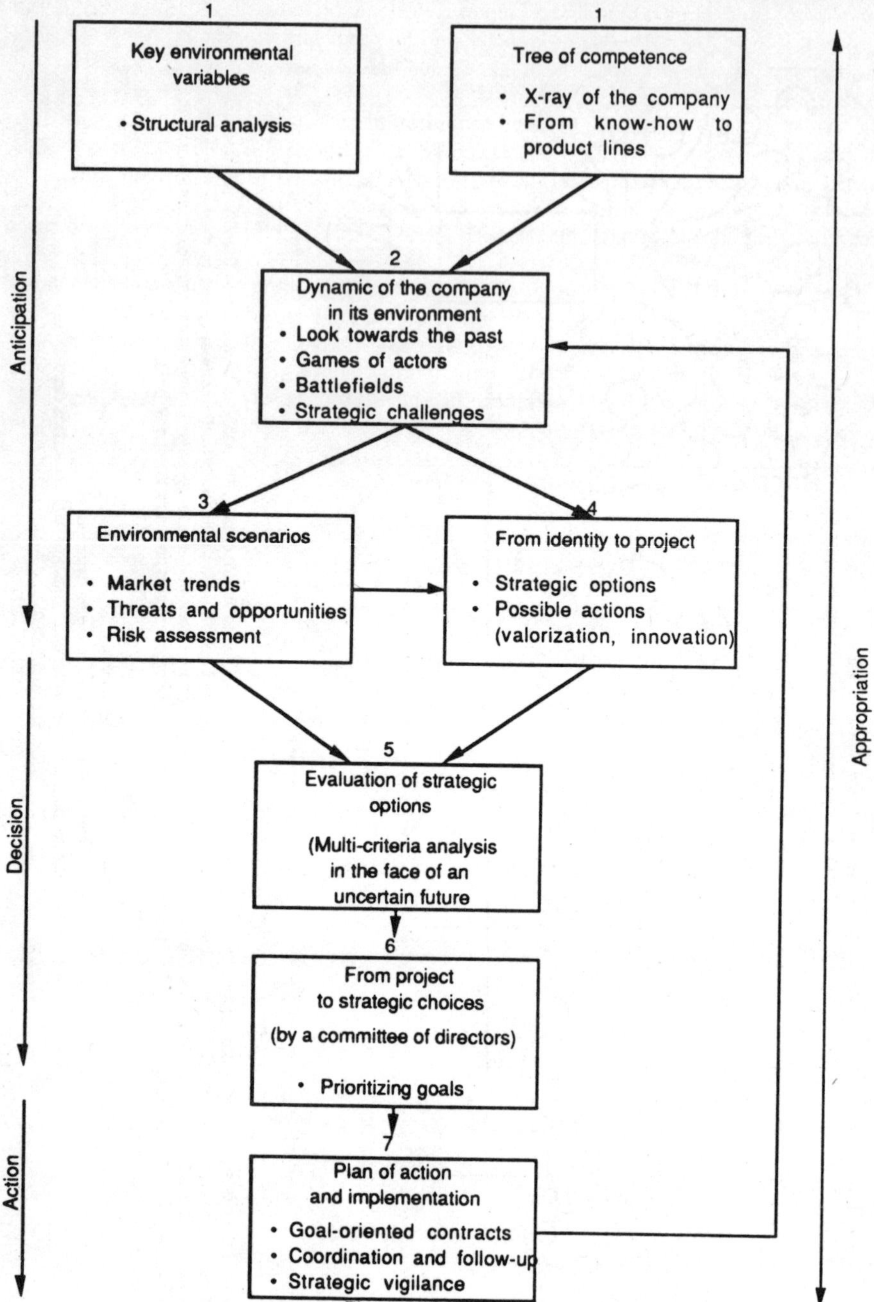

Figure VIII-2

Integration of prospective and strategic approaches

Source : Marc Giget (Euroconsult) and Michel Godet (CNAM), 1989

In all cases, choice of methods depends not only on the nature of the problem, but also on the available resources (financial and human), and we should not forget that time constraints are probably the most restricting.

The marriage between prospective and strategy is still too recent to bear fruit, but the union seems promising ! In this integrated scheme, the rational skeleton does not prevent the circulation of irrational marrow. Collective appropriation serves to prepare for effective action without, however, opposing the restricted, partly confidential nature of strategic decisions.

As we see it, the rationalist and heuristic schools of thought are simply two sides of the same reality. It is pointless to look, for example, to theories of deterministic chaos and bifurcations for 'scientific' explanations which are not directly transposable to the social sciences. The advances made in determinism may push back the frontiers of chance, but they will never eliminate it, and the possibility of 'bifurcation points' confers on human action a degree of freedom to exercise will and express desires in the face of the range of possible futures. In short, between chance and necessity there is room for mutineers and mutants bearing change.

CHAPTER IX

PEOPLE AND ORGANIZATIONS MAKE THE DIFFERENCE

How can we not conclude with the essential point : 'It is people and organizations which make the difference'. Tools of prospective and strategy are nothing without the hand which uses them ; they can equally well lead to better or worse - it all depends on the mind which directs the hand.

As we come to the end of this book, two dangers are worth stressing. The first arises out of excessive rationalism, leading to a blind and mechanical reliance on tools which are designed primarily to stimulate thought and imagination, and to facilitate communication, but never to substitute for the human mind. The second danger, almost symmetrical, would be to succumb to excessive arrogance : inadequate tools do not prove that the mind is adequate. In other words, it is good to increase the human mind's powers of analysis and synthesis by using the lever of tools which it has constructed.

This last chapter will proceed in three stages. First, we shall show how and why people are at the heart of the difference between a winning and a losing organization. The second stage will be devoted to company and team projects - the importance of these should not blind us to the pitfalls. The third stage will discuss the metamorphoses in structures and behaviour which are necessary for companies to face up to change.

1. Quality of leaders and winning teams

Throughout this book we have constantly referred to the human and organizational factor as *the* key out of the thousand and one keys to excellence (and also to failure). We have thus (re)discovered the principle of contingency. That which created yersterday's success may well be the cause of tomorrow's failure. In order to adapt to a changing world we must know how to change our structures, behaviour, and habits.

A far-seeing manager is one who regularly introduces factors to break habits. In order to remain motivated a person needs to be permanently diverted and stimulated by challenges. Such challenges are more mobilizing if they are new, and more relevant if they form part of a coherent trajectory. This is how we should understand apparently disjointed attempts to mobilize the intelligence of organizations : leadership by objectives, participative management, quality circles, company plans...

All these attempts are marked by success and failure... which goes to show that the bottle alone does not cause drunkenness, it all depends on the conditions of application. This is how it is with prospective and strategy : in order to move from anticipation to action, appropriation is a compulsory step.

For people to be really good at doing something they have to understand it. As Henri Fayol stressed : 'If to govern is to foresee, to obey is to understand'. Mary Parker Follett's famous first-class manager does not give the orders but, rather, instigates the initiatives which move towards implementing the orders he could have given. The quality of leaders is a determinant factor : without a good captain there can be no winning team.

During the course of our consultancy work in companies and public administrations we have come across a number of these first-class managers - more often (although not exclusively) in small organizations than in large ones and more often in companies in difficulty than in companies in apparent good health. When all is going well a company can afford the luxury of mediocre or unnecessarily domineering managers (a general should not fight his own army).

We shall present just a few cases because of their exemplary nature, without naming names. The careful reader will easily be able to locate them.

Firstly, there is the case of Sollac, which made a spectacular recovery in iron and steel making. In a few years it was able to emerge from the red, while remaining in the same business, simply by moving from a production logic to a commercial logic. Today it is the leading, most profitable European manufacturer of steel products, with over half of its production going to export.

According to Sollac's directors, almost 80 % of the increase in productivity achieved in recent years has been due to human and organizational factors. Among the levers used, were the company plan and shared vision, the development of a common culture, total quality, the customer action plan, training, and, more generally, the 'crisis' itself seized as an opportunity to leap forward, etc.

Another example of a remarkable recovery during the 1980s is a small company in the iron and steel making business : FFM (La Fabrique de Fer de Maubeuge). As the chairman proudly declared, 'What saved us was the fact that we had never had any state aid'. Here again, recovery was achieved without significant material investment, but with considerable reinforcement of non-material investment, mobilizing thinking around the themes of quality, flexibility, and responsibility, as well as innovation.

It was a joy to discover the Crédit Agricole de Haute Normandie, which showed us that the reality of the world in general and companies in particular sometimes exceeds the ideal fiction of books on strategy and management.

Here we met competent, open, listening and simply contented managers, surrounded by happy executives who were praising their bosses even behind their backs. We were also impressed by the high level of strategic culture. What a contrast with so many large organizations paralysed by their gigantism, where most internal energy is devoted to quarrels over territory, and battles between bosses for power.

There remains public administration. Our last example demonstrates our belief in people and our hope for the evolution of structures and behaviour. It concerns the French Ministry of Equipment, and more precisely the Moselle Departmental Director of Equipment (DDE). Faced with the new competitive challenges resulting from regionalization in France and the opening up of Europe, and despite its iron collar of administrative rules and regulations, the DDE set itself the task of inventing new ways of working.

It was a matter of doing better with fewer resources. The apparatus put in place comprised a whole panapoly of measures : keeping a look-out collectively by means of an observation network made up of every individual ; problem-solving groups ; training groups ; and quality circles aptly named ARC (Active, Responsible, Creative). So we can see that despite the administrative iron collar there do exist degrees of freedom, and these must be appropriated or even created.

The strengths of the above examples also constitute their weaknesses : a number of highly charismatic people were able, at the opportune moment, to stimulate the adhesion and even enthusiasm which saved the organization. They must take care not to depart prematurely and thus nip in the bud what are still fragile dynamics.

2. Yes to the plan and shared vision, no to its pitfalls

Let us declare our own belief straight away : it is better to devise a company plan and shared vision without saying so than to talk about it without really making one ; small concrete projects are better than one grand, illusory plan and shared vision, for the process of appropriating the plan and shared vision counts for more than the plan and shared vision itself.

We believe in the necessity of the plan and shared vision as a beneficial point around which to mobilize the company's intelligence, and as a decisive trump card in the search for competitiveness and excellence. This is precisely why we are afraid of seeing this 'passionate obligation' obliterated by unfortunate or desultory experiments.

Talk among managers, the desire for internal communication and the (real or supposed) genius of consultants are not enough to justify a company plan and shared vision or to ensure its success ; what is also required is serious initial reflection, real conviction at all levels and many precautions in its use. Fashion, for the company plan and shared vision, is not 'ready-to-wear' but 'made to measure' : it is up to each company to define the timing, forms and content of the plan and shared vision(s) which best suit it.

A company plan and shared vision normally comprises four aspects : a vision of the future ; collective resolve ; a system of shared values ; and major medium-term strategic objectives (cf Jacques Giroire 1985) :

- An ambitious future vision, in terms of main aims and overall objectives, which should be subject to broad debate. More than one main thrust is possible, but it is also necessary to take environmental uncertainties into account. For example, a large company may adopt the long-term objective of becoming the market leader in certain markets for certain products, services or techniques. Ambitions are often expressed openly and qualitatively. This is the indispensable role of dreams in helping to create reality.

- A collective resolve to maintain course even more firmly if the storm blows harder. This means that each partner must speak the same language and be open and responsible under all circumstances, including in conflictual situations. This resolve to attain objectives which correspond to corporate aims is everyone's business, to be adhered to at all times, and in a real and practical way at all levels.

PITFALLS TO AVOID IN A COMPANY PLAN
(Vision for the future)

1. *Lack of real content.*
In this case, the project is a communication gimmick for the directors, who are not really involving the company's vital forces in a process of reflection and collective questioning. There is thus the danger that those who respond to the initial appeal are demobilized for a considerable time. A good way of avoiding this trap is occasionally to undertake a company plan without saying so, and to set the process in motion without initially holding out bright prospects for the result.

2. *Considering the company plan as an end rather than a means.*
The main benefit of a company is that it is an opportunity for structured reflection and collective debate on the company's strengths and weakness in the face of the threats and opportunities of its present and future environments. For the project, as for the company plan, the process is more valuable than the result.

3. *Sub-contracting a 'ready-to-wear' company project* assembled in kit form by specialists outside the company who are experienced in the art of reducing complexity to simple, well-fitting images. If we wish to clarify too much, we are in danger of blinding ourselves. The idea of adopting an à la carte project based on the company's own culture can be attractive. However, is it reasonable to engage the company's future on the strength of a blueprint which is probably ephemeral and which may be debatable ? Would it not be more suitable to examine provocative changes in the environment, and changes in individuals' aspirations and behaviour ?
This type of examination, focused on connecting mechanisms and contrasting forces of change with forces fo inertia, is indispensable in order to arrive at an understanding of the inevitable resistances to change, and to identify the levers of action which are capable of bringing about the necessary transformation of structures and behaviour.

4. Setting up a company project in the hope of *avoiding the metamorphosis of structure and behaviour* which the project implies and which it will bring about. The company project imposes on managers and directors a real 'revolution of the mind' ; its aim is that authority should no longer be based on function and title, but on competence and ability to develop initiative and responsibility among subordinates. To say that the future belongs to flexible structures which are decentralized around projects, on a human scale, autonomous and responsible, is also to say that there will be fewer hierarchical levels, and consequently fewer managers.

If these pitfalls are not avoided, the company project is in danger of going out of fashion. This would be a shame for companies, which will have lost an opportunity and will have to look for other ways of initiating the necessary metamorphosis of structure and behaviour in the face of major change.

- A shared system of values among the company's partners with respect to : recognition of individual rôles and differences ; the virtues of dialogue and mutual comprehension ; dissemination of information ; mutual trust in responsible behaviour ; pride in belonging to the same team, in producing quality goods, in being competitive, and in playing a leading rôle in innovation in the face of technical, economic and social change.

- Some major objectives to be set as short- and medium-term priorities (such as self-financing, investment, market share, training, working conditions, etc) and also as longer-term priorities (eg, R&D, diversification, etc). As was expressed so well at the Crédit Agricole de Haute Normandie, 'Profit is not sufficient as an ambition ; however, one should keep an eye on the profitability of ambitions'.

In other words, a company plan and shared vision is not simply the declaration of aims ; it is also the expression of corporate resolve to reach these goals, the recognition of a shared system of values, and mobilization around these objectives, which are more fully accepted if the corresponding main aims have been clearly set out and have been the subject of broad debate.

3. Metamorphosis of structures and behaviour

Analysis of environmental changes must not lead us astray. If we train our projectors on externalities we run the risk of leaving the interior in the dark. It would be illusory to believe that the future of a company could depend solely on good external strategic choices without making any changes to internal structures and behaviour.

Mastering change is achieved by breaking habits and having the courage to face up to certain issues which are often avoided or evaded, such as :

- job security
- the adequacy of existing qualifications for meeting future needs
- effectiveness of systems of communication, training and research
- criteria for evaluating performance and promotion
- ways of designating and legitimizing managers and higher executives in the company
- the crisis in trade unionism : causes and consequences.

Should the company subordinate its strategy to the maintenance of existing manpower levels, structures and behaviour ? If the answer is yes, what developmental objectives should be favoured, what results should be expected from them, and what strategic deadlocks should be considered acceptable ? If the answer is no, on the other hand, what consequences will the demands of the chosen strategy have for manpower levels, qualifications and structures ? The fact that the question is being asked indicates an inclination to find the answer.

3.1. Adaptable or anticipatory structures ?

Ideally, structures should not only adapt to environmental developments but also anticipate them, for structural inertias necessarily give rise to a delay in adaptation.

This debate is not new. It was popularized by A. Chandler (1962), for whom adaptation of internal structures was achieved 'by trial and error', following changes in the environment (products, markets, technologies...). In such a process, the majority of companies submit to change rather than manage it. This delay effect means that structures are constantly inadequate to cope with an environment which is changing with ever increasing rapidity. Here we have the classic opposition between forces of change and forces of inertia (structures), which are the source of so many crises.

In the 1970s there was a realization that such rapid obsolescence of structures had to be avoided and that necessary internal changes had to be carried out with each new change in strategic direction. But structures take much longer to evolve than the environment. This is why Igor Ansoff proposed inverting Chandler's sequence of events. For him, internal evolution can precede external change and this is precisely what strategic management consists of : setting up structures through anticipation, not solely through adaptation.

Adaptive or anticipatory - this is still an open debate. The dual structure proposed by Ansoff - where new forms coexist with older ones - seems to us the most realistic option, especially as the evolution of structures depends not only on strategic and environmental imperatives, but is also the complex result of the firm's history and culture.

As D. J. Hall and M. A. Saias (1980) state 'Structures result from the complex interplay of factors other than strategy : culture, values, the past and present functioning of the organization, the history of successes and failures ... there is, therefore, no reason to subordinate structure to strategy'.

Behind the organizational structure there is a corporate concept covering its policy and objectives, its inherent priorities and power games. To be effective under these conditions, the structure must be adapted to the corporate culture and behaviour patterns. It is not possible to refer to structure without associating behaviour and management. There is no ideal structure and the most dynamic companies have simply found some kind of harmony between strategy, culture and structure.

Finally, in place of the much too linear theoretical diagram (I) of company behaviour, proposed by R. E. Caves (1980), we propose substituting diagram (II), where all relationships are reciprocal. If future performance depends on harmony between strategy, culture and structure, past performance in turn conditions strategy, is wedded to structure, and shapes culture.

It is commonplace to recall that formulae which enable companies that are already performing well to improve their results still further are not necessarily suitable for companies in difficulty : generally, a balanced meal for a healthy person has little in common with the diet that an ill person should be given.

For a company in difficulty, it is rarely appropriate to behave as if it were in good health, if only because the economic and financial situation is different. On the other hand, companies which have always had an easy time are more fragile than others when difficulties suddenly emerge. There are several possible explanations for this phenomenon : times of hardship are character building, and individuals are self-selected, whereas easy times hardly encourage a capacity for reactivity. In addition, it requires a different type of management to manage growth and to overcome crisis.

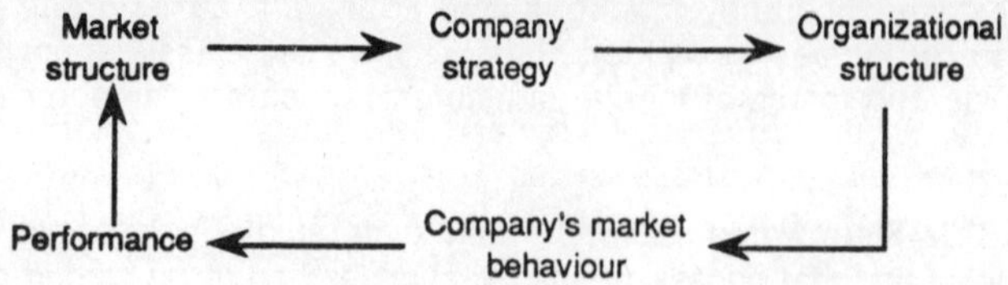

Diagram I

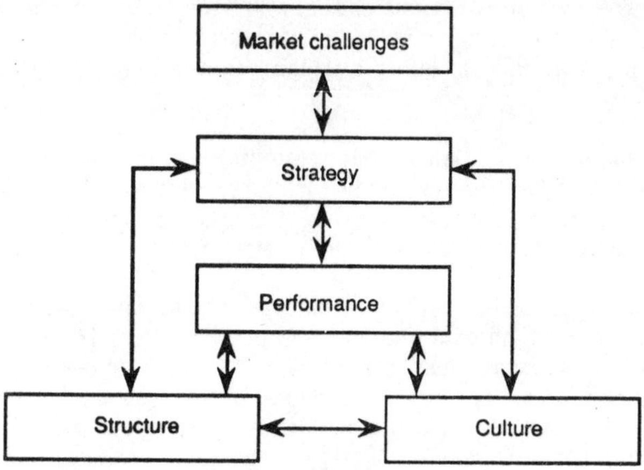

Diagram II

3.2. Simple, lean structures

How can this harmony between strategy, culture and structure best be realized ?

First of all, we note that in the structures-power-environment trilogy, power is attacked by environmental developments and defends itself by means of structures. One characteristic of structures is that they become the property of those who set them up, and this is a source of rigidity.

Any structure risks sclerosis if it is not regularly subjected to a reorganization exercise, redistributing responsibilities and power. As far as possible, habit-breaking factors, as mentioned above, should be introduced into structures. Somewhere between a state of rigidity-sclerosis or unrest-alibi, which give rise to anxiety and ineffectualness, it is necessary to find the appropriate speed of transformation which can respond to environmental developments without pointlessly upsetting established equilibria. The search for harmony presupposes an intentional step which takes into account time and its inertia - inertias are weaker if one is dealing with simple, lightweight structures.

Companies are confronting an increasingly complex competitive and strategic environment. Increasing the size of the company and consequently its internal complexity is not the best way to respond to external complexity. For a company to function well it must remain simple and comprehensible to all concerned.

Operational structures (responsibilities allocated by product line and market structure) seem to be preferable to functional structures (responsibilities allocated by major function : design, methods, purchasing, production, sales), and the least effective structure is to attempt to cross the two with so-called matrix organizational structures. The smaller the structure the better its health. Not only is 'small beautiful', it can also be profitable. The organization of a company into small, human-scale operational units is the *sine qua non* for an ability to adapt constantly, and the key to innovation. A system of shared values within the framework of a company plan and shared vision is essential to act as living cement between these small units, for if flexibility is to be effective it requires a certain rigour.

3.3. Strategic centralization and operational decentralization

A form of the 'subsidiarity principle' could be applied to the company : decentralize everything that can be decentralized, and centralize everything that has to be centralized. In order to attain this strategic centralization and operational decentralization, rigour and flexibility have to be reconciled ; this means the coexistence of a firm managerial line and maximum individual autonomy.

Here we find once again, implicitly and under another name, the well-known debate on decentralization. This signifies more than autonomy and delegated responsibility ; it presupposes a certain amount of central coordination for the overall coherence and effectiveness of the company, without at the same time transforming decentralization into deconcentration.

Decentralized structures are better adapted to complex, dispersed and evolving situations. The functional set-up for this type of structure may require a preliminary centralizing operation. The keys to successful decentralization are :

- strongly to assert the central managerial line on certain fundamental values (quality of production and service, basic internal policy rules) ;

- to base individual and group autonomy and responsibilities on rules that are clear and respected (negotiation of objectives, evaluation of results, profit sharing, sanctions, etc).

Responsibility, for example, means that quality control is incumbent upon every individual, and is not the sole responsibility of a specialist department. Autonomy also means the development of a certain amount of internal competition.

In view of the complexity of the decisions to be taken and the aspiration of the majority towards better control over all aspects of their functions, traditional Taylorian compartmentalization needs to be questioned. Gathering experts together around the same object (such as a product or a resource), and sharing common objectives, strategies and information are essential. One must avoid diluting responsibility, however, whilst at the same time choosing structures which encourage a synergy of skills.

3.4. Strategic consequences of environmental changes

Without claiming to be exhaustive, we have considered nine main trends which characterize changes in the general corporate environment and we have shown some of the consequences for corporate organization and strategy. We shall comment briefly on the following table.

Environment	Strategic consequences
1. Uncertainty	Flexibility Versatility Actor's project
2. Interdependence and complexity	Global vision and simple structures
3. International imbalances	Regulation by 'world systems'
4. Globalization	Redeployment of activities Internationalization of management
5. Slow, irregular and unequal growth	Battle for market sectors, productivity, quality, diversification
6. Technological change +	Automation
7. Deregulation	New competitors
8. Economy of diversity Mass production of variety +	'Small is profitable' Responsible, autonomous teams
9. Autonomy, diversification	Entrepreneurs, intrapreneurs
END OF HABITS, MENTAL REVOLUTION	

Note : the reader looking for a deeper analysis may refer to Chapter X.

The uncertainty of the environment certainly demands flexibility and versatility, but also reinforces the need for a plan and shared vision, if only in order to take one's bearings in relation to the objectives.

The growing interdependence of phenomena makes understanding them a more complex task. In addition, action increasingly requires a global vision. In order to tackle this environmental complexity, it is no use equipping oneself with complicated structures ; simple, lean forms are far preferable.

The persistence of international imbalances (geopolitical, demographic, environmental, economic...) and the absence of global regulators are partially compensated for by new forms of regulation, new 'world systems', to coin Fernand Braudel's phrase. Thus, the international financial network functions 24 hours a day, from one end of the globe to the other. Multiple international disturbances and non-tariff barriers to trade have not prevented a trend towards globalization of activities (processes-products-markets) : every year since 1945 exports of manufactured products have increased faster than production. Companies have to deploy their activities at the global level, which is also happening through a degree of internationalization of management.

Three trends (slow and irregular growth, technological change in processing, and deregulation) are combining to organize competition and the battle for market sectors becomes the search for the best quality-price ratio... Companies have simultaneously to diversify, to automate in order to boost productivity where possible, and to confront new competitors.

The human and organizational factor is crucial for competitiveness, so it is wise to take advantage of new information technologies and communication networks to move towards being 'small, beautiful and profitable'. We have entered the age of the economy of diversity ; in other words, the future trend is towards mass production of variety and small-scale profitable production. This techno-economic evolution is taking place in step with the transformation of individual needs and aspirations towards more autonomy and diversification. For companies this means setting up small, autonomous teams of responsible intrapreneurs. Thus new forms of management, attitudes and behaviour are gradually emerging at all levels of the organization.

MIDES* : the beginnings of a mental revolution at Renault in 1983.

1. Mides : a necessity

The performance of a company is directly related to its organization, its management, and to the prices and quality of the products and services it puts on the market. Experience today shows that these parameters are largely determined by the dynamics of working relationships and quality of life within the company.

To remain in the top league of world manufacturers means constantly improving our competitiveness (better prices, better quality). This depends on our simultaneously taking into account different developments : in technology, in the economy and in business...

...But also and above all on our capacity for innovation and adaptation, ie on the way in which each one of us transforms the life of the company through our work, thus facilitating the company's development in a changing world.

2. Mides : a resolve

If we do not immediately mobilize our energy, in all sectors and at all levels of the company, the world will change without us and perhaps against our interests.

Because we want it to change with us, because our future is our business, we have to develop within the company, through our daily activity of preparing for our future, a widespread, constant, concerted effort : we have to learn to live and to work differently.

3. Mides : a state of mind

'The Mides spirit' is based on a number of simple principles :

Openness and anticipation

Understanding better what is happening around us and knowing how to distinguish between the constraints and the opportunities in our environment, in order to influence them or adapt ourselves to confront them.

Pluralism and concerted action.

Recognizing and accepting our differences, taking conflicting opinions into account, knowing how to listen -these form the basis of concerted action. Knowing how not to abandon options or responsibilities in the course of concerted action- this is the basis of relationships within the company.

Method and imagination

Stating problems clearly before trying to resolve them, promoting individual self-expression, stimulating imagination and creativity, displaying all possible choices and their advantages and drawbacks, associating all the actors involved at all levels of analysis and decision-making. These are the principles which guarantee that responses correspond closely to the problems and needs of those concerned.

Autonomy and responsiblity

Taking better account of people's aspirations in the practical organization of daily work (the desire to manage their time better, to work in small groups, to know what we are manufacturing, etc).

Basing authority on the capacity to motivate people and unite their skills.

These are the principles which guarantee everyone an area of autonomy in keeping with the responsibilities conferred upon them.

* Mides stands for 'Mutations Industrielles et Dynamique Economique et Sociale' (Industrial change and economic and social dynamics). This box summarizes the content of the Mides brochure N°1, issued in 1984 by Renault. This operation to promote a collective awareness of change was not able to be completed, owing to difficulties experienced by Renault in 1984 and a change of Chairman. However, it played a useful role in the development of the internal company mentality, and involved almost 3000 people. The operation, led by Jean Lagasse, then the highly charismatic Director of Research, deserves a place among the management classics.

3.5. From an end to habits to a mental revolution

Developments in the environment require that a company has a capacity for rapid response and flexibility, which is largely dependent on structures. From now on, structures will have not only to adapt to environmental developments but also to anticipate them, for structural inertia causes a delay in adaptation. The future belongs to flexible structures, which are decentralized around projects, on a human scale, and autonomous. Autonomy means responsiblity, and consequently being subject to market sanctions or to assessment of performances in relation to objectives.

This trend towards the appropriation of the company by individuals or groups of intrapreneurs demands new qualities from executives and managers. For many companies in difficulty, the shipwreck is due more to internal management inadequacies than to the storm which is raging outside. What other explanation can there be for the fact that other companies thrive under the same conditions ?

Among these managerial inadequacies, absence of power features just a much as constant power struggles which paralyse action. It is not so much the notion of power which is in question as its misuse : the pleasure of dominating others is all too often sought as an end in itself, to the detriment of the power of domination over oneself, and the power of creativity and realization of projects.

Let us reiterate Mary Parker Follet's message : the real power of a leader cannot be measured in terms of his or her domination over others, but in terms of his or her ability to develop initiative and responsibility among subordinates. This obliges executives and managers to participate in a true 'mental revolution' which aims no longer to base authority on function and job titles, but on competence and the ability to motivate.

Authority in general is the renouncing of autonomy, which is conceded to someone else in exchange for something (eg, salary, security, expertise). It is a contract. The authority of someone at a particular level in a hierarchy must be based on competence, an ability to synthesize, and plenty of responsibility and autonomy. Authority is open to criticism when it is not based on competence or when it is exercised in an abusive way. The notion of 'little chiefs' represents abusive authority which is no longer adapted to fellow workers' qualifications and type of work. It is more an authority to delegate based on superiority in the hierarchy than authority through competence : it forms a filter, and poses the problem of possible recourse against abuse of authority. Such possible measures include the following : definition of functions, the formal right (or not) to appeal to level N+2, having recourse to trade unions, quality circles, office or shopfloor committees.

On the other hand, an executive who can base his authority on competence and motivation can let his fellow workers take the initiatives ; he no longer needs even to negotiate objectives, as these emerge naturally. The principle of subsidiarity is stated at every level of the organization : this operational decentralization presupposes contracts over objectives, and evaluation and control a posteriori. With this new way of allocating responsibility in terms of skills, staff can receive higher remuneration as the number of hierarchical levels is reduced (the German model). In order to install such a model, which is open to communication and change, the size of production units is important (not exceeding 300 people per industrial or administrative unit, for example, is a target which some companies already aim for).

Responsiblity is no longer hierarchical but collegiate ; however, neither the boss nor authority have disappeared. The manager commands respect solely for himself and his ability to mobilize, arbitrate and successfully manage human conflicts and economic risks in a positive way. He is coopted rather than appointed. Management is open and plural ; in other words it no longer questions traditions, beliefs and values but relies on them in order to adapt itself to national and regional particularities, like a fish in water.

The whole organization of the company is feeling the effects of this mental revolution. The company is a vast arena of social experimentation. The rules of the bureaucratic game are being swept away by executives who wish to take on the same responsibilities within the company as they have in society. Economic effectiveness is not incompatible with aspirations when it is achieved via autonomy and, consequently, initiative and responsibility.

The new role of management

	YESTERDAY	TOMORROW
SCALE	LARGE	SMALL
TASKS	DIVIDED	COMPLEX
COMPETENCES	LIMITED	POLYVALENT
AUTHORITY	DERIVED FROM STATUS	DERIVED FROM COMPETENCE
RELATIONSHIPS	HIERARCHICAL DIRECTIVE	AUTONOMOUS: RESPONSIBLE COMMUNICATION
SUCCESS	THROUGH DEVOTION	THROUGH INITIATIVE AND REACTIVITY
OBJECTIVES CONTRACTS	IMPOSED	NEGOTIATED, STIMULATED
ACTIONS	CONTROL A PRIORI	CONTROL A POSTERIORI

But how to reconcile aspirations towards autonomy and security ?

Security is found mainly in large private companies or in public administrations or companies, which are hierarchical systems par excellence ; autonomy, on the other hand, is found mainly in less formal, more exposed forms of work, such as self-employment or craft companies.

From the point of view of social innovation, all possibilities are worth exploring, except those which lay claim to universality but which in reality only make change uniform, thus threatening to constrain change or introduce new rigidities. The flexibility we dream of involves an reexamination of non-reversible career paths, promotion by seniority, and the principle of increased responsibilities with age ; responsibilities, and the advantages and disadvantages that go along with them, are thus dissociated from age and cease to be the object of social envy, as a symbol of power. New castes emerge, but this time they are alive, open and constantly renewed, because they are made up of people who have proved themselves socially and economically. Having once passed a highly competitive examination no longer counts for much.

We should not dream too much ! The ravages of 'diploma disease' have only just begun. It will probably take major upheavals before a new division of work is established, breaking the sequential rhythm of education, work and retirement, and setting up flexible, alternated formulae : for example, each year of work could entitle people to free time to dispose of as they wished, both later in life and also at 30 or 40 years of age, in order to become a student again, to travel, to educate their children or to devote themselves to any other activity that interested them.

In the meantime training, in this instance renamed 'intellectual investment', has become fashionable. It is legitimate to ask ourselves whether the educational mirage has not simply replaced the technological mirage of the early 1980s. As Pierre Caspar remarks, (1989) : 'Spending a lot on training does not necessarily mean making real investments'. Training is certainly essential for the mental revolution, but only so long as it promotes, as far as possible, collective self-education, for it is by teaching that we learn ; in addition, periods of passive education need to be abolished, and training needs to be accompanied by action which allows theoretical knowledge rapidly to be accompanied by action which allows theoretical knowledge rapidly to be put into practice.

In fact, any training which is not followed up by action is wasted effort. The function of internal training should also be entrusted to the best staff, for example to executives who are awaiting promotion, as at IBM. Without exception, taking on the function of trainer should be no more than one (or several) phase(s) of one's career.

How are we to distinguish those companies where the mental revolution is already under way from those where it has not yet begun ? We propose a simple test : ask informally, at the beginning of the week, 'How are things ?' If the answer is 'As you'd expect for a Monday', the company is in a bad way. Happiness cannot be comparmentalized. To be happy in society, a person needs also to flourish at work, and the reverse is also true ; the company cannot ignore the issues of the society around it.

In the face of the major changes taking place as we near the end of the century, people must agree to acquire new attitudes and practices. The metamorphosis of structures and behaviour has already begun. It is up to each one of us to decide whether we wish to submit to or to lead the mental revolution - whether or not we wish to change the present by conspiring for the future.

CHAPTER X

THE DAWN OF THE 21st CENTURY

1. Multiple uncertainties linked to the absence of a regulator

2. A quasi-certainty : Europtimism

2.1. From Europessimism to Europtimism
2.2. Europe 1993, the dream and the reality

3. Eleven likely trends

3.1. Demographic imbalance and South-North and East-North migratory flows
3.2. Threats to the physical environment and the negative legacy of past growth
3.3. A lawless and turbulent international environment
3.4. Slow, irregular, unequal and interdependent growth
3.5. New energy price rises, beneficial if they are gradual
3.6. The flood of new technologies : a new competitive order
3.7. Deregulation associated with new international and regional regulation
3.8. Economic competition on a global scale with states playing a key rôle
3.9. Decline in industrial jobs and rise of service industries
3.10. Crisis of the Welfare State
3.11. New forms of exclusion

4. Three major uncertainties

4.1. Will the rate of diffusion of new technologies be as rapid as forecast ?
4.2. Metamorphosis of work and employment
4.3. Evolution of lifestyles and social organization in developed countries

5. The lie of the land in the year 2000, in brief

5.1. Probable trends
5.2. Major uncertainties
5.3. Possible discontinuities (examples)

Without for a moment claiming to construct real scenarios of the environment, it seemed useful to us to throw some light on strategic thought through a synthesis of the probable trends, major uncertainties and risks of discontinuity for the developed countries in the 1990s.

This synthesis does not claim to be exhaustive. Some questions would require in-depth study, which we have not yet been able to undertake. Among the areas not tackled the ex-Soviet Union and Eastern Europe stand out. This omission has at least spared us the diagnostic errors which are so common on these topics.

Although a deadlock situation is impossible in the geopolitical arena, it is more evident in economics, in so far as the ex-socialist countries represent in total less than 10% of international trade. For the same reasons, economic questions relating to the Third World countries will receive little attention here. Whether we like it or not, by the year 2000 three-quarters of the world's solvent demand will be in the developed countries of the North America-Europe-East and Southeast Asia triad. Our attention will focus particularly on the political, demographic, social and environmental aspects which could have greater repercussions in the developed countries[1].

One could question this rather restrictive choice of coverage. We would emphasize that, although it may be limited, this area remains very broad and that 'first we must put our own house in order'. As regards the developing countries, we consider the concept of the 'Third World' to be more or less obsolete. It is not wealth of natural resources or the extent of external domination which makes the difference between nations, but the mobilization of the population and the quality of their leaders. Too often Third World aid only serves to prolong the lives of corrupt regimes and translates into a chain of perverse effects. For example, food aid ends up modifying consumption habits or gives rise to a collapse in prices - ie, it has quite the opposite effect to that which is necessary to stimulate local production. In short, we despair of certain Third World countries, and the principle of non-interference, although it allows us to denounce apartheid in South Africa, throws a chaste veil over the male-female racism which prevails in the Islamic republics.

Thus, the right to difference, taken to the extreme, throws into question those apparently accepted universal principles. In such a context, the best service one can render certain peoples is not to help their leaders to maintain their oppression, their obscurantism or quite simply their wastage.

Europe as such will receive specific attention, since we devote a whole section to this theme. This paper is divided into five parts of unequal length, but logically following on one from another. In the introduction we set out the multiple geopolitical uncertainties linked to the lack of an international regulator. Second, we identify a

[1] In the concluding tables, we have considered the changes as a whole without restricting these to geographic regions.

quasi-certainty: Europtimism. Third, we note eleven probable trends in the national and international environments of the 1990s. Fourth, we note three major uncertainties. As a conclusion, we propose a list synthesizing the probable trends, major uncertainties and risks of possible discontinuity beyond the year 2000.

1. Multiple uncertainties linked to the absence of a regulator

The world is changing ; the geopolitical, monetary, energy, technological, economic and social environments which we will face in the next 10 or 15 years will also undergo profound upheavals. By definition, prospective thinking up to 1995 is easier than up to the year 2000. Notably, it enables us to disregard the consequences of the main change in the coming decades, which is of a demographic nature - at the beginning of the next century the European Community will have fewer inhabitants than the Muslim countries of the South Mediterranean basin, whilst the population of Brazil and Nigeria combined will be comparable to that of Europe.

Looking to 1995, leading experts rightly put forward hypotheses which would have seemed improbable some years ago :

- a low inflation rate of less than 5% ;
- positive real interest rates ;
- relatively low growth.

Reading between the lines, however, one sees that these hypotheses are fragile : independently of the 1990 Gulf crisis, one could expect new oil shocks between now and 2000. Furthermore, growth could be sustained for several years on vivid memories of the recession of the early 1980s; but fundamentally the conditions for a lasting and steady recovery of the world economy are not all present. In an increasingly interdependent world, the lack of international regulation makes itself cruelly felt. A new 'world economy' (to use Fernand Braudel's term) will not take over tomorrow.

The absolute value of power does not prevent the relative decline of power itself. The USA today represents only 22% of world GNP and 37% of the total GNP of industrialized market economy nations, compared with 40% and 57%, respectively, in 1955. The USA is no longer sufficiently powerful to impose itself as the regulator (of a bipolar world), but is still sufficiently powerful to play a disruptive role. It retains a minority freeze on the world system and is thus capable of preventing any other regulator taking its place (in a multipolar world)[2].

In other words, fluctuations in US economic policy could themselves be enough to trigger off worldwide inflation again. In the meantime, we share the uncertainty expressed by some economists over exchange rates, with the dollar between 4FF and 10FF. We may regret the scale of this uncertainty, but it would be irresponsible not to take account of it.

---

[2] This theme of the relative decline of the USA follows on from our analysis in *'United States: renaissance or concealed decline"* Futures, June 1985

For its part, Japan has no desire to become the centre of a new 'world economy'. The myth of Japan at the centre of a Pacific Rim which would definitively relegate the Atlantic Old World, and consequently Europe, to its periphery is without foundation :

- at most, from now until 2000, Japan will account for only 12% of global GNP, as compared with 10% today - ie, roughly half that of the USA or Europe. Certainly the growth of the Southeast Asian NICs is spectacular, but it is primarily a catching up phenomenon (GNP per capita in South Korea is six times less than in Japan) ;

- Pax Nipponica will not take over from the defunct Pax Americana, for, in any case, Japan lacks the military power. US-Japanese co-management of the global system would be a more realistic hypothesis, on the condition, however, that the USA managed to reindustrialize. The Japanese are working on this through investment, but they believe less and less in the USA's ability to maintain its leadership, and criticisms of US economic and monetary policies, which are incapable of ensuring exchange rate stability, are increasingly intense.

The Japanese might in fact find much more responsible partners in Europe, particularly in Germany. Will Japan's slogan become *'Out of America, into Europe'*? This is an open question. We should already applaud Japan's renewed interest, which gives European countries an additional stimulus to modernize their production systems.

Due allowance being made, some strategic and military giants are economic dwarfs (eg, Russia) and some economic giants (eg, Japan, Germany) are military dwarfs. This imbalance is a source of tension. The bipolar world no longer exists, but will the multipolar world be able to emerge without profound upheaval ?

In fact, there is a risk that the combined effects of demographic and political impacts, unequal rates of development, growing nationalism and the absence of regulators will engender conflicts and feed a climate of international insecurity. In these conditions the management of growing interdependence has little chance of working by means of dialogue, foresight and planning.

Defence issues are central. Will the West and the East combine their forces to become the police force of the UN ? Will Europe remain oriented towards the Atlantic for defence and towards the EC for its economy ? The opening up of the East European nations to the market economy has not yet been achieved. An eventual failure of internal reforms in the ISC (Independent State Community) would be extremely serious for Europe. In history external war has often served as an outlet for a country's internal contradictions. Russian military potential remains colossal and Europe should not let down its guard.

Let us propose a medium-case scenario : as a counterpart to increasingly heavy Western aid, Russia could refocus on the internal problems of ISC republics and leave the USA and its allies the task of plugging the breaches which will inevitably erupt among Third World countries. Since it is impossible to eliminate uncertainty it is necessary to master its consequences. Country risk is an evolutionary key variable, which demands prospective thought. Taking account of uncertainty also means not seeking salvation in an ideal development of the situation, but preparing oneself for survival in the most unfavourable circumstance (the worst-case scenario).

2. A quasi-certainty : Europtimism

The Old World has not uttered its last word, as one would believe.

2.1. From Europessimism to Europtimism

What has happened to the Cassandras who, only yesterday, were predicting the inexorable decline of Europe ? With the centre of world gravity shifting almost inevitably from the Atlantic to the Pacific, the Old World was, according to them, doomed to become a peripheral zone, tagging behind the United States and Japan.

In fact, it was only a few years ago, at the moment of the flash in the pan of the American recovery and when the dollar was at its highest, that it was almost automatic to point to the technology gap in Europe, Europe's weak economic growth, endemic unemployment and social and political rigidities. It also appeared as though the word "crisis" had disappeared from the North American vocabulary and was replaced by "Euro-pessimism".

The analysts of Euro-sclerosis had forgotten that a crisis can be a harbinger of hope provided that it jolts a nation into overcoming the forces of inertia and habit which slow change and adaptation.

It is in this manner that the majority of the European countries have learned over the past few years to win the battle against inflation by reducing wage escalators, apply the value added tax in a manner more favourable to business, acquire flexibility (although still insufficient) in matters of employment and salary, and establish limits on protectionism.

We have seven good reasons to hope. This belief is in particular built upon the following considerations :

1) Like a sea serpent, the theme of the decline of Europe resurfaces periodically. Already in the '60s a false alarm was sounded with *"The American Challenge"* by J.-J. Servan-Schreiber. Nonetheless, Europe experienced a rate of growth even stronger than that of the United States during the period between 1967 and 1973. Since then, economic growth in the two regions has been comparable ;

2) Europe has maintained its position as a turn-table of international trade : more than one third of international commerce is conveyed through Europe, and Europe is the principal supplier and the principal channel for trade for most of the other regions of the world (except Japan) ;

3) Even if one excludes in this instance the United Kingdom, it is clear that European countries have had the good sense to significantly reduce energy dependence :

up to 53% in France and Germany. Europe has thus done better than Japan which continues to be dependent for over 80 % of its energy ;

4) Europe also had the good sense, with the European Monetary System, to endow itself with relative monetary stability in a turbulent international environment ;

5) Europe possesses the strongest scientific potential in the world and showed with the Airbus and Ariane that cooperative research and development can be profitable ;

6) Industrial renovation in the Old World is being accompanied by a higher level of investment and higher productivity gains than are being realized in the United States (this is the counterpart of less job creation). Europe had the sense to gain strategic positions in key industrial sectors (aeronautics, space, nuclear, communication), and it also reinforced its place in traditional sectors (agriculture, chemicals, textiles) ;

7) Last but not least, the socio-cultural diversity of the European countries, often seen as a barrier to Europe's cohesiveness and as an element of weakness, represents a potential advantage for adapting in the face of future uncertainty. The odds are that the tours organized for leaders in the direction of California and Japan are now turning towards Southern Germany and Northern Italy.

2.2. Europe 1993, the dream and the reality

Europe, the greatest (solvent) market in the world, is put forward as the new El Dorado for European enterprises in the 1990s. The Euro-pessimism so prevalent until the mid-1980s is no longer in fashion. Europe had previously seemed to be stagnating in a phase of decline and rigidity, incapable of emerging from crisis and unemployment ; the world's focal point was supposedly shifting from the Atlantic to the Pacific. The strong dollar and the Japanese economic triumph were irrefutable evidence of this apparent shift. But today, Europe, the world's leading trading power, has once again become the economic focus for the end of the 20th century. What has happened?

The announcement of the great internal market of 1993 did not have an immediate effect. Indeed, the signing of the Single European Act by the European Council of heads of state in December 1986 in Luxembourg passed almost unnoticed, with the Council's deliberations marked by dissension and apparent failure. This historical context has been strikingly analysed by Jacques Nemrod[3].

In Nemrod's book we learn that in addition to the Single European Act there is also a Final Act (which is never publicly mentioned), composed of 20 declarations, some made jointly and some made unilaterally, which express many reservations.

---

[3] Nemrod J. (1987) : "*Le mal européen*", Rivages les Echos, Paris. See also Godet M. "*Europe: the dream and reality*", Futures, April 1989

Among the joint texts adopted we find that : *"Fixing the date of 31 December 1992 does not have any automatic juridical effects"*. Reservations are also expressed, notably by West Germany and the UK ; these reservations are concerned with maintaining national sovereignty over areas such as health, consumer protection, the environment, and so on. Nemrod states that *"Most of the infringements of the principle of free circulation of goods rest on these pretexts... if we do not change anything, why do we wish to persuade people that everything is going to change ?"*.

In fact, the Treaty of Rome in 1957 envisaged the full realization of a Common Market by 1 January 1970. It is therefore highly unlikely that on 1 January 1993 the great European internal market will be fully realized. Nevertheless, the goal of "Europe 1992" plays a beneficial mobilizing role, since it encourages people to think about coming changes, and about habits which will have to be called into question.

The road to the realization of these ambitions is now harder than ever. The easiest part has been done, and in order to achieve further progress, states will have to agree to give up part of their national sovereignty, which does not seem likely. For instance, Germany will never accept the idea of a Central European Bank whose operations would to a greater or lesser degree be influenced by political forces. The Germans do not wish to import inflation at any price, and they already feel they are paying more than their due for Europe.

Limiting the costs

It is probable that the internal market will not be achieved in the short term. While awaiting the putative benefits, we should take care to limit the costs of a single Europe. The establishment of a single market with universally accepted norms could benefit Japanese and US businesses first, which, moreover, will enjoy dominant positions in their own countries with complete impunity. The benefits of the European market must not be bestowed on the rest of the world without compensatory measures. New competition within Europe must be balanced with greater protection from external competition.

Let us therefore take care that the Euro-illusion does not sow the seeds of disillusionment, otherwise the mobilization of minds could turn against its initial objective.

3. Eleven likely trends

At the heart of the numerous uncertainties bearing down on the future of Western societies, several very probable trends can be discerned :

- Demographic imbalance and South-North and East-North migratory flows
- Threats to the physical environment and the negative legacy of past growth
- A lawless and turbulent international environment
- Slow, irregular, unequal and interdependent growth
- New energy price rises, beneficial if they are gradual

- The flood of new technologies : a new competitive order
- Deregulation associated with new international and regional regulation
- Economic competition on a global scale with states playing a key role
- Decline in industrial jobs and rise of service industries
- Crisis of the Welfare State
- New forms of exclusion

3.1. Demographic imbalances and South-North and East-North migratory flows

A population explosion in the poorest countries, and relative, followed by absolute, population decline in the richest countries, this is the marked trend which, if it continues for two or three more decades, will alter the map of the world and cause upheaval in our societes. By 2020, for example, the population of Europe will be comparable to that of Nigeria or Brazil. In 1990 the population on the southern shores of the Mediterranean exceeded that of the northern shores ; in 2030 if current trends continue, ie, without discontinuity, it will be twice as great.

The near-stagnation of population levels in the developed countries is the result of a fall in birth-rates which began in the mid-1960s in both the West and the East. The USA, Japan and Europe are no longer securing the replacement of generations and are ageing in the face of Third World countries which are increasingly young and densely populated. The prospects of migration waves coming from Eastern countries will certainly increase the pressure to control and limit the flows, and pose new problems to East-West relationships.

Beyond the inevitable questions concerning pension provisions and health expenditure, it is the problems of integrating people of the 'third' and 'fourth' ages which will be raised (will we be able to continue excluding people from economic activity, through retirement, when they can expect to live for another 20 or 30 years ?). At stake is the capacity of our societies to demonstrate dynamism and imagination in the face of increasingly complex global problems.

Of course these projections are not forecasts and are unlikely to correspond to future reality, if only because of migratory pressures. By 2030, some of today's minorities could represent one-fifth of the total population in countries such as Germany, France or the UK. Is this a passing phenomenon or a lasting concern ?

3.2. Threats to the physical environment and the negative legacy of past growth

The environment once again is the focus of attention, and it has taken accidents like Seveso, Three Mile Island and, especially Chernobyl to mobilize opinion. Is this a passing phenomenon or a lasting concern ?

At the start of the 1980s it was believed that the environmental policies of the preceding decade had borne fruit. The improvement in air and water quality, facilitated by resituating certain primary activities which were among the most polluting (chemicals, steel-making) gave the (illusory) impression that most environmental problems could be solved. Today this calm assurance is no longer apparent, for several major future environmental problems have burst onto the scene and are fuelling a number of controversies. What are they ? What should we make of them ?

Firstly, it is thought that the regular increase (by over 10% in the last 25 years) in the levels of carbon dioxide in the atmosphere will gradually cause the atmosphere to become warmer (the greenhouse effect). Estimates of average temperature increase give a range of between +2 C and +6 C between now and the middle of the next century ; this would not be sufficient to cause a melting of polar ice, but could increase rainfall in certain regions such as the Mediterranean and could even cause some deserts to recede. Will yesterday's worries come to be considered as a hope for tomorrow ? Although most experts are in agreement over the trend, they are much more divided over the degree of significance of the phenomenon and the scale of its eventual consequences (the same applies to the ozone layer). The subject demands reflection and thought needs to be given to regional agricultural specializations which could find themselves overturned.

Secondly, the degradation of the environment in the Third World is a very worrying phenomenon because it will affect the daily lives of hundreds of millions of people. The unconsidered development of human activities, unplanned demographic and urban explosions, excessive deforestation, overexploitation of land, the perverse effects of irrigation (soil salinization) - all these trends hold the beginnings of a number of crises : over water, firewood and arable land. This environmental degradation in the countries of the South will only aggravate the consequences of certain natural phenomena such as drought and floods (see below).

Thirdly, the risk of a reduction in biological diversity is severe, owing to the rapid rate of disappearance of animal and plant species, particularly in the tropical forests, whose still considerable surface area is expected to shrink dramatically (by as much as one-third between now and the end of the century). Here again, it is information that is lacking ; all those spectacular figures such as 'one million of the 5-10 million species or living organisms will disappear' (Global 2000, 1980) are almost meaningless : how can we appreciate a reduction in stock which seems to be five times smaller than the margin of error on the size of the stock itself ? It is the stock of species -ie, our heritage- which we have to understand better and record in order to preserve the future by conserving threatened stock.

Fourthly, acid rain and its catastrophic effects on the lakes and forests of Europe and North America is a typical example of a problem identified long ago, but without foreseeing preventative action nor even enough research to allow the real causes to be identified - they still remain the subject of controversy. Some scientists believe it would be unreasonable to set up expensive control systems which would have no effect on this phenomenon of transborder pollution, whose sources are diffused and multiple (eg, exhaust fumes). Conversely, some ecologists fear that proof of links between causes and effects will not become evident until it is too late: after all, 25% of German forests were affected before there was any reaction.

Environment and the Third World :
after the looting, the massacre

In the coming decades Third World countries will reap the harvest of the counterproductivity of previous output in many fields. One could call this "the Aswan effect", after the Aswan dam in Egypt, where there now appear to be so many problems of such magnitude that present and future drawbacks (soil salinization, diminished downstream fertility due to decreased siltation from flooding, a drastic fall in fish catches in the Nile delta...) could sweep away the benefits derived from irrigation in the past.

Bad or over-exploitation of land, together with soil erosion, salinization and calcification, will bring about a gradual spread of desertification everywhere. According to some estimates the increased spread of desert regions in the world could amount to an area the size of France between now and the end of the century. Some countries, in order to pay food and energy bills and to service their debts, have no option but to export primary materials (ores, wood, tropical products) and industrial products. They are forced to overexploit and irreversibly destroy their stock of natural resources.

Thus, at the current rate of exploitation, 30 % of tropical forests will have disappeared between now and the end of the century. The prospects are particularly worrying as regards firewood since, by the year 2000, demand could be 25 % higher than the supply normally available. In underdeveloped countries, confronted with considerable demographic, urban and social problems, there is a great risk that we shall see environmental problems taking a back seat as an unaffordable luxury.

In particular, anarchic urbanization will put extra pressure on space and we must expect a quadrupling of urbanized areas at the expense of agricultural areas. Coastal regions (60-80 % of which depend on fishing) and forested areas are the most vulnerable.

The situation is expected to deteriorate because industrialization and hunger give rise to a rural exodus (aid always arrives in the towns first), not to mention the fact that having a large family is protection against poverty and unemployment (when jobs are scarce, having several children increases the chances of securing one or several sources of income for the extended family).

Poverty, violence, insecurity, disease - this will be the lot of an ever-increasing number of human beings crowded into enormous megalopolises (about 30 million inhabitants in Mexico City in the year 2000). It is not difficult to imagine the scale of the problems posed to urban living conditions and environmental conditions : pollution is the price of poverty.

Finally, some of the environmental problems which are emerging today are a result of the vulnerability and negative fallout of environmental protection policies carried out up until now : we would point to the damage caused by filtering devices, the concentration of treated waste, the transfer and diffusion of pollution. We should also mention the consumption-destruction of certain protected spaces such as overexploited nature parks, not to mention the widespread invasion of open spaces,and the massacre of landscapes, particularly by industrial or agricultural buildings. We could also cite the concrete belt along the coast...

Beyond the need for information and scientific knowledge, which is hugely lacking in the environmental field, and which renders politicians blind, the major problem for the environment is primarily a problem of anticipation, prevention and responsibility towards future generations. The behaviour and practice of economic calculation is in question.

Let us take a sad example of short-term vision : the pollution of groundwater by nitrates from agricultural fertilizers. The phenomenon is slow and almost irreversible. Nothing is done as long as the critical threshold has not been reached, and afterwards it is too late to fight the effects of nitrates distributed in the subsequent 10-20 years. Is it not urgent to apply to agriculture the polluter-pays principle to which industry has been subjected for years ? Past growth has planted time bombs under our feet. Let's not wait for them to explode - let's defuse them.

3.3. A lawless and turbulent international environment

The lack of regulators (mentioned in § 1) appears all the more critical as we have to expect internal social explosions within the Third World and an upsurge in the number of regional or local conflicts.

The seeds of tomorrow's social eruptions are buried in today's trends : rapid population increase, glaring inequalities (where luxury sits side-by-side with poverty), massive urbanization in gigantic megalopolises which are nearer to slums than to cities.

Beyond the multiple uncertainties of the lawless and turbulent international environment, two permanent factors can be discerned :

- international monetary instability (currency reflects geopolitics), and particularly the persistence of a strongly fluctuating dollar in relation to other currencies ;
- the 'self-centred' development of themselves by the developed countries (for most products and services, four-fifths of solvent markets will remain within the triad).

3.4. Slow, irregular, unequal and interdependent growth

Interdependence is not a fiction but a reality which can be measured by means of many indicators, such as the ever increasing proportion of national production devoted to export. This increasing openness to the outside means that no country can claim to be in sole command of its own growth : the accelerator is international and only the brakes remain national.

Because of the impossibility of establishing international and national structures and rules adapted to the new context of interdependence and technical and economic change, a new phase of general, concerted economic growth seems to us unlikely. We would add that population ageing is hardly likely to stimulate growth.

It is irregularity, rather than slowness of growth, which will have serious consequences for investment decisions, as it will lead to forecasting errors and to erratic behaviour shifting from optimism to pessimism and vice versa. Periods of recession will be followed by periods of recovery as if the powers of recall were acting to maintain growth rates around a low average of about 2% - which, considering levels of development, is considerable - four to five times higher in absolute terms than an average year in the last century.

The gaps in development between countries of the South are becoming accentuated. There is no longer 'one' but 'many' Third Worlds. This unequal development, which explains the emergence of a North movement within the South, is expected to be another source of tension between neighbouring countries, some of which are developing rapidly, with medium population levels, while others are prey to the difficulties of underdevelopment and overpopulation.

3.5. New energy price rises, beneficial if they are gradual

Expensive energy is abundant and rising prices encourage economy measures and energy substitution, Unfortunately, the fall in the real value of oil prices in the 1980s makes further sudden price rises (shocks) more likely after the mid-1990s. Already in 1990 one detonator (Iraq's invasion of Kuwait) has been enough to trigger off a price explosion.This new shock will prove all the worse if we let up on our efforts.

3.6. The flood of new technologies : a new competitive order

New techniques of production and organization bring hope (of productivity gains, new products and services) but also threats (to jobs, freedom...) : it will all depend on the political and social choices which are made in these new technologies and on their rate of diffusion (we shall return to this point, which constitutes a major uncertainty).

Competitive differentials between companies will increasingly stem from the quality of organization and mastery of the information systems which surround new technologies. After the hardware and software, the 'org-ware' will be a determining productivity factor for a company's competitive position.

Five major trends, which have serious consequences, are at work for the coming years :

- mass production of variety, by small-scale production systems ;
- the comparative advantage of low salaries becoming less and less important as a determining factor ;
- flexibility of production equipment, indispensable for adapting to the fluctuations which characterize changing markets ;
- the need for alliances and cooperation with other companies at the level of pre-competitive research, or development and industrialization, owing to the globalization of markets which alone will enable expenditure on technology to be profitable ;
- a stronger coupling between scientific research and marketing, within the framework of an efficient strategy for managing a company's technological resources.

3.7. Deregulation associated with new international and regional regulation

The process known as 'deregulation' which started in the USA almost 15 years ago is being reproduced throughout the world. In reality it is an evolution rather than a disappearance of regulations. This evolution is taking place along two fundamental axes, each with its own specific consequences.

Firstly, the opening up to competition of certain types of activity (transport, telecommunications, or more generally, services), of certain types of market (certain public markets, for example), or of geographic regions (Japan) which until now have in fact been excluded. It is an extension of the field of industrial competition, in terms of physical space and sectors of activity.

Secondly, the increased effectiveness of regulations on hygiene and health (for consumers and workers), safety and environment. The current trend is to make regulations more coherent and precise in order to improve their effectiveness. On the whole this does not lead to a relaxation of constraints - quite the contrary - but it does guarantee that the same rules are applied universally, and this makes their development easier to forecast correctly - which also makes international harmonization easier.

At the European level, regulation and the introduction of standards will be a factor reducing uncertainty over the rules of the game, but also generating new areas of competition and hence of turbulence. The international competition to which, until now, manufacturing industries have especially been exposed, will extend to activities such as services (banks, insurance...), which have until now been 'protected'.

Finally, the methods of instituting these new regulations are themselves evolving; the strategic decision-making bodies are increasingly the EC, international organizations such as GATT, or even the American Congress. Moreover, companies have a greater say in these processes, as they have the expertise and as they are recognized as being fully responsible for all the consequences of their activities.

3.8. Economic competition on a global scale with states playing a key rôle

Keen industrial and commercial technological competition between companies to acquire parts of a market which has become global will continue. The transnational arena is the place for this competition between the large multinationals which are tending to form global oligopolies through broad sectors of activities. To this competition will be added increasing cooperation and strategic alliances, for example, in the technological field, which will tend to reinforce still further barriers to entry for companies not coopted into the oligopoly. Those multinationals which function as global information systems have, furthermore, two characteristics which distinguish them from other companies.

Firstly, the ability to take the results of fundamental research and transform them into adaptable technologies. These results, which we shall call 'strategic basic research' are produced and published by the scientific community of the world's universities, and by virtue of this they are free ; this capacity for transformation is due to the quantitative and qualitative levels attained by the laboratories of these multinational companies.

Secondly, the ability to have access to the world capital market, a huge source of finance, which moreover allows the continuous fluctuations in interest rates and exchange rates to be used as an opportunity.

These multinationals interact with many smaller companies, often small and medium-sized enterprises, which are rooted in regional, social and economic realities. These regional companies are specialized sub-contractors and product innovators and often maintain a symbiotic relationship with the multinationals, each needing the other to ensure its competitiveness and longevity.

Between the transnational and the regional, the national level often determines very different comparative advantages through three distinct mechanisms. In the first place, a nation's public policies on training, standards and public markets define the technical environment of the companies. Secondly, national social dynamics determine collective attitudes towards distribution of value-added, towards the rules of the game between social groups and towards the individual's relationship to work and the company.

These three factors determine the social environment and the company's working conditions. Thirdly, monetary realities, as manifested in exchange rates and interest rates, constitute the company's financial environment. These three mechanisms contribute to the 'structural competitiveness' at national level ; increasingly, it is the interface between the transnational, national and regional space which forms the basis of a company's competitiveness.

3.9. Decline in industrial jobs and rise of service industries

The decline in industrial jobs, which started in the early 1970s in Europe (between 1970 and 1990 industrial output rose by 40% in Europe, and at the same time employment fell by 30%), is expected to spread to all developed nations (numbers of industrial jobs have been declining noticeably in the USA since 1980, and in Japan have remained constant since 1973). It appears that what happened in the agricultural sector is being reproduced in the industrial sector: because of technical progress an increasingly small proportion of the population is sufficient to produce growing quantities of industrial goods.

This uncoupling of production and classical industrial jobs could reach the point where, as in agriculture, the labour of 10% of the active labour force is adequate for production needs. It is the 'knowledge workers' who will take over - they will become more numerous, even within industry, than traditional blue- and white-collar workers.

Services, ie, commercial and financial activities, transport, leisure, utilities (water, electricity) public administration, education and health, today employ 55-65% of the active labour force in the industrialized nations; this growth of employment in services is as huge as it is recent. The proportion of household consumption spent on services is growing continually (45% of the total) and it appears that expenditure on health and education can only continue to grow in future.

As for companies, functions other than production are developing rapidly. At each stage, from raw material to finished product, activities involving organization, stock control, maintenance, repair, coordination and information have increased to the extent that they now make up the most significant proportion of product cost.

This 'tertiarization of the secondary sector' also affects the product itself (often made up of an integrated whole of products and services), and investment is becoming increasingly 'non-material' (training, software, R&D, marketing...) and is growing at four times the rate of material investment. This development of services both within and outside the firm is central to performance improvement.

However, this rise in services is running into three different kinds of limitation which are mortgaging its growth in the medium term... First, collective services see their development limited by public finance problems ; financial restraints, moreover,are bringing to a head the problem of the growing differentiation of some consumer services (health, social security, education) as they are privatized. Second, the growth of services in the home is reaching its limits as consumers produce these services themselves by purchasing the product which performs the service (eg, buying a washing machine instead of using a laundry service) ; there are also limits to the amount of free time devoted to consuming services.

Finally, and more fundamentally, technological advances have still not produced a new wave of activities which go beyond mere gadgets and which satisfy real needs. Prospects are starting to shape up, however, for some services to companies, where information technologies play a key role. But this will only emerge after a period of social learning and the installation of major infrastructures (telematic networks), which means that they remain hypothetical for the present.

In fact, services are creating three times fewer jobs in France today than 15 years ago, and do not compensate for the reduction in jobs in agriculture and industry ; thus, the 'white tide' has not managed to submerge unemployment,... So will opportunities arise out of strengthening service exports ? (France is well placed on this score, ranking second in the world, just behind the USA). Tourism makes up a large part of this item. When a country does not have enough products to export, it sells its landscapes, its way of life - another reason to preserve them.

3.10. Crisis of the Welfare State

In most developed countries (in Europe, the USA and even in Japan) the size of compulsory deductions (taxes and social security payments) in relation to GDP has increased sharply since 1973, and now, in Europe, often represents 45% of national product. This percentage, which has climbed by 10-15 points in the space of 10 years cannot grow indefinitely without damaging general economic activity. In many cases, limits are imperative, particularly in Europe, where social security is facing an exponential growth in health expenditure.

Reducing the scale of compulsory contributions and at the same time diminishing the role of the state in the economy would seem indispensable in order to help restore companies' ability to finance themselves and to avoid penalizing those who wish to work more and thereby earn more. If this reduction in the tax burden is to happen without worsening the budgetary deficit, it can only be at the cost of either a reduction in the wage bill of public employees or by imposing limitations on social transfers - the choice has to be made. Contributions are only one aspect of the problem. Public expenditure must also be considered. In France in 1990 this represented 52% of GDP, and public debt rose from 20% to 40% of GDP in a few years. This will have to be repaid, and the return of inflation, *'That momentary agreement in reported confusion'* (according to Pierre Massé) could prove politically convenient.

Beyond the financial crisis there is also a crisis in the legitimacy of the Welfare State. With the presence of a strong, dominant and omni-interventionist state, it becomes more advantageous for citizens to seek to manipulate (or to take possession of the state apparatus) than to base their relationships on mutual reciprocity, creating an optimal social increase in value. The logic of the state, whether Right or Left, can only be 'corporatist'. Some social groups are better placed than others to apply pressure and obtain extra benefits from the state, to the detriment of the collectivity. In the struggle of redistribution the state becomes party to the law of the strongest.

The state must, however, support the infantry of the economic machine and tend those wounded and left out for the count by the savagery of the market. To preserve social peace it must brandish the imperatives of solidarity and give a quasi-wage to the unemployed, ready to recoup the corresponding costs (unemployment, benefits, national insurance payments) through taxation.

Finally, there is a crisis of effectiveness : the administrative machine is no longer accountable. The state is the worst of bosses. Financial crisis is forcing it to accept the relative impoverishment of public employees. In many administrations absenteeism has increased threefold since 1980; as one administrative director commented : 'Civil servants have compensated for their reduced buying power by taking time off'. Perhaps what is needed is fewer, better paid civil servants - except that some see the civil service as being rather like a day hospital.

We also recall the French government giving lessons on wage policy to the Peugeot group in autumn 1989. Some categories of worker were better paid in one establishment than another, despite being equally qualified. But the state would do well to put its own house in order - after all, it currently pays the same Central Administration Director 50% more if he works in the Ministry of Finance than if the works in the Ministry for National Education ! And members of ministerial cabinets receive cash subsidies - which are not subject to any kind of taxation. The example of what not to do comes from above - not to mention those political parties which vote to amnesty their financial misdeeds and bribes. How dare they still put people in jail for stealing apples ?

When taxation kills work, when the state holds its civil servants in contempt and sets a bad example for its citizens, when the state plays a disruptive rather than a regulatory role, then it becomes intolerable. We would add that the crises of effectiveness and of legitimacy are merging. In reality, power is in the hands of a state aristocracy which is very few and happy. Hence several thousand families seemingly by chance have a monopoly hold over the best jobs from one generation to the next.

3.11. New forms of exclusion

In order to break down the ramparts of resistance and rigidity built up by the social oligopoly (organized pressure groups) towards any change which could call into question benefits acquired in the past in another context, there will probably be a high price to pay in terms of crises and unemployment. However, in a world where everything is changing, advantages must also change. Unfortunately there is good reason to believe that in this clash between the forces of change and the forces of inertia, some people will fall by the wayside in a rearguard battle - young people, older workers...

The unemployed are often excluded from the job market by those who control the education system. Unemployment is very destructive in a world where work has become the essential channel for social recognition and value, and where the overworked man or woman is the symbol of success. Exclusion from the job market is a form of social death.

4. Three major uncertainties

If the above trends seem probable, what exactly would result from a conjunction or confrontation between them is a question full of uncertainties. Here we call attention to three uncertainties which it would seem important to take into account.

4.1. Will the rate of diffusion of new technologies be as rapid as forecast ?

In answer to this question we can only postulate that generally progress will remain slow, due to inertia inherent in production and social systems. We could note numerous cases of resistance to the effective introduction of new technology.

Resistances are perhaps even stronger in the tertiary sector, in so far as this sector has so far been less affected by the stimulus of international competition. At the end of the 1970s it was believed that in a few years' time new office technology systems would take over all service industries (banks, insurance companies, administration, etc). Today we realize that this has not been the case at all. Many factors combine to explain the slow rate of this penetration. In the first place there is the question of reallocating time freed by new techniques (of production, organization, etc). What is the point of investing in order to obtain productivity gains which cannot be translated into expanded production (due to saturated markets or slow growth rates), or into staff reduction ? The staff are there, and must be kept busy, and a reduction in working hours can only be gradual (if it is to be equitably shared out between sectors).

In the second place the generalization of office technology means that the world of work becomes relatively transparent, which works against established hierarchies. Information technologies are not neutral vis-à-vis power structures. It is therefore hardly surprising that certain actors at the heart of companies (often managers) feel threatened and resist innovation.

Furthermore, we should not forget that what is technologically possible is not necessarily economically profitable (we should beware of creating a Concorde in the field of telematics) or socially desirable. As evidence we can take the issue of teleworking and homeworking. It is unlikely that homeworking will develop to the point that a significant amount of office work disappears. Several factors militate against this maximalist hypothesis. For one thing, the actual physiognomy of urban housing estates in France - their pokiness, lack of comfort and the mediocrity of the environment - makes it unlikely that they will be lived in for whole days at a time. Moreover, we should take into consideration the fact that work is a social activity and meets a need for communication which is satisfied to a lesser degree elsewhere.

4.2. Metamorphosis of work and employment

Unemployment today affects 10% of the active labour force in France - tomorrow it may well affect 15%, then 20% or more if there is no change in structures, organizations, rules of the game and behaviour. This means we are heading for a dual society - with a growing proportion of the population (the young and the old - who are becoming younger and younger) - excluded from the labour market. Such a scenario can only be explosive.

Ultimately, there is only one way out - a sharing out of work and income, matched with greater mobility of existing jobs (if there are only four jobs for five workers, this is not a problem if the jobs are rotated - but rather an opportunity to increase creative breaks from work). If a continuation of the secular trend towards a reduction in working hours seems probable and desirable to us, it does not have to mean a decrease in hours of real activity. People do not want to work less, but to work differently. Reducing the working hours of one's main activity in fact means opening the door to a variety of activities.

In order to avoid the dual society, we must promote the pluralistic society (where each individual could have several jobs and where each job cold be occupied by several people).

4.3. Evolution of lifestyles and social organization in developed countries

The most persistent question concerns the evolution of values and ways of life. At this level, conjecture fails, as futurists do not see clearly and sociologists have difficulty in understanding the present or even the recent past. As for analyses in terms of lifestyle, these have no predictive value. They record changes without explaining them. Lifestyle studies do not explain household purchase behaviour, but rather traditional socio-demographic categories. In technical terms, the percentage of 'variables' explained by 'lifestyles' is almost systematically negligible, and in all cases is 10 times less important than any socio-demographic indicator such as the level of education of the housewife or her profession.

After World War II new values emerged to replace the traditional values of fulfilling one's duties, of making one's efforts pay, of saving, and of hierarchies. These new values were to become dominant during the 1960s - they gave priority to consuming, to the attraction of novelty, and to the importance of keeping up appearances.

From the end of the 1960s, however, this model, which had been taken on board by the majority and even become hegemonic, found itself challenged by the emergence of new values, characterized by the rejection of the criterion of social excellence, and of the motives of status, large organizations and bureaucracy, in order to give importance to conviviality, personal and cultural life, relationships, quality of the environment (personal and collective),. decentralization, small groups, autonomy and self-realization.

Were the values of the 'post-materialist' society about to sweep away those of the consumer society, just as 15 years earlier these had supplanted traditional, rural, bourgeois values? The 1970s were to bring many surprises, and in particular they were to strip this question of its meaning.

As they spread, the new values amalgamated in a heterogeneous way with the values of the consumer society, which assimilated them. Conviviality was translated into Club Méditerranée, autonomy into the suburban detached house, and self-realization into hi-fis. Beyond a small minority fringe, were the new values to become anything more than gadgets, simple avatars of the consumer societies ?

Double social fragmentation

Beyond the current phase of adjustment of demands and behaviour to new opportunities and new constraints, it seems that we are heading towards a double fragmentation of the social scene:

- deepened and renewed fragmentation at the level of the classical major social partnerships (employers, unions, the state, socio-professional actors), who are negotiating over the way revenue is shared out, and over the status and development of the Welfare State. We have a social oligopoly, whose game will be further complicated by the appearance of new social partnerships and the often unstable institutionalization of minorities or groups representing other values ;

- fragmentation of the representatives of 'new values' into many groups and minorities, expressing different values or even different interfaces between common values and varied opportunities and constraints. This juxtaposition between the believers in moral excellence (the 'militants'), the small, more or less closed groups (even sects), the 'new consumers', those who live for the moment, the minority who have a satisfying job, the 'new agriculturalists', those without work (or without declared work), etc, will translate into growing disparities in lifestyles, demands and behaviour.

In this variety we shall find all the possible degrees of compromise between partially contradictory trends developing in parallel, such as the search for both autonomy and security, for both freedom and a sense of roots.

5. The lie of the land in the year 2000, in brief

The main fields which we tackle here are as follows : international environment ; energy ; economy, technology and industry ; ways of life and socio-economic organization.

It is best to treat the terms 'uncertainties' and 'discontinuites' as if there were a question mark at the end of each variable. These terms indicate propositions subject to doubt and controversy, whereas the term 'trends' corresponds to probable developments, even quasi-certainties. We ask the reader to excuse the sometimes pleonastic and incomplete nature of this Prévert-like list.

5.1. Probable trends

Lawless and turbulent international environment

- absence of an international regulator (the old bipolar order is dead but the new multipolar order is not yet ready to be born) ;
- international monetary instability : strong fluctuations in exchange rates ;
- worldwide demographic pressure - 5 billion people in the world today, at least 6,5 billion in the year 2000, then 8-12 billion during the first decades of the next century ;
- demographic concentration in developing countries (70 % of the Third World population concentrated in eight countries) ;
- development inequalities between countries in the South increasing more rapidly (greater economic and ecological inequalities) ;
- a minority in the South (400 million inhabitants) with access to western-style consumption patterns ;
- explosive and anarchic development of the megalopolises of the Third World (Mexico City will have 30 million inhabitants in the year 2000) ; domestic pollution, destitution, violence ('polluted poverty') ;
- general overexploitation of our heritage (forests, water, petroleum, ores, agricultural land, fish, etc) in order to satisfy local needs and to obtain, at any cost, export earnings or import substitutes ;
- development of nationalism, growing number of regional conflicts ;
- nuclear proliferation and sophisticated arms (several countries will acquire nuclear armaments in the 1990s) ;
- rise of religious -particularly Islamic- fundamentalism ;
- international migratory pressure ; flow of illegal immigrants and refugees.

Energy

- rising energy prices (in the order of a doubling in real value up to the year 2000) ;
- decelerated increase in global energy consumption (about 1-2 % per year in volume) ;
- strong inertia in production and consumption structures ;
- variety and heterogeneity in energy policies among developed nations.

Economy, technology and industry

- increasingly interdependent economies, despite protectionist threats and increasingly global market ;
- four-fifths of the solvent world markets situated within the triad of North America, Europe and Japan ;
- slow, irregular growth in the North, unequal growth in the South ;
- painful new industrial restructuring (eg, the car industry, electronics) ;
- process innovation (automation) rather than product innovation ;

- new era of growing profits (earnings from capital and labour) ;
- development of small, decentralized, formal and informal production units, allowing mass production of variety ;
- industrialization of tertiary activities and tertiarization of secondary activities ;
- deregulation and new regulations in services (banks, insurance, transport, distribution) ;
- continued decline of the numbers of jobs in industry ;
- scarcity of professionals in traditional areas of employment (services, building industry) ;
- persistent unemployment and rise in social tensions.

Ways of life and socio-economic organization

- attitudes and behaviour evolving more slowly than economic and technological developments ;
- disappearance of the peasantry and rise in the power of retired people (the 'grey panthers') ;
- new forms of inequality (qualitative, status, lifestyles) increasing together with inequalities in income and wealth ;
- new forms of frustration and exclusion as a result of the perverse effects of the rise in the number of diplomas- 'the diploma disease' ;
- growing burden and declining effectiveness of the Welfare State ;
- extension of the market to collective goods and services : education, health, environment, culture.

Socio-economic trends

- ageing population and increasing health costs ;
- increasing dichotomy between workers assessed by their status or qualifications and the rest, exposed to risk, competition and insecurity or excluded through unemployment ;
- worsening of unemployment until the end of the 1990s.

Trends in lifestyle and aspirations

- growing heterogeneity and differentiation in lifestyles ;
- development of contradictory trends - the need for security (social protection, job...) and aspirations to autonomy ;
- growing feelings of insecurity - individuals withdrawing into themselves or into the nuclear family ('the family as social shock absorber') ;
- new forms of social, cultural and technological exclusion (computer illiteracy, the perverse effects of the race for diplomas)...
- increasing incompatibility between aspirations, training and jobs ; demotivation for work ;
- qualitative extension of the 'third age' (people are old at an increasingly young age and young at an increasingly advanced age, it is difficult to find

work after the age of 45, and yet people are fit for longer).

Trends in city life and transportation

- inertia of urban forms ;
- rejuvenation of town centres and small villages ;
- social segregation in urban areas and decay of certain areas ;
- saturation point reached in car parks ;
- more hours spent on transport ;
- long and frequent journeys ;
- continuation of the rapid development of air transport.

Trends in tourism

- search for new tourist sites - including the rediscovery of what there is in one's own country ;
- spread of the tourist ghetto phenomenon in Third World countries, particulary on the coast ;
- differentiation of holidays and the development of business.

5.2. Major uncertainties

International environment

- significant immigration flows into Europe from the South and the East ;
- economic renewal of the ex-Socialist countries ;
- break-up of the Soviet empire and consequences for European security.

Energy

- gradual or graduated oil price rises ;
- another Chernobyl-type nuclear accident ;
- future of nuclear power and coal.

Economic, technology and industry

- de-industrialization of certain developed countries (USA, UK) ;
- rate of diffusion of new technologies and associated products and services ;
- impact of robotization and automation on the size of production units -end of gigantism, "small is profitable" ;
- return to their northern birthplace of certain industrial activities which have emigrated to the South (such as textiles) ;
- new export opportunities (construction, environmental industy) ;
- decline of the traditional wage-earner (with one, full-time job) ;

- rise in multi-occupations and entrepreneurship.

Ways of life and socio-economic organization

- reinforcement of inequalities in income and particularly in wealth and lifestyles ;
- reduced, increased or flexible retirement age ;
- new forms of work organization ;
- job sharing, part-time work, legalization of moonlighting ;
- emergence of aspirations to order, due to feelings of insecurity ;
- far-reaching revision of fiscal systems and levying of social taxes ;
- importance of the social power of people of the "third" and "fourth" age ;
- measures taken to reduce the burden of public expenditure ;
- impact on professional mobility of the need for a sense of roots (living in the country) ;
- future of inner cities and dense peri-urban areas ;
- development of multiple home ownership ;
- role of spirituality in advanced societies ;
- integration of immigrants/emergence in Europe of American-style urban ghettos ;
- privatization and regionalization of the education system.

5.3. Possible discontinuities (examples)

International environment

- fierce US protectionism ;
- serious social conflicts in Japan ;
- break-up of the EC ;
- blockade of the Persian Gulf and embargo on petroleum exports, political and economic blackmail and embargoes through technical and industrial embezzlement.

Energy

- nuclear accidents and a sudden stop to nuclear programmes ;
- technological breakthrough in fields such as fusion, gasification of coal, geopressure... ;
- discovery of huge oilfields outside the Middle East ;
- harsh and lasting rupture in supplies from the Persian Gulf.

Economy, technology and industry

- changes in means of production (carbon chemistry, chemistry of wood) ;
- revolutionary breakthroughs in bio-industries ;

- major accidents ;

Ways of life and socio-economic organization

- self-organization of the unemployed (huge demonstrations) ;
- pogroms, new religious wars, conflicts between cultural communisties ;
- resurgence of religious practices in advanced countries.

BIBLIOGRAPHY

ACKOFF R. L. (1973) : *Méthodes de planification de l'entreprise*, Editions d'Organisation.

AFCET - AFPLANE (1990) : "Vers une école européenne du management stratégique", Actes du colloque des 31 janvier et 1er février 1990,*AFCET*, Paris.

ALBA P. (1988) : "Prospective et stratégie d'entreprise", *Futuribles*, février.

ALLAIS M. (1989) : "La philosophie de ma vie", *Annales des Mines* : gérer et comprendre, N° juin.

ALBERT K.J. (1983) : *The Strategic Management Handbook*, Mcgraw Hill.

AMARA R. (1984) : "New directions for futures research - setting the stage", *Futures*, August.

ANCELIN C. (1983) : "Analyse structurelle : le cas du vidéotex", *Futuribles*, n° 71.

ANSOFF I. (1965) : *Corporate strategy*, Mcgraw Hill.

ANSOFF I. (1975) : "Managing strategic surprise by response to weak signals", *California Management Review*.

ANSOFF I. (1976) : *From strategic planning to strategic management*, John Wiley, New York.

ANSOFF I. (1978) : "Corporate capability for managing change", *SRI report* n° 610, Business Intelligence Program.

ANSOFF I. (1979) : *Strategic Management*, Macmillan, New York.

ANSOFF I. (1984) : *Implanting strategic management*, Prentice Hall International.

APOSTOL P. (1972) : "Marxism and the structure of the future", *Futures*, September 1972.

ARCHIER G., SERIEYX H. (1984) : *L 'entreprise du 3ème type*, Seuil.

ASHBY W.R. (1956) : *An introduction to cybernetics*, Chapman Hall, London.

ASSELAIN J.C. (1984) : *L'histoire économique et sociale de la France du XVIIIè siècle à nos jours*, Le Point, Seuil.

ATLAN H. (1979) : *Entre le cristal et la fumée,* Seuil, Paris.

ANTOINE J. (1988) : "Pour une prospective du deuxième âge", *Futuribles* n° 123, juillet-août.

AVENIER M.J. (1985) : *Le pilotage stratégique,* Presses du Cnrs

AYRES, R. (1969) : *Technology Forecasting and Long Range Planning,* Mcgraw Hill, New York.

BARRAND J. , GUIGOU C (1984) : " Analyse structurelle", Mémoire du DEA 120, Paris IX Dauphine.

BAREL Y. (1971) : *Prospective et analyse des systèmes,* La Documentation Française, février, collection TRP (Travaux et Recherches de Prospective).

BARRET PH. (1977) : "Objet et méthode de la prospective", numéro hors série *Futuribles.*

BATTLE A. (1986) : *Les travailleurs du futur,* Seghers.

BEAUFRE A. (1963) : *Introduction à la stratégie,* Ifri-Economica, réédition en 1985 du livre publié en 1963 aux Editions Armand Colin.

BELL D. (1973) : *The coming of post-industrial society - a venture in social forecasting,* (Basic Books, N.Y. 1st edition 1973, 2nd edition 1976).

BERGER G. (1964) : *Phénoménologie du temps et prospective,* Puf.

BERGER G. (1967) : *Etapes de la prospective,* Puf.

BERTHO C. (1981) : *Télégraphes et téléphones : de Valmy au microprocesseur,* Livre de poche, librairie générale française.

BERTIER P., de MONTGOLFIER J. (1978) : *Approche multicritère des problèmes de décision,* Hommes et Techniques.

BLUET J.C., ZEMOR J. (1970) : "Prospective géographique : méthode et direction de recherches", *Metra,* Vol. IX n° 1.

BOUDON R. (1979) : *Effets pervers et ordre social,* Paris, PUF.

BOYER L., EQUILBEY N. (1990) : *Histoire du management,* Editions d'Organisations.

BRAUDEL F. (1980) : *Civilisation matérielle, économie et capitalisme,* XVè - XVIIIè siècle, Armand Colin, troisième édition.

BRUTER C. (1977) : "Deux remarques sur les rapports entre économie et mathématiques", Actes du colloque Analyse de système, *AFCET.*

BOSTON CONSULTING GROUP (1981) : *Les mécanismes fondamentaux de la compétitivité,* Hommes et Techniques.

CAHIERS FRANCAIS (1987) "Vers l'an 2000 et après ?", n° 232, juillet/septembre, *Documentation Française.*

CARRERE D'ENCAUSSE, H (1979): *L'empire éclaté,* Flammarion.

CASPAR P. (1989) : *L'investissement intellectuel,* Economica.

CAVES R.E. (1980) : "Industrial organization, corporate strategy and structure", *Journal of Economic Litterature,* March.

CAZES B. (1986) : *Histoire des futurs, les figures de l'avenir de Saint Augustin au XXIè siècle,* Seghers.

CETRON M. et DAVIES O. (1989) : *American renaissance, our life at the turn of the 21st Century,* St Martin's Press, New York.

CHANDLER A. (1962) : *Strategy and structure,* MIT Press, Cambridge.

CORNISH E.S. (1979) : "Planting Seeds for the Future", *World Future Society, Washington.*

CROZIER M., FRIEDBERG E. (1977) : *L'acteur et le système,* Seuil.

DARWIN Ch. (1859) : *The Origin of the Species,,* reissued by Découverte in 1985.

DALKEY N, HELMERT O (163) : " An experimental application of the Delphi method to the use of experts", *Management Science,* N° 9

DALKEY N. (1972) : "An elementary cross impact model", *Technological Forecasting and Social Change,* vol. 3 n° 3.

DATAR (1971) : *Une image de la France en l'an 2000, (scénarios de l'inacceptable),* collection TRP n° 20, Documentation Française.

DELATTRE P. (1985) : *Système, structure, fonction, évolution, essai d'analyse épistémologique,* 2è édition, Maloine.

DRUCKER P. (1959) : "Long-range planning a challenge to management science", *Management Science,* April.

DUCOS G. (1980) : "Two complementary cross-impact models : MIP1 et MIP2", *Futures,* October.

DUCOS G. (1983) : "Delphi et analyse d'interactions", n° 71, *Futuribles.*

DUPERRIN J.C., GODET M. (1973) : "Méthode de hiérarchisation des éléments d'un système", Rapport économique du CEA, R-45-41.

DUPUY J.P. (1982) : *Ordres et désordres*, Seuil.

DURAND Th. (1985) : "Evolution de la pensée stratégique et pratique d'entreprise", *Futuribles*, September.

DUVAL A., FONTELA E., GABUS A. (1974) : "Cross-impact : a handbook on concepts and applications", Institut Batelle (Geneva, Dematel reports) cf. also FONTELA et GABUS : "Events and economic forecasting models", *Futures*, August 1974.

ECKELAND I. (1984) : *Le calcul, l'imprévu : les figures du temps de Kepler à Thom*, Seuil, Paris.

ENZER S. (1980) : "Interax : an interactive model for studying future business environment", *Technological Forecasting and Social Change*, Vols. 2 et 3.

EYMARD J. (1975) : "Un modèle markovien d'impacts croisés", *Metra* vol. XIV, n°2.

FAYOL H. (1916) : *Administration industrielle et générale*, Dunod, réédition en 1979.

FORESTER Jay W. (1971) : *World Dynamics*, Wright Allen Press, Cambridge.

FREEMAN C. (1974) : *The economics of Industrial Innovations*, Penguin, London.

GAUDIN T. (1988) : *Les métamorphoses du futur*, Economica.

GAUDIN T. (1990) : *2100, récit du prochain siècle*, Payot.

GENTRIC B. ET LECLERC P. (1990) : "La sécurité en Europe", Fedn, dossier 32,

GIGET M. (1989) : "L'identité de l'entreprise. Préalable à la réflexion stratégique" et "Arbres technologiques et arbres de compétences : deux concepts à finalité distincte", *Futuribles* n° 137, novembre.

GIRI J. (1984) : *Le Sahel demain; catastrophe ou renaissance*, Karthala.

GLEICK J. (1987) : *Chaos*, Viking Press, New York.

GLOBAL 2000 (1980) : *Report to the President : entering the twenty first century*, Washington D.C. US Government, Printing Office (Barney).

GODET M. (1974) : "SMIC : a new cross impact method" *Futures*, August.

GODET M. (1975) : "Les scénarios du transport aérien à l'horizon 1990, analyse stratégique par la méthode SMIC", Metra, Vol. XIV n° 1.

GODET M., MAALOUF A. (1977) : "Nucléaire tout est joué sauf si...", Economica, N° 38, novembre.

GODET M, (1977) : *Crise de la prévision, essor de la prospective,* Puf.

GODET M. (1980) : *Demain les crises : de la résignation à l'antifatalité,* Hachette.

GODET M. (1985) : *Crises are opportunities,* Gamma Press, Montreal.

GODET M. (1987) : *Scenarios and strategic management,* Butterworth.

GODET M. (1991) : *L'avenir autrement,* Armand Colin.

GONOD P.F. (1990) : *Dynamique de la prospective,* Etude Cpe Aditech n° 136.

GORDON T.J., HAYWARD H. (1968) : "Initial experiments with the cross imact Matrix Method of Forecasting", *Futures,* December.

GOUX Ch. (1969) : *L'horizon prévisionnel,* Cujas.

GRIMALDI N. (1971) : *Le désir et le temps,* Puf.

GUERNY J, GUIRIEC J.C (1979) : *Le plan d'entreprise,* Delmas.

HALL D.J., SAIAS M.A. (1980) : "Strategy follows structure", *Strategic Management Journal,* Vol. 1.2., April-June.

HELMER O. (1972) : "Cross impact gaming", *Futures,* June, Vol. 4.

HELMER O. (1981) : "Reassessment of cross impact analysis", *Futures,* October.

HELMER O. (1982) : *Looking forward, a guide to futures research,* Sage Publications, London.

HOLL J.C., PLAS J.P., RIOU P. (1973) : *Les choix d'investissement dans l'entreprise,* Puf, Collection Sup. l'Economiste, n° 35.

INTERFUTURS (1979) : *Face aux futurs,* OCDE, 1979.

JANTSCH E. (1967) : *Technological forecasting in perspective,* Paris, OECD.

JOUVENEL H. de (1982) : "La prospective pour une nouvelle citoyenneté", Futuribles.

JOUVENEL H. de (1988) : "Prospective et politique", Futuribles, n° 122, juin.

JOUVENEL B. de (1964) : *L'art de la conjecture,* Editions du Rocher.

JULIEN P.A., LAMONDE P., LATOUCHE D. (1975) : *La méthode des scénarios,* TRP n° 59, Documentation Française.

KAHN H., WIENER A. J. (1967) : *L'an 2000,* Robert Laffont, Paris.

KANE J. (1972) : "A primer for a new cross impact language KSIM", *Technological Forecasting and Social Change,* vol. IV.

KAHN H. (1984) : *"The resourceful earth : response to global 2000".*

KAPFERER J.N. (1987) : *"Rumeurs, le plus vieux métier du monde",* Seuil.

KARSKY M. (1984) : "La dynamique des systèmes", *Enjeux* n° 47, mai 1 984.

KERVERN G.Y. (1986) : "L'évangile selon St Mac", *Annales des Mines, Gérer et comprendre,* n° de mars.

KERVERN G.Y., PONSSARD J.P. (1990) : "L'entreprise définie comme un réseau", *Revue Française de Gestion,* n° de juin.

KLEIN G. (1986) : " Prévision, probabilité, prospective", *Revue Réseaux(N°* 50-51-52).

LANDIER H. (1987) : *L'entreprise polycellulaire,* Entreprises Modernes d'édition.

LEBOULANGER H., ROY B. (1969) : "L'entreprise face à la sélection et à l'orientation des projets de recherche : la méthodologie en usage dans le groupe SEMA", revue *Metra,* Vol. VII, n° 4.

LEFEBVRE J.F. (1982) : "L'analyse structurelle, méthodes et développements", thèse de doctorat de 3ème cycle. Université de Paris IX Dauphine.

LESCA H. (1982) : *Structure et système d'information, facteurs de compétitivité de l'entreprise,* Masson.

LESOURNE J. (1981) : *Les mille sentiers de l'avenir,* Seghers.

LESOURNE J., MALKIN D. (1979) : "L'exercice interfuturs, réflexion méthodologique", *Futuribles* n° 26-27, septembre-octobre.

LESOURNE J. (1989) : "Plaidoyer pour une recherche en prospective", *Futuribles* n°137.

LESOURNE J , GODET M. (1985) : *La fin des habitudes,* Seghers.

LESOURNE J. (1990) : *"L'économie de l'ordre et du désordre",* Economlca.

LORENZ E., (1963) :"Deterministic nonperiodic flow", *Journal of the Atmosphere Science,* n° 20.

LINSTONE H.A., SIMMONDS C. (1977) : *Futures Research, New Directions,* Addison, Wesley publishing.

LUSSATO B. (1981) : *Les structures de l'entreprise*, Editions d'Organisation.

MARTINO J.P. (1975) : *Technological forecasting for decision-making*, Elsevier.

MASSE P. (1965) : *Le plan ou l'anti-hasard*, Idées Gallimard.

MEADOWS D.H., RANDERS J., BEHRENS W.W. (1972) : *The limits to growth*, Universe Book, New York.

MENDELBROT B. (1989) : *"Les objects fractals"*, Flammarion.

MERRILL H.F. (1970) : *Les classiques du management*, Bibliothèque du Management, Paris.

MINTZERG H. (1982) : *The Structuring of Organizations : A Synthesis of Research*, Prentice Hall, New York.

MIRENOWICZ Ph., CHAPUY P., LOUINEAU Y. (1990) : "La méthode Delphi - Abaque appliquée à la prospective du bruit", *Futuribles* n° 143, mai.

MONTBRIAL TH. (1990) : *Que faire ? : les grandes manoeuvres du monde*, La Manufacture, Paris.

MORGENSTERN O. (1963) : *On the Accuracy of Economic Observations*, Princeton University Press, Princeton, NJ.

MOUSLI M. (1985) : "L'entreprise à visage humain", *Futuribles*.

OUCHI W. (1983) : *La théorie Z : faire face au défi japonais*, Paris, Interéditions.

ORGOGOZO I. (1987) : *Les paradoxes de la qualité*, Editions Organisation.

PAM (1977) : *Bilan d'une expérience prospective*, ouvrage collectif de l'équipe de Prospective et Aménagement (PAM) collection TRP, N° 71, Documentation Française.

PASCALE R.T., ATHOS (1984) : *Le management est-il un art japonais* ?, Paris, Editions d'Organisation.

PETERS T., WATERMAN R. (1982) : *In Search of Excellence*, Harper and Row.

PETERS T. and AUSTIN N. (1985) : A *Passion for Excellence*, Random House, New York.

PETERS T. (1989) : *Le chaos management*, Interéditions.

PHILIPART E. (1986) : "La prospective aux Etats-Unis", Revue *Réseaux*, N° 50-51-52.

PONSSARD J.P. - SARRAZIN J. (1981) : "Fondement des nouvelles méthodes d'analyse stratégique : le critère de part de marché relative", *Annales des Mines*.

POINCARE H. (1902) : *La science et l'hypothèse*, Flammarion, Paris.

POINCARE H. (1908) : *Science et méthode*, Flammarion, Paris.

PORTER M.E. (1980) : *Competitive Strategy*, The Free Press, New York.

PORTER M.E. (1985) : The Free Press, New York, traduction française : *L'avantage concurrentiel*, Paris, Interéditions (1986).

PRIGOGINE I., STENGERS I. (1979) : *"La nouvelle alliance"*, Gallimard, Paris, nouvelle édition en 1987.

PRIGOGINE I. (1989) : "Le chaos et l'enthousiasme", *Science et Technologie* n° 19, Paris, octobre.

PRIGOGINE I. (1990) : "Loi, histoire et désertion", article dans l'ouvrage collectif sur "La querelle du déterminisme", *Le Débat*, Gallimard.

REGNIER F. (1989) : *Annoncer la couleur*, Institut de la Métrologie qualitative, Nancy.

RIBOUD A. (1988) : *Modernisation, mode d'emploi*, UGE 10x18, Paris.

RUELLE D., TAKENS F. (1971) : *"On the Nature of Turbulence"*, Communications on Mathematical Physics, vol. 20, pp. 167-192.

SAINT-PAUL R., TENIERE-BUCHOT P.F. (1974) : *Innovation et évaluation technologiques : sélection des projets, méthodes et prévisions*, Entreprise Moderne d' Edition.

SAPOWAL, B. (1990) : *Les fractales*, CPE, Aditech.

SCHERER F.M. (1981) : *"Innovation and Growth-Schumpeterian perspectives"*.

SERIEYX H. (1982) : *Mobiliser l'intelligence de l'entreprise*, Entreprise Moderne d'Edition.

SERIEYX H. (1989) : *Le zéro mépris*, Interéditions.

SICARD C. (1987) : *Pratique de la stratégie d'entreprise*, Hommes et Techniques.

SIMON H. (1974) : *Administrative Behavior - A Study of Decision-Making Processes in Administrative Organization*, Macmillan, New York.

SRI (1982) : "Royal Dutch Shell Experience with Scenarios", *SRI Business Intelligence Programs* - report n° 669.

SISSA, J. (1987) : *Le corps virginal*, Vrin.

SUN TZU (1972) : *L'art de la guerre*, Flammarion.

TAYLOR F.W. ( ) : *Direction scientifique des entreprises,* réédition en 1979, Dunod.

TENIERE-BUCHOT P.F. (1973) : "Modèle "Popole" *Analyse et Prévision*, n° de février-mars.

TENIERE-BUCHOT P.F. (1989) : *L'ABC du pouvoir,* Editions d'Organisation, 1989, Paris

TODD E. (1983) : *La troisième planète : structures familiales et systèmes idéologiques* , Seuil.

TOFFLER A. (1970) : *Future Shock,* Random House N.Y.

TOFFLER A. (1980) : *La troisième vague,* Denoël.

TOFFLER A. (1984) : *Les cartes du futur,* Denoël.

THOM R. (1989) : *Paraboles et catastrophes,* Flammarion, Paris.

THOM R. (1990) : "Halte au hasard, silence au bruit", article dans l'ouvrage collectif sur "La querelle du déterminisme", *Le Débat,* Gallimard.

VILLE J. (1937) : *Etude critique de la notion de collectif,* Gauthier-Villars.

WACK P. (1985) : "Scenarios uncharted waters ahead", *Harvard Business Review,* September-October.

WALLISER B. (1978) : "Méthodes multicritères : arbres de pertinence", Revue *RCB.*

WEISS D. (1988) : *La fonction ressources humaines,* (collectif sous la direction de), Editions d'Organisation.

WOOT Ph. de (1988) : *Les entreprises de haute technologie et l'Europe,* Economica.

ZWICKY F. (1947) : "Morphology and nomenclatura of jet engines", *Aeronautical Engineering Review,*June